CLASS, CONTENTION, AND A WORLD IN MOTION

DISLOCATIONS

General Editors: August Carbonella, *Memorial University of Newfoundland*, Don Kalb, *University of Utrecht & Central European University*, Linda Green, *University of Arizona*

The immense dislocations and suffering caused by neo-liberal globalization, the retreat of the welfare state in the last decades of the twentieth-century and the heightened military imperialism at the turn of the 21st century have raised urgent questions about the temporal and spatial dimensions of power. Through stimulating critical perspectives and new and cross-disciplinary frameworks, which reflect recent innovations in the social and human sciences, this series provides a forum for politically engaged, ethnographically informed, and theoretically incisive responses.

CLASS, CONTENTION, AND A WORLD IN MOTION

Edited by Winnie Lem and Pauline Gardiner Barber

Berghahn Books
NEW YORK • OXFORD

First published in 2010 by
Berghahn Books
www.berghahnbooks.com

© 2010, 2013 Winnie Lem and Pauline Gardiner Barber
First paperback edition published in 2013

Library of Congress Cataloging-in-Publication Data

Class, contention and a world in motion / edited by Winnie Lem and Pauline
Gardiner Barber.
  p. cm.
Includes bibliographical references and index.
  ISBN 978-1-84545-686-3 (hbk.)--ISBN 978-0-85745-794-3 (pbk.)
  1. Human beings—Migrations. 2. Migrations of nations. 3. Culture
and globalization. 4. Emigration and immigration—Political aspects.
5. Emigration and immigration—Economic aspects. I. Lem, Winnie.
II. Barber, Pauline Gardiner.
  GN370.C54 2010
  304.8—dc22   2009042386

British Library Cataloguing in Publication Data
A catalogue record for this book is available from the British Library

Printed in the United States on acid-free paper

ISBN 978-0-85745-794-3 Paperback   ISBN: 978-0-85745-827-8 Retail Ebook

Contents

Part III | Complicity and Compliance

Acknowledgments

The editors would like to thank Gus Carbonella, Don Kalb, Bruce Barber, Gavin Smith, Vivian Berghahn, and Marion Berghahn for their encouragement and support in making this volume possible. Chapters by Barber, Leach, Lem, Però, and Zontini are revised versions of articles that were previously published in *Focaal: European Journal of Anthropology,* vol. 51, 2008. We extend our thanks to Berghahn Books and the editors of Focaal for permission to include these works. We also gratefully acknowledge the reviewers of this volume for their insightful comments, criticisms and enthusiasms. For their careful work in helping to prepare this manuscript, we thank Luisa Steur and Catherine Bryan. A final note of thanks is owed to Melissa Spinelli and Mike Dempsey for their diligent work in overseeing the production of this book.

INTRODUCTION

Winnie Lem and Pauline Gardiner Barber

This book brings together the work of scholars who are concerned with illuminating the relationship between capitalist transformation and the configurations of class in global migration. The contemporary dynamics of transformation under capitalism tend to be encapsulated by the overused but nonetheless apposite gloss of globalization. Globalization encodes the multiple and varied social, economic, political, as well as cultural processes through which nation-states are traversed and weakened. Contemporary migration is itself deeply implicated in globalization as both a product and part of this process. This book therefore focuses on migrants both as subjects of and participants in the processes of globalization. Our point of departure is to undertake an analysis of migration by questioning the ways in which the formation of classes within capitalist transformation intervenes in the spatial movements of populations. We address this problematic by focusing on the multiple ways in which migrants are produced as political subjects. We do this by problematizing the relationship between political mobilization and the class locations of women and men who must continually negotiate and the social conditions under which they make a living as migrants. In each of the chapters, therefore, the analytics of class are brought to the forefront in studying the question of spatial mobility.

Our concern with class is driven by the ways in which globalization has been conceptualized in the discipline of anthropology. At the risk of oversimplifying, we hazard that there are, at least, two broad approaches to the study of globalization in anthropology. On the one hand, global processes and transformation tend to be emphasized as cultural flows.[1] On the other, globalization is emphasized as a political project of globally imposed marketization (see, for example, Kalb 2005a, Friedman 2003, 2004). It is a matter of argument to suggest which holds more sway. But nonetheless, in the former there is a tendency to focus on culture in globalization and globalization as culture. Where class appears it does so as an afterthought. In the latter approach class appears as a consideration, but it does so among a series of other considerations in a material and historical structural—or world system—view of globalization. While there are notable exceptions to this tendency,[2] few anthropologists have placed class at the forefront of the analysis of globalization. We hazard that this is particularly evident in the studies of globalization and migration that direct our attention toward cultural questions,[3] rather than to questions of how the processes of capitalist transformation produce populations that are differentiated into mobile and non-mobile groups, economically, politically, socially, and also spatially.

Arjun Appadurai (1990, 1996), for example, set the tone for many globalization research agendas with an innovative articulation of the paradoxes of cultural flows that are associated with transnational imaginaries. Following Benedict Anderson's (1983) conceptualization of "imagined communities," such imaginaries are linked to differentiated and disjunctive flows termed *scapes*. This is a metaphor drawn from the idea of landscape with its connotations of vistas, sentiment, memory, and temporality. Appadurai is careful to acknowledge that populations are socially and economically differentiated. He notes too that historical migratory interactions are often initiated by powerful elites; economic transactions, he proposes, are factored into "financescapes." Nonetheless, cultural flows associated with "the image, the imagined, the imaginary" (1996: 31) are given a privileged place in conceptualizing and understanding the movement of commodities, resources, and also of people over space. This model provided a hugely influential yet culturally circumscribed research agenda for translocal scholarship. While we train our sites on Appadurai's work, it is but one example in which studies of globalization and mobility are emphasized as cultural flows and in which class, when acknowledged, appears under the long shadow cast by culture (see also Inda and Rosaldo 2002; Tsing 2002; Ong 1999).

In what we have characterized here as an alternative approach, class appears less as a contingency and is integrated more as a fundamental analytical category stressing the material, structural implications of globalization. For example, anthropologists who have theorized globalization through the analytical lens of historical structuralism have noted that class polarization is in fact embedded into the very nature of globalization processes (Friedman 2003, 2004). Similarly, class is acknowledged in some work and stresses a transnationalist perspective in understanding globalization and migration (Glick Schiller 2004; Olwig 2007). In these approaches migration itself is seen to embody the process of globalization insofar as it is held that this kind of mobility is enabled through the increasing permeability of national borders (Basch, Glick

Schiller, and Szanton Blanc 1994; Szanton Blanc 1997), albeit more so for some would-be migrants than for others (Barber 2008; Cunningham and Heyman 2004). So, increasing numbers of people and the resources they mobilize move with increasing frequency and velocity both within the national context and also internationally (Glick Schiller, Basch, and Szanton Blanc 1992; Glick Schiller 1999). Migration is also seen as a product of globalization. One of the factors that induces increasing numbers to move has been the liberalization of economies to create conditions hospitable to capitalist markets and the development of capitalism itself (see Gledhill 2004; Harvey 2005). Moreover, others have noted that one of the systematic outcomes of globalization is the ongoing proletarianization of the world population, and proletarianization includes the accelerated transformations of the peasantry into informal and mobile labor (Kalb 2005a).[4]

The implications of these observations form the point of departure for our book. Our underlying premise is that the development of capitalism in industry, in agriculture, and the crises intrinsic to capitalist accumulation, foster social and economic differentiation, class polarization, dispossession, and the extrication of people from livelihoods. These forces spur geographic mobility in the form of transregional and also transnational movements of people.[5] We contend that an understanding of the ways in which migrants are embedded in the relations of class while forming part of the class structure of the societies of provenance and also relocation, is critical to apprehending the processes that are involved in the spatial mobility of populations.[6] We also argue that in contending with the formation and accumulation of capital, different classes of migrants—laborers, entrepreneurs, service-sector workers, reserve army of laborers—are further differentiated by gender and racialization and, as such, they engage in confrontations to contest those processes in a multiplicity of ways. The chapters in this book then are dedicated to exploring the complexities of these confrontations as the authors conceptualize migrants, and also their non-mobile counterparts, as members of what Marx might have defined as a relative surplus population (1976: 531–532).

In much of the literature on the anthropology of globalization, claims are made to have liberated the discipline from place-bound studies (Gupta and Ferguson 1997), to have moved beyond what has been called methodological nationalism and the fixation on nations, place, territories, and ties to places (Wimmer and Glick Schiller 2003). Implicit in this view is that the study of mobility in its own right has become unbound and displaced, emphasizing the forces that produce mobility while drawing attention away from forces that produce immobility, or the fixity of people in places (Mintz 2000; Friedman 2004). Class and culture, as well as mobility and the fixity of people in place, are often presented as oppositional lenses though which to view global trans-formations. However, as Zygmunt Bauman (1998) reminds us, a more profound understanding of the global forces at work in contemporary capitalism, in its varying manifestations, requires a consideration of the forces that produce mobility as well as immobility, that produce mi-grants *and* categories of people who remain tied to particular locations. An assessment of globalization and the unevenness of those processes that accompany modernity, including forms of human mobility, so Bau-man asserts, should be counter-posed simultaneously with those whose mobility remains restricted. Speaking of modernity's "outcasts," Bau-man (2004) argues that we should proceed sociologically with atten-tion to the political implications of continuities as well as dislocations. Bauman's insistence on the social, material, and geographic intercon-nectedness between those who are mobile, or aspire to be, and those who remain "condemned" to immobility and perpetual impoverish-ment, provides a powerful antidote to classless narratives of mobility (see also Massey, Goldring, and Durand 1994; and Giles and Narotzky in this volume).

The work of anthropologists who are concerned with the social dy-namics of place-making and social reproduction captures the classed tension between fixity and movement in the geographies of capitalism (Escobar 2001; Kalb 2005a, 2005b; Narotzky and Smith 2006; Sider 2003). For us, these interventions are salutary and they position class with all its complexities—material, social, subjective, and political—in histori-cal and spatial configurations that are amenable to ethnographic enqui-ry. For example, Don Kalb is explicit in calling for a research program that is "theory driven, comparative, and in search of explanations of di-vergent spatial and temporal outcomes of universal processes" (2005b: 176). The chapters in this volume reflect this project. We thus advance the proposition that migration and the forces that produce and shape geographic mobility are also the forces that produce and reproduce class distinctions and differentiations in different locations. Moreover, we suggest that the experiences of those processes in the past and in the present, and in different national contexts, play a significant role in situating migrants within the political space of nations, at the border, and beyond. The ethnographic project of this book then is to examine and illustrate the political implications of continuities and changes in configurations of capital and labor, in livelihoods, and in political ex-pressions. It also illustrates the disruptions, political quiescence, and dislocations, and the way in which global structures and processes condition migrants' mobilization and demobilization. Below we present an outline of the forces that shape contemporary global migration.

Neo-Liberalism and the Anthropology of Migration

Over the past few decades, in anthropology as in many other disciplines, there has been a proliferation of research on migrants and migration (Foner 2003; Kearney and Nagengast 1989; Kivisto and Faist 2007; Portes and DeWind 2007; Sassen 1998; Zlotnik 1998). The upsurge of interest in migration has emerged in response to what is considered by some analysts an unprecedented scale, intensity, and novelty in forms of transnational movements of people in the last half of the twentieth century (Castles and Davidson 2000; Cohen 2006).[7] Referred to as the "age of migration" by some analysts (Castles and Miller 2003), this period of people's heightened mobility across national borders followed on the heels of the oil crisis in the 1970s. The subsequent economic upheavals precipitated a series of transformations linked in discourse and practice to doctrines of neo-liberalism in international political economies. Neo-liberalism is associated with a series of interlocking reforms to impose a relatively standardized vision of a minimalist state and the transformation of state (society) economy relations to accommodate the imperatives of the market (Peck and Tickell 2002). These reforms have resulted in different transformations of the state and varying logics of governance (see, for example, chapter 8) that are adopted both in advanced capitalist contexts and in countries considered to be "developing" (see, for example, chapters 3 and 10). In developing economies it has meant the imposition of structural reforms under the aegis of multilateral institutions such as the World Bank and the International Monetary Fund. Increased spatial fluidity of capital accompanied the rise of a further iteration in the international division of labor (Cohen 2006), represented in geographically decentered production regimes based on flexibility (Harvey 1995, 2005; see also chapters 2, 9, and 10). It has also meant the development of improved telecommunications technology, further facilitating the transnational connectedness of people, along with the mobility of products (see chapter 7). In many economies, the concentration and centralization of enterprises within the framework of the nation-state shifted to the reconcentration and dispersal of economic enterprises across the globe. Mass production in state-regulated enterprises in agriculture and industry diminished in favor of production in small-scale, self-regulated privately run enterprises (Sassen 2001; Tsing 2002). The role of the nation-state as the governor and regulator of economies and polities has been redefined. Emboldened by the ideology of neoliberalism, its role in governance has been adapted to better accommodate the global integration of markets and the attenuation of borders in support of increased capital and trade flows.

Neoliberalism then serves as the dominant ideological rationalization for globalization, which itself includes a array of processes—social, economic, political, and cultural—through which sovereign nation-states are criss-crossed and undermined (Beck 2000; Peck and Tickell 2002). From both within anthropology and outside the discipline, globalization is also thought of as a geopolitical process of the transnationalization of the Western state (in part), colluding with similar though heterogeneous transnationalizations of other states (Kalb 2005b). It is also seen as a fragmentation of nations rather than states, coupled with the dislocation of industrial production (Friedman 2003). Instead of seeing the geopolitical and institutional shifts taking place under globalization as the outcome of a conflict between free markets/economics and the state/politics, such approaches relate these global shifts to transnational class formations that reveal changes in power structures and centers (see Kalb 2006). Transnationalism is seen then as one facet of globalization, where commodities, capital, and also *people* are increasingly moving between nations facilitated by governments subscribing to the ideologies of neoliberalism and the practices of liberalization. This has meant in some cases the revision of national emigration and immigration policies, which once posed barriers and constraints impeding the movement of people across regions and national borders.[8] In other cases it has meant the creation of supranational forms of citizenship and the attenuation of borders in the creation of trade zones, which has resulted in the higher degree of mobility of labor across national borders as transnational migrants.[9]

However, we stress in this book that borders are not necessarily traversed with more ease for all migrants, across the globe. It is evident that those whose provenance is the developing regions of the globe, who seek to work and often to gain citizenship in economically privileged nations, are a clear exception. Exceptions then are marked by class and often national differences. These exceptions are embedded in historical political and economic arrangements stemming from the colonial period and carried on in post-colonial divisions of labor under varying regimes of capital accumulation, be they capital-receiving for the exploitation of local workers, primarily labor exporting, or a mixture of both. As with capital moving offshore in search of malleable, low-cost labor, or "greenfields" (Collins 2003) for production sites, wealthier nations exhibit various specialized labor markets where the demand for "cheapened" immigrant labor is intense and there is no shortage of workers socially, economically, and even culturally predisposed to travel to such insecure, intensively exploitative forms of employment (Cohen 2006; Sassen 1998, 2000; Sayad 2004). Such migration flows, racialized and gender differentiated, are facilitated by both societies of provenance and relocation. And, as always, the bearers of capital (economic, social, and cultural) continue to seek citizenship privileges in multiple locations (Ong 1999, 2006).

The volume of scholarship on migration across the disciplines certainly grew during this "age." However, before the early to mid 1990s, anthropological insights into migration were typically embedded in more comprehensive ethnographic work, not necessarily intended to focus upon migration per se. For example, Margaret Mead's work in New Guinea in the 1930s contained observations about migratory practices (Brettell 2003), but the attention was not analytically sustained. Still, while the volume was small in the pre-1990 period, some ethnographic studies that focused on migration made a significant contribution to the thinking on important questions in the discipline. For example, the pioneering work of Godfrey and Monica Wilson (1968) on the social changes associated with mining in the African Copperbelt contributed important insights into ethnicity, social conflict, and social-network analysis. Similarly, Stuart Philpott's (1973) work on Caribbean migration was a precursor to studies of transnational migration, having been almost unique among early studies of migration that focused on what we have called here societies of provenance and relocation. As many have pointed out, the study of the mobility of people from *place to place* before the 1990s seemed to have been overshadowed by the study of people *in place* (see, for example, Brettell 2000) and the methodological nationalism to which we referred earlier. As Liisa Malkki (1995) has suggested, mobility was eclipsed by a prevailing "sedentarist bias" that ensured the hegemonic status of studies of locality and the local.[10]

This bias inclined many anthropologists to overlook what is crucial for anthropology of migration: the observation made by Eric Wolf in *Europe and the People without History* (1982) that few locales have been untouched historically by the mobility of people.[11] Wolf demonstrated how the powerful and powerless, socially differentiated into different classes of people, have traversed the globe through history. European colonizers and imperialists, compelled by the imperative to accumulate, circumnavigated the globe at least since the fifteenth century, setting in motion the now familiar circuits of people, commodities, information, and ideas. Capital and labor also moved in the past, as in the present. "New laborers" moved to capital while capital itself sloughed off workers in one locale after another, relentlessly seeking new, cheaper sources of labor. As the histories of slave rebellions, peasant uprisings, and worker revolts have shown in the era of the formation of capitalism, and in the contemporary era of the reformulation of capitalism, capital's relation to labor—the relations between classes—has rarely been one of quiet accommodation.

Part I: Configurations of Class

The essays in the first section of the book draw on Marx's notion of class as a relational concept while considering the forces that have produced migrants and refugees as members of the global mobile proletariat. In chapter 1 Wenona Giles calls for the reconceptualization of refugees in studies of migration and forced migration. She argues that refugees must be understood as workers who are often rendered as members of the surplus labor force in capitalist societies and that only through an exploration of the ways in which refugees are actively engaged in making a living through precarious work can the depth of understanding of long-term refugee situations be achieved. Giles's attention then is directed toward the ways in which refugees are incorporated into a subterranean or "illicit' informal economy in urban centers in Iran. The shift in conceptualization also allows an understanding of the work undertaken by refugees as a livelihood strategy that has the political consequence of individualized and sometimes collective struggle against the state of immobility imposed by national refugee regulatory regimes. Josiah Heyman, in chapter 3, also addresses the question of the regulation of mobile populations. He examines the way in which closely enforced rules of movement and residence have produced an important series of subdivisions among working people, between citizen, legal migrant, guest worker, and the unauthorized migrant. In problematizing the notion of "legality" and "illegality," Heyman asks whether such a distinction facilitates the exploitation of Mexican workers at the US border. He further explores the ways in which risk-constituted state-society relations interact with class by considering how the unequal governance *over* and practice *of* movement affects class relations at the US-Mexico border, a border zone where state surveillance and policing is extensive but not omniscient and omnipresent.

Frances Abrahamer Rothstein's essay (chapter 2) also focuses on Mexican migration and the question of the forces that produce certain categories of people as workers. She documents (as does Marie France Labrecque in chapter 10), how globalization in the Mexican case has accelerated the proletarianization of women in an agrarian context. Her long-term transnational study illustrates the principle of "cumulative causation" (Massey, Goldring, and Durand 1994: 1498) in which migration generates new consumption and class aspirations. This process has resulted in an increased flow of women, as workers in their own right, into the United States, a point understated in the current literature, which has tended to view women migrants as wives more than as workers and class subjects.

The conceptualization of migrants as a population differentiated by class is common to all contributions to this volume. Susana Narotzky (chapter 6), Belinda Leach (chapter 9), and Labrecque (chapter 10) all focus on migrants as workers in the industrial capitalism whose experiences and political practices are shaped by a history of working within and contending with forces that situate migrants in deskilled, racialized labor markets and occupational niches. Davide Però (chapter 4), Elisabetta Zontini (chapter 5), and Pauline Gardiner Barber (chapter 7) focus on public and domestic service workers, and Winnie Lem (chapter 8) explores migrants as members of the petty capitalist class. By emphasizing how class acquires a different social and material complexion in one location relative to another (Tilly 2001), we align ourselves with writers who have been concerned with analyzing the consequences of class formation, its politics and transformation in and through spatial processes (see Carbonella 2005; Kalb 1997; Narotzky and Smith 2006; Roseberry 1989; Wolf 1982.) The question of class politics and mobilization is addressed by the essays in part II.

Part II: Migrants and Mobilization

The chapters in this section explore the ways in which migrant agency can be converted into collective action. This is a point that is strongly emphasized by Però in chapter 4. By focusing on the organizations and activities that have been formed among Latin Americans working in the domestic service industry in England, Però points out that in public debate on social integration immigrants have generally been considered objects to be managed, controlled, disciplined, and exploited. The arena of public debate is one that is characterized by a mounting neo-assimilationist and anti-multicultural offensive. This is a theme echoed in citizenship debates throughout Europe, North America, and Australasia. Però argues that both assimilationist and multiculturalist visions of citizenship fail to address the conditions of exploitation under which migrants work. This in fact fosters the act of "misrecognition" of new migrants (see also chapter 1). As Però points out, the issue of exploitation, however constrained by citizenship debates, does not remain in a realm outside the formal political sphere. Popular organization and collective grassroots political movements seek recognition and address the nature of the relations between classes.

Nancy Fraser (2000, 2005) has argued that struggles against misrecognition must be joined with struggles against misrepresentation in seeking social justice (again a point relevant to Giles's chapter). In drawing on this argument the authors in part II (and throughout) explore the possibilities for the translation of particularized concerns of local claims into the broader collective mobilizations of class activism, as well as nationalist claims and struggles for entitlement as denizens within defined polities. They do this by attending to the relationship between such a conversion and the political and geographic continuities as well as locations, and dislocations experienced by migrants. Zontini (chapter 5), for example, attempts to understand the question of how such a translation may occur by focusing on the everyday political actions of Filipino and Moroccan women in two locations, Bologna and Barcelona. She argues that anthropologists and feminist scholars have pressed for a redefinition of the "political" as part of a political project to understand the effectiveness of feminist political strategies. They have done this by offering alternative definitions that reach beyond formal institutions to include broader power relations within the workplace, and family and households. However, despite their efforts there has been a failure to identify the needs and claims of important new actors—migrant women—who live and work within the context of the political and economic changes that are specific to the twenty-first century in contemporary Europe. Her chapter focuses therefore on the main concerns of immigrant women, as well as the different concrete strategies of resistance that are used to improve their everyday conditions. Through her contribution and also in the essays by Narotzky (chapter 6) and Barber (chapter 7), the varied class, gender, and cultural components of identity formation are made explicit as the authors question how and why political struggles and activism may, or indeed may not, be carried forward in border crossings (geographic and social), as well as in different citizenship and migration scenarios.

Narotzky's chapter considers the ways mobility and fixity are articulated in the experience of class and implicated in the production of its conscious political expression. She explores two life histories of women workers to show how material economic conditions and the production of coherence in personal circumstances explain different forms of political activism despite similar migratory experiences. She argues that because of differences in local historical and personal contexts the conditions for and possibility of class resistance and activism were very different in the two women's lives. Her exploration of a nexus of politics, history, experience, and politics is undertaken by using Pierre Bourdieu's idea of "habitus" (Bourdieu 1977). She uses the notion to examine the durable dispositions that condition expectations and provide the tools for envisioning the transformation of existing structures (Bourdieu 2003). In a similar vein, Lem's essay (chapter 8) also uses Bourdieu's idea of habitus. However, she does this to explore the possibilities for living within rather than transforming structures in order to explore the politics of compliance.

In chapter 7 Barber also addresses the question of the politics of compliance. She focuses on the conditions in gendered labor export markets under which Philippine women in domestic service comply with the expectation of docility and subordination, *and* the conditions under which such compliance might translate into defiance. She argues that the individualizing forces of the labor market induce what can be construed as a classed "performance" of compliance. This performance does not necessarily extend beyond the context of the labor market and domestic service. But the consciousness of class, she argues, is also shaped through the staging of the migration process, the experience of labor market deskilling as well as the demoralizing class subjugation associated with the labor process. It is further shaped, so Barber suggests, through the many transnational political dialogues about migration that occur in the diaspora and the Philippines. Still, the translation from subordinated subjectivity to militant political expression is extremely difficult as the compliant face of class is more visible. Barber illustrates the ways in which this consciousness is reinforced through the stretching of the demands of familial social reproduction across a transnational social field to the overseas workplace of commodified domestic labor. But also, she identifies the possibilities for migrants' alternative understandings through consideration of how cellular phone technologies enhance the capacities for organized and personal resistance by Filipino workers while also contributing to the contentious reproduction of the migrant labor force.

The essays by Zontini (5), Narotzky (6), and Barber (7) in this section and the chapters by Labrecque (10) and Rothstein (2) all draw on and illuminate issues raised in the current discussion on the feminization of migration (Hondagneu-Sotelo 1994; Jones-Correa 1998; Pessar and Mahler 2003; Piper 2008; Werbner 1999). In this body of literature class is often acknowledged as a feature of gendered migration worthy of further attention. However, attention to it is sometimes more cursory than sustained. In much feminist work that focuses on the production of global commodities, attention is directed at the forms of subordination experienced by the women migrants *qua* women than as migrants and members of the laboring classes (see, for example, Anderson 2000; Ehrenreich and Hochschild 2003; Parreñas 2001; Sassen 2000). Class is elided into other social forms of collective identity. Moreover, it is the disciplining qualities of the emotionally charged labor processes of care-giving work, particularly when it is home-based, combined with

gendered cultural politics favoring feminized docility and familial loyalty, which have enabled the elision of class in the ethnographic literature on women migrants.[12] Migration research including the work on the
feminization of migration, then, often risks becoming preoccupied with
narrowly constituted discourses about disciplining migrants whether as
women, or as neoliberal subjects and citizens.

In this book we focus too on the forces that produce disciplined
workers, but we place an emphasis on power and the class-like dynamics of familistic regimes. Such power dynamics become transformed
and may under certain political and social conditions be carried across
transnational (and intranational) borders. Rothstein suggests that in the
case of Mexican women migrants, they do not. She argues that women
must be seen as full agents for purposes of migration because they
take initiative in intra- and international migration and because of this
are able to elude the regimes of family and male power. By contrast,
Lem (8) observes that younger Chinese women in France find themselves contending with patriarchal conditions of the familistic enterprise. In these regimes the power of elder males to command and control is ideologically and materially supported by, although not produced
by, the prevailing political economy of neoliberalism. These issues are
further investigated in the chapters by Barber (7), Zontini (5), Narotzky
(6), and also Leach (9). Our interventions here represent an attempt to
reconceptualize the social process of migration and its connection to
dynamics of power in relation to class formation, as well as gender and
ethno-racial formation. This analytical framework, we propose, illumi-
nates the ways in which women and young adults contend with the expressions of patriarchal control and capitalist discipline over their labor
power in migration under post-Fordist capitalism (see also Nonini 1997;
Ong and Nonini 1997).

With our emphasis on placing class at the forefront of research into
power, discipline, and gender in divisions of labor, we contribute, in our
view, a necessary analytical dimension to the body of literature on the
feminization of migration. Toward this end, we address not only the class
complexities that attend disciplining regimes but also how such regimes
inhibit, deflect, or provide opportunities for activism. This focus unites
the papers in the third section of the book.

Part III: Complicity and Compliance

This volume advances our premise that any instance of activism and also
its absence requires the problematization of the politics and economics

of its production and reproduction. Leach (chapter 9), for example, discusses the mechanisms that impose discipline in the context of the auto industry in Canada. Her analysis focuses on the forces that produce the acquiescence of different groups of migrants to labor-process discipline and she suggests that this must be understood as produced by the neoliberal transformations that have impinged upon the work context. By detailing these processes and locating the different histories of migration to Canada in different periods of the development of Canadian capitalism, Leach argues that because older histories of migrations have come to be privileged in working-class culture, they subordinate and emphasize the differences, rather than similarities, in histories of dispossession. Their class-based, masculinist, and nationalist ideologies bolster neoliberal agendas and pave the way for super-exploitation and the pitting of worker against worker with a resulting antagonism between immigrants and non-immigrants. Such negative interactions mitigate the practice of class-based politics. Leach's contribution then explores the ways in which the disciplinary regimes of neoliberalism promote docility and passivism while repressing defiance and activism.

While Leach explores the question of its absence, Lem (chapter 8; and to some extent Narotzky and Barber discussed above) provides examples of the contingency of militancy. The chapters by Leach and Lem both address the question of the political and economic changes that produce contentiousness in some cases and quiescence in others. Lem's chapter explores the political and economic conditions that produce compliance and contention among different classes of migrants in urban France. Noting that neither Chinese migrants nor the French-born children of Chinese migrants participated in the urban protests and demonstrations in France in the fall of 2005 and spring of 2006, Lem addresses the problem of the political quiescence among certain denizens of France. She does this by examining the relationship between livelihood and citizenship. From her observations about the organization and ideology of petty entrepreneurship, she argues that in neoliberal regimes petty capitalism and entrepreneurship are seen as a means by which immigrants can become integrated into host societies and disciplined into citizens. It is both encouraged by the state and often taken up by migrants themselves in the face of exclusion and discrimination in the labor market. Lem argues that under neoliberalism, such strategies for promoting integration and civic participation also ultimately produce political submission and docility in the face of exploitation, with the end result of an erosion of the entitlements of citizenship. Leach, Lem, and also Narotzky (chapter 6) all shed light on the ways in which history and experience are linked to political mobility and also immobility.

The question of history and experience is also discussed by Labrecque in chapter 10. In a comparison between Chihuahua and Yucatán, Labrecque shows how in a globalized economy, the transnational capital underlying *maquiladoras* is able to adjust to the sociohistorical specificities of different places and to turn to its advantage some of the changes currently underway. In the two states compared here, the processes of fragmentation and segmentation of the labor force—which are both causes and effects of worker demobilization—were already well underway and even quite advanced when the maquiladoras arrived, either because of corporatist unionism or *charro* (in the case of Chihuahua) or because of the negative reputation that unionism had earned itself because of charro (in the Yucatán). In this sense, to answer the question laid out in the beginning of this chapter, worker demobilization clearly cannot be explained by new forms of work organization alone; rather demobilization may explain why these new forms were introduced into maquiladoras in the first place. As to whether unionism is obsolete in maquiladoras, the question must be reformulated in Mexico taking into account corporatist unionism or charro.

Conclusion

In this volume we contend that class relations and class politics under contemporary capitalism and the transformation glossed as globalization are rendered more complex through the process of migration. The classed character of the process of migration and understanding migrant livelihoods is merely the starting point for a critical examination of how migration and class are mutually constitutive, in complex ways. Our concerns over the deficit of examining class relations in migration and class mobilizations apply beyond the discipline of anthropology to migration studies in general.[13] But it is beyond the scope of this volume to review the paradigms of migration studies in other disciplines. Within our own, a critical transnational perspective (see Glick Schiller 2006) has been important in examining the question of how class travels and the consequences that this has for the political mobilization of migrants. However, to return to the insights offered by Andreas Wimmer and Nina Glick Schiller (2003), methodological nationalism has persisted through several iterations of transnational scholarship and a "communitarian" bias often prevails in this body of work. This bias, so they argue, produces the tendency to over-represent the commonality of migrants' experiences. It is a methodological procedure that replicates a bounded community logic supposedly dislodged through the translocal orientation of studies following the conceptualization presented in the work of theorists of globalization and culture. In our effort to analyze the experiences of migrants differentiated by class, we hope to have circumnavigated the fallacy of methodological nationalism in studies of migration. Moreover, it is by now abundantly clear that the focus of this volume is on migrants as subjects of history and all the authors have been concerned to explore the agency of migrants as classed subjects. The ethnographic examples recorded here serve as ballast to a tendency to present migrants as objects of abstract political and economic forces made concrete in the disciplinary regimes of states and economies,[14] and we explore the engagements of migrants socially, politically, and economically in the contemporary world of neoliberalism.

Our attempt to place class and class analysis at the forefront in anthropological studies of migration and indeed globalization is part of a program that calls for a regalvanization of considerations of class in analytical frameworks in anthropology. Kalb (2005a), among others,[15] suggests, for example, that this program must avoid a reductionist reading of class a priori as a form of consciousness determined by relations to the means of production. Rather it should be thoroughly investigated through an ethnographic research program of historically sensitive local-global enquiry.[16] By making this inquiry in this volume we take a step toward moving class out from the shadow of culture.

Notes

1. See, for example, Appadurai (1990, 1996), and also the articles in Inda and Rosaldo (2002).
2. Some exceptions to this in anthropological studies of migration are Ong and Nonini (1997), Rouse (1995), Heyman (2001), Barber (2004, 2008), and Lem (2007).
3. At least until the middle of the twenty-first century.
4. According to Zhang (2003: 162) the proletarianization of peasants is a long-term phenomenon. In 2001 China's population of rural laborers was estimated to be 482 million and 382 million were engaged in agricultural production. That number is expected to increase by over 8 million over the next five years and about 150 million rural laborers are not employed. From 2001 to 2010 there will be 63.5 million new rural laborers and joining the WTO will result in the loss of at least 20 million jobs in agriculture.
5. This discussion draws on Lem (2007) and was written during the economic turmoil caused by the global financial crisis of 2008–2009.
6. We prefer to use the terms "societies of provenance and relocation" over "sending and receiving countries" and "countries of immigration and emigration" or "destination" counties to signal the complexity, multidirectionality, and often impermanence of the global movement of populations. This also avoids the mechanist implications of neoclassicism in theories of migration (see, for example, Borjas 1989).

7. There is in general a lack of agreement over these issues. Foner (2000), for example, argues that the forms that contemporary migration takes are not novel. On the question of scale there also tends to be some disagreement. Staring (2000), for example, has argued and presented empirical evidence to show that in scalar terms, contemporary migration shows continuity with the past.

8. One example is the case of China, where the relaxation of national restrictions on emigration and population mobility within the country has accompanied the country's transition to a market economy.

9. In Europe, of course, the emergence of the Schengen Agreement in the context of the expanding European Union has permitted the freer movement of people within its boundaries.

10. While there is a case to be made that a turning point in the volume of studies of migration in anthropology was made in the 1970s with the publication of *Migration and Anthropology* edited by Robert Spencer, as Brettell (2000) notes, its impact on the discipline was rather narrow. Later works authored by Glick Schiller, Basch, and Szanton Blanc (1992); Glick Schiller (1999, 2006); Gamburd (2000); and Rouse (1995) had a broader impact both within and beyond the discipline of anthropology in part due to the problematization of locality in terms of migration and setting this current "age of migration" in the context of global history.

11. This is a point that is also made by Mintz (1998).

12. Exceptions to this are present in the work of Barber (2004, 2008); Gamburd (2000); George (2005); and Gibson, Law, and McKay (2001).

13. Apart from the well-known work of Sassen (1998), Sennett (1998), and others concerned to link migration, political economy, and issues in contemporary capitalism, there is often an emphasis on the regulation of migration, the disciplining regimes of citizenship, and the management of migration. For an overview of theoretical approaches to migration studies see Castles and Miller (2003) and Massey (1993; et al. 1999).

14. This tendency appears less in anthropological work than in studies of migration that appear in economics, political science, and sociology. For an overview of some of this work see, for example, Hammar et al. (1997).

15. For a recent commentary on this see *Anthropology News* 47 (8), November 2006.

16. Tilly (2001: 299) concluded that anthropology had "lost its prominence as a source of general ideas about inequality" when he located only 19 out of 337 essays discussing this topic in the *Annual Review of Anthropology* from 1984 to 2000.

References

Anderson, Benedict. 1983. *Imagined Communities*. London: Verso.

Anderson, Bridget. 2000. *Doing the Dirty Work? The Global Politics of Domestic Labour*. London: Zed Books.

Appadurai, Arjun. 1990. "Disjuncture and Difference in the Global Economy." *Public Culture* 2 (2): 1–24.

———. 1996. *Modernity at Large: Cultural Dimensions of Globalization*. Minneapolis: University of Minnesota Press.

Barber, Pauline Gardiner. 2004. "Contradictions of Class and Consumption When the Commodity is Labour." *Anthropologica* 46: 203–218.

———. 2008. "The Ideal Immigrant? Gendered Class Subjects in Philippine–Canada Migration." *Third World Quarterly* 29 (7): 1265–1285.

Gamburd, Michelle. 2000. *The Kitchen Spoon's Handle: Transnationalism and Sri Lanka's Migrant Housemaids*. Ithaca: Cornell University Press.

George, Sheba Mariam. 2005. *When Women Come First: Gender and Class in Transnational Migration*. Berkeley: University of California Press.

Gibson, Katherine, Lisa Law, and Deirdre McKay. 2001. "Beyond Heroes and Victims: Filipina Contract Migrants, Economic Activism and Class Transformations." *International Feminist Journal of Politics* 3 (3): 365–396.

Gille, Zsuzsa, and Seán Ó Riain. 2002. "Global Ethnography." *Annual Review of Sociology* 28: 271–295.

Gledhill, John. 2004. "Neoliberalism." In *A Companion to the Anthropology of Politics*, eds. David Nugent and Joan Vincent, 332–348. Oxford: Blackwell Publishing.

Glick Schiller, Nina. 1999. "Transmigrants and Nation-States: Something Old and Something New in the U.S. Immigrant Experience." In *The Handbook of International Migration: The American Experience*, eds. Charles Hirschman, Philip Kasintiz, and Josh DeWind, 94–119. New York: Russell Sage Foundation.

———. 2004. "Transnationality." In *A Companion to the Anthropology of Politics*, eds. David Nugent and Joan Vincent, 448–467. Oxford: Blackwell Publishing.

———. 2006. "Introduction: What can Transnational Studies Offer the Analysis of Localized Conflict and Protest." *Focaal: European Journal of Anthropology* 47: 3–17.

Glick Schiller, Nina, Linda Basch, and Cristina Szanton Blanc, eds. 1992. "Towards a Transnational Perspective on Migration: Race, Class, Ethnicity and Nationalism Reconsidered." *Annals of the New York Academy of Sciences* Vol. 645 (July).

Gupta, Akhil, and James Ferguson, eds. 1997. *Anthropological Locations: Boundaries and Grounds of a Field Science*. Berkeley: University of California Press.

Hammar Tomas, et al., eds. 1997. *International Migration, Immobility and Development: Multidisciplinary Perspectives*. Oxford and New York: Berg.

Harvey, David. 1995. "Globalization in Question." *Rethinking Marxism* 8 (4): 1–17.

———. 2005. *A Brief History of Neoliberalism*. Oxford: Oxford University Press.

Heyman, Josiah. 2001. "Class and Classification at the U.S.-Mexico Border." Human Organization 7 (1).

Hondagneu-Sotelo, Pierrette. 1994. *Gendered Transitions: Mexican Experiences of Immigration*. Los Angeles: University of California Press.

Inda, Jonathan Xavier, and Renato Rosaldo, eds. 2002. *The Anthropology of Globalization: A Reader*. Oxford: Blackwell.

Jones-Correa, Michael. 1998. "Different Paths: Gender, Immigration and Political Participation." *International Migration Review* 32 (2): 326–349.

Kalb, Don. 1997. *Expanding Class: Power and Everyday Politics in Industrial Communities, the Netherlands, 1850–1950*. Durham: Duke University Press.

———. 2005a. "'Bare Legs Like Ice': Recasting Class for Local/Global Inquiry." In *Critical Junctions: Anthropology and History Beyond the Cultural Turn*, eds. Don Kalb and Herman Tak, 109–133. New York: Berghahn Books.

———. 2005b. "From Flows to Violence: Politics and Knowledge in the Debates on Globalization and Empire." *Anthropological Theory* 5 (2): 176–204.

———. 2006. "Stones through the Window." *American Anthropologist* 108 (3): 524–528.

Kearney, Michael, and Carol Nagengast. 1989. *Anthropological Perspectives on Transnational Communities in Rural California*. Davis: California Institute for Rural Studies.

Kivisto, Peter, and Thomas Faist. 2007. *Citizenship: Discourse, Theory and Transnational Prospects*. Malden and Oxford: Blackwell.

Lem, Winnie. 2007. "William Roseberry, Class and Inequality in the Anthropology of Migration." *Critique of Anthropology* 27 (4).

Malkki Liisa H. 1995. "Refugees and Exile: From Refugee Studies to the National Order of Things." *Annual Review of Anthropology* 24: 495–523.

Marx, Karl. 1976. *Capital*, Vol. 1. London: Pelican

Massey, Doreen. 1994. *Space, Place and Gender.* Minneapolis: University of Minnesota Press.

Massey, Douglas, et al. 1993. "Theories of International Migration: A Review and Appraisal." *Population and Development Review* 19.

———, et al. 1998. *Worlds in Motion: Understanding International Migration at the End of The Millennium.* Oxford: Clarendon.

Massey, Douglas, Luin Goldring, and Jorge Durand. 1994. "Continuities in Transnational Migration: An Analysis of Nineteen Mexican Communities." *American Sociological Review* 99: 1492–1533.

Mintz, Sidney, 1998. "The Localization of Anthropological Practice: From Area Studies to Transnationalism." *Critique of Anthropology* 18 (2): 117–133.

———. 2000. "Sows' Ears and Silver Linings: A Backward Look at Ethnography." *Current Anthropology* 42 (2): 169–90.

Narotzky, Susana, and Gavin Smith. 2006. *Immediate Struggles: People, Power and Place in Rural Spain.* Berkeley: University of California Press.

Nonini, Donald. 1997. "Shifting Identities, Positioned Imaginaries: Transnational Traversals and Reversals." In *Ungrounded Empires: The Cultural Politics of Modern Chinese Transnationalism*, eds. Aihwa Ong and Donald Nonini, 1997. New York: Routledge.

Olwig, Karen Fog. 2007. *Caribbean Journeys: An Ethnography of Migration and Home in Three Family Networks.* Durham: Duke University Press.

Ong, Aihwa. 1999. *Flexible Citizenship: The Cultural Logics of Transnationality.* Durham: Duke University Press.

———. 2006. *Neo-Liberalism as Exception: Mutations in Citizenship and Sovereignty.* Durham: Duke University Press.

Ong, Aihwa, and Donald Nonini, eds. 1997. *Ungrounded Empires: The Cultural Politics of Modern Chinese Transnationalism.* New York: Routledge.

Parreñas, Rachel. 2001. *Servants of Globalization: Women, Migration, and Domestic Work.* Stanford: Stanford University Press.

Peck, Jamie, and Adam Tickell. 2002. "Neoliberalizing Space." *Antipode* 34 (3): 380–404.

Pessar, Patricia, and Sarah Mahler. 2003. "Transnational Migration: Bringing Gender In." *International Migration Review* 37 (3): 812–846.

Philpott, Stuart. 1973. *West Indian Migration.* London: University of London Press.

Piper, Nicola, ed. 2008. *New Perspectives on Gender and Migration: Livelihood, Rights and Entitlements.* New York: Routledge.

Portes, Alejandro, and Josh DeWind, eds. 2007. *Rethinking Migration: New Theoretical and Empirical Perspectives.* New York and Oxford: Berghahn Books.

Roseberry, William. 1989. *Anthropologies and Histories: Essays in Culture, History, and Political Economy.* New Brunswick: Rutgers University Press.

Rouse, Roger. 1995. "Thinking through Transnationalism: Notes on the Cultural Politics of Class Relations in the Contemporary United States." *Public Culture* 7: 353–342.

Sassen, Saskia. 1998. *Globalization and its Discontents: Essays on the New Mobility of People and Money.* New York: The New Press.

———. 2000. "Women's Burden: Counter-Geographies of Globalization and the Feminization of Survival." *Journal of International Affairs* 563 (2): 503–524.

———. 2001. "Spatialities and Temporalities of the Global: Elements for a Theorization." In *Globalization*, ed. Arjun Appadurai, 260–278. Durham: Duke University Press.

Sayad, Abdelmalek. 2004. *The Suffering of the Immigrant.* Cambridge: Polity Press.

Sennett, Richard. 1998. *The Corrosion of Character: The Personal Consequences of Work in the New Capitalism*. New York: W.W. Norton and Co.

Sider, Gerald. 2003. *Between History and Tomorrow: Making and Breaking Everyday Life in Rural Newfoundland*. Peterborough: Broadview Press.

Staring, Richard. 2000. "Flows of People: Globalization, Migration, and Transnational Communities." In *The Ends of Globalization: Bringing Society Back In*, eds. Don Kalb et al., 203–215. Lanham: Rowman & Littlefield Publishers, Inc.

Szanton Blanc, Cristina, ed. 1997. *Towards a Transnational Perspective on Migration: Race, Class, Ethnicity and Nationalism Reconsidered*. New York: New York Academy of Sciences.

Tilly, Charles. 2001. "Introduction: Anthropology Confronts Inequality." *Anthropological Theory* 1 (3): 299–306.

Tsing, Anna. 2002. "The Global Situation." In *The Anthropology of Globalization: A Reader*, eds. Jonathan Xavier Inda and Renato Rosaldo, 453–485. Malden: Blackwell.

Werbner, Pnina. 1999. "Political Motherhood and the Feminization of Citizenship: Women's Activism and the Transformation of the Public Sphere." In *Women, Citizenship and Difference*, eds. N. Nira Yuval-Davis and Pnina Werbner, 221–245. London: Zed Books.

Wilson, Godfrey, and Monica Wilson. 1968. *The Analysis of Social Change: Based on Observations in Central Africa*. Cambridge: Cambridge University Press.

Wimmer, Andreas, and Nina Glick Schiller. 2003. "Methodological Nationalism, the Social Sciences, and the Study of Migration: An Essay in Historical Epistemology." *The International Migration Review* 37 (3): 576–610.

Wolf, Eric. 1982. *Europe and the People without History*. Berkeley: University of California Press.

Zhang, Mei 2003. *China's Poor Regions: Rural Urban Migration, Poverty, Economic reform and Urbanization*. London: Routledge Curzon

Zlotnik, Hania. 1998. "International Migration 1965–1996: An Overview." *Population and Development Review* 24 (3): 469–510.

Part I

Configurations of Class

— *Chapter 1* —

LIVELIHOOD AND AFGHAN REFUGEE WORKERS IN IRAN

Wenona Giles

In many parts of the world today, refugees work illegally in vulnerable types of jobs that pay low wages. Tied to specific locations for extended periods, they are among the most precarious workers globally. It is difficult to say which group—those within refugee camps or without—is worse off. Both groups of refugees confront continuing processes of imperialism and "empirism" manifest in the geopolitics of their home and "host" countries. However, the geopolitical and spatial separation that exists in the world today conceals the fact that many refugees are also workers. The relationship between forced exile and the international organization of labor relations reveals itself more clearly, when we link so-called refugee issues to globalization. This approach also allows for an exploration of class inflexions on global geopolitical arrangements, specifically those related to industrial militarism and international corporate capital. It is important to state herein my agreement with Inderpal Grewal (2005: 169), Liisa Malkki (1995), and others concerning the ways in which a "refugee crisis" cloaks or mystifies the more fundamental crises generated by global forms of industrial militarism.

Globalization is described in a variety of ways.[1] Cindi Katz's definition is among the most relevant for this essay. She includes several phenomena in her definition that are important to my focus on class and livelihood: labor, uneven development, and spatial scales. Katz writes: "Globalization has been the signature dish of capitalism—a system of social relations of production and reproduction nourished by uneven development across a range of spatial scales from the local or regional to the national or supranational" (2001: 1213). Globalization and its associated politico-economic wars have affected some groups of people more negatively than others. Those who have been in long-term exile situations, inside and outside of camps, in poor regions of the world are among the more seriously affected by these militarized conflicts. And, as Henk Overbeek points out, the political and the economic coincide in the refugee (1995: 27): "Political violence is often triggered by worsening economic conditions, and economic hardship often results from the exercise of repressive political power, thus relegating the distinction between the political and economic migrant, or between the forced and the voluntary migrant to the realm of ideology and manipulation." Zygmunt Bauman's "far-away locals" (1998: 76) are those who are deprived, degraded, and feared in a globalized world in which "mobility is the main stratifying factor" (2). He argues that the denial of mobility—of mass migration—to the poor majority of the world, to places where food and livelihood may be more plentiful, is an essential part of globalization. Paradoxically, corporate globalizers must deny freedom of movement to the majority of the world's population, while eulogizing mobility "as the topmost achievement of the globalizing world" (76). In chapter 3 of this volume Josiah Heyman argues that while "the pattern of perils in mobility affects a wider range of crucial resources and relationships," mobility poses great risk for the undocumented workers' lives that he explores. The travel of immigrants and refugees is described by Bauman as surreptitious, dangerous, and often "illegal" travel, through "the walls built of immigration controls, of residence laws," etc. (1998: 89). The spatial and bureaucratic alienation of refugees is one side of Janus-faced globalization; the other side is the way the global resonates with the local.

Forced migrations generate complex social relations. For example, in many countries those defined as *refugees* have formerly been migrant or temporary workers from neighboring regions and these earlier migrations were marked by class, gender, and ethnic relations that may or may not spill over to periods of forced migration. A series of wars marks some countries (e.g. Afghanistan, Lebanon, the region of the former Yugoslavia), each conflict expelling different ethnic and class groups from their homes. Thus definitions and descriptions of forced migrants defy the substitution of a homogeneous refugee victim discourse with that of a unitary definition of class. For example, educated, middle-class refugees often find their lives (and class relationships) further downgraded because of shifts in policy and attitudes toward refugees in the country of exile.

Until recently the principal focus of forced migration research has mainly pertained to issues concerning recognition and representation, particularly as these relate to legal status and cultural identity. Not enough attention has been paid to redistribution and thus also to class. This chapter focuses on class, work, and livelihood among refugees, cognizant that the other two realms of research (i.e. recognition and representation) are also important. The case of long-term refugee situations constitutes the main focus of this essay; in particular, the situation of Afghan refugees in Iran provides an anchor for my theoretical approach. Afghans in Iran present a challenging circumstance, due not only to the diverse nature of their migrations, which include seasonal work-related migrants, religious exiles, and forced migrants. In addition, government policies concerning these several migrant groups overlap, as do their everyday livelihood strategies. Thus Overbeek's argument above, regarding political and economic migration, applies equally to the case of Afghan refugees in Iran, wherein the situation of "refugees" is often indistinguishable from other types of migrants who also lack rights.

Targets of Anguish

The size of the group broadly defined as *refugees* has increased rapidly as anguish over personal safety and security has intensified, leading up to and following 9/11. Bauman argues, "Refugees have become . . . the epitome of that extraterritoriality in which the roots of the present-day precariousness of the human condition—first on the list of present-day human fears and anxieties—are sunk" (2002: 85). The continuing expansion of this extraterritorial group is related to the production of social fear. As it becomes increasingly difficult for those fleeing violence and other disasters to access asylum in the West, and in the continued absence of a political strategy (84)—short of all-out invasion and war—to assist these "foreigners," refugees have become a ready target of Western fear.

There are now significant numbers of refugees (as defined by the United Nations) and internally displaced populations living in long-term refugee situations and eking out bare livelihoods in the world today. At the end of 2008, 8.5 million worldwide had been sequestered for ten years or more in long-term refugee situations (i.e., in refugee camps or beyond; USCRI 2009a). This is 63 percent of the 2008 global refugee population of 13.5 million (USCRI 2009b). These refugees fall under the 1951 UN Refugee Convention definition. In addition, there are now 25 million people who are defined as *internally displaced* (IDPs), who have been ousted from their homes and local communities due to civil wars, but who remain within their home country borders.[2] These refugees and IDPs are among the most insecure people in the world today. There are now thirty-three so-called protracted refugee situations[3] in the world (exile of five or more years) according to the United Nations High Commissioner for Refugees (UNHCR; Campbell 2006) and these are "growing in number and lasting longer without being resolved" (Loescher and Milner 2005: 154).

The location of the majority of refugees in poorer regions of the world demonstrates the linkage between the global economics of wealth and a Western culture of fear. This global space of wealth and fear is reflected in the dialectical relationship between uneven development and the locality of refugee-like situations. Uneven development on a global scale is a result of imperial and neo-imperial relations of power, combined with the more recent expansion of "international trade in goods and services based on the concept of 'comparative advantage'" (Ellwood 2002: 14–15). Ensuing inequalities have left some regions and peoples of the world exposed to impoverishment. Poverty exacerbates conditions of forced migration and exile, no matter which economic class, ethnic group, or gender is involved.

This is not a new argument but the depth and persistence of this relationship bears revisiting. Even the UN has pointed out that less-developed countries are both the major source and destination of refugees: 86 percent of refugees originated in these areas and 72 percent of the world's refugees are provided with asylum in these regions (UNHCR 2002: 24–25). Countries in the West admit a minority of the world's refugees and would like to keep it that way. For example, in 2008 Canada accepted 10,804 people who were defined as "bona fide" refugees from abroad and these were among the almost 14 million defined as "in need of protection" at that time, worldwide (this latter figure does not include internally displaced populations; USCRI 2009c, USCRI 2009b). The care of refugees in developing regions "implies a significant additional cost to an already fragile economy" in most cases (UNHCR 2002: 65). The economic effects of hosting refugees (numbers of refugees in relation to economic resources) "are mostly felt in Africa"—in particular, Sierra Leone, DR Congo, Tanzania, Ethiopia, Burundi, Rwanda, Eritrea. Pakistan, Syria, and Iran are among the principal countries outside Africa where "the economic impact of refugees on the local economy is significant" (UNHCR 2002: 65; USCRI 2008: 29). This separation—both geographical and bureaucratic—between wealthy, industrialized countries and those pushed into exile by war, development-induced displacement,[4] and environmental disasters may increase into the future with the establishment of new "zones of protection" (Isin and Rygiel 2007; Hyndman and Giles forthcoming 2010). Two types of zones have been promoted by the European Commission, Denmark, the Netherlands (Betts and Milner 2006), and Australia (Hyndman and Mountz 2008): third country processing centers (e.g., Eastern Europe) and regional protection areas, normally close to countries of refugees' origins (e.g., the Great Lakes region of Africa; Hyndman and Giles forthcoming).

I will address the matter of Afghans in Iran below—suffice it to say here that Iran has its own serious problems related to high unemployment and poverty,[5] as well as other well-known geopolitical struggles with the

West. Despite this socioeconomic situation, Iran accepted the third largest number of refugees in the world in 2006 and 2007[6]—mostly from Afghanistan and Iraq (USCRI 2007; USCRI 2008: 29). In 2004 Iran was described as the main asylum country in the world by the World Food Program (WFP)—accounting for 11 percent of all those under the UNHCR's mandate. By far, the largest group of exiles in Iran is Afghans. In 2007 there were 915,000 registered Afghans and an estimated 1 million unregistered Afghans living in Iran (Ashrafi 2007: 1).

The large number of stateless people living in exile outside their countries of origin for long periods of time and the fact of their location in poor regions of the world are interrelated global phenomena that are evocative of Bauman's description of prisons as sites of "forcible perpetuation of estrangement" (1998: 106). Today, solitary confinement in prisons—and he gives the example of Pelican Bay Prison in the US—means that it doesn't matter what inmates do in their cells (because they do little beyond eating and defecating; 108). "What *does matter* is that *they stay there*" (113; emphasis in original). Many long-term refugee situations are extreme sites of spatial confinement that immobilize and estrange the other, isolating them from productive, mobile lives. What is important to wealthier regions of the world is that the great majority of refugees stay where they are.

Vicious Circles:
Politics, Economics, and Status

By way of providing a theoretical context, I refer to research by Nancy Fraser regarding globalization and justice. Her work is helpful in thinking through a methodology for the study of the refugee situation in the world today. Fraser argues that there are three intertwined dimensions that are of concern in social justice claims: redistribution, recognition, and representation. She writes: "Efforts to overcome injustice cannot, except in rare cases, address themselves to just one dimension. Rather struggles against maldistribution and misrecognition cannot succeed unless they are joined with struggles against misrepresentation—and vice versa. Where one puts the emphasis, of course, is both a tactical and a strategic decision" (2005: 79). Following Fraser, I am arguing for a methodology in which all three—recognition, representation, and redistribution—inform one another in research and policy on refugees. What is missing in refugee research and policy perspectives, in any significant way today, is attention to redistribution, which includes, for example, mobile access to productive, protected, and so-called legal forms of work, wages, and self-support. Let me first define what I mean by these three areas as they pertain to refugees and forced migrants and thus their importance to my study of refugees as a workers.

To date, legal and cultural recognition has played a major role in research and policy analysis, as well as in the development of remedies to misrecognition or status subordination (Fraser 2000: 113). Fraser refers to a "status model" of recognition whereby injustice is redressed via "a politics aimed at overcoming subordination" toward full membership in the society in which one lives (113). Refugees easily fit Fraser's definition of a misrecognized group, i.e., those who have been "denied the status of a full partner in social interaction, as a consequence of institutionalized patterns of cultural value that constitute one as comparatively unworthy of respect or esteem" (113–114). The rectification of the subordinate status of refugees has been a principal goal of national and international humanitarian and human rights instruments, interventions, and policies. Exclusion, stigmatization, and violent policing practices as these pertain to a particular group are examples of the denial of recognition (114). Sequestration to refugee camps, lack of access to education or livelihood, and control of mobility and travel are some examples of misrecognition that pertain to many stateless extraterritorial groups. The goal of the status model of recognition is always "reciprocal recognition and status equality" (114). The extent to which these are achievable goals is dependent on possibilities and developments around refugee representation and economic redistribution. A focus solely on recognition tends to treat refugees as passive recipients of remedies and is often linked to homogenous definitions of refugees as victims.

The nature of the refugee situation in which people lose access to their original citizenship and experience exclusion from any political community has led to questions and research about representation. Fraser describes this as the political dimension of justice, which concerns the existence of space to express "their claims and adjudicate their disputes" (2005: 75). For refugees this space is extremely delimited, particularly so if they are located in refugee camps, but also when they are living outside of camps as part of a precarious workforce. The issue of the "voice" of refugees has been raised in research and policy on refugees; i.e., where can refugees safely air their concerns; who represents refugees; are some groups of refugees completely denied the possibility of expressing their rights? In her discussion of representation, Fraser refers to the extreme case of those who are "excluded from membership in any political community. . . . Deprived of the possibility of authoring first-order claims, they become non-persons with respect to justice" (77). This definition certainly seems to "fit" the situation of most long-term refugees. However, even in totalitarian situations, some refugees manage to find spaces of political protest, whether covert and therefore important, but less effective, or on more public terrain. Despite ever-diminishing margins of freedom, is it expectations of a better future that encourage resistance to exploitation among some refugees (as per Susana Narotzky's discussion of Bourdieu's *habitus* in chapter 6). Narotzky argues that the more uncertainty in people's lives, the less likely they will be able to orient themselves toward future expectations, as in the cases of women migratory workers in Spain that she explores. In the case of refugees who resist, are their expectations linked to hopeful lingering memories from past lives or to the dire sequestered certainty of their present lives?

Consider, for example, the plight of Sudanese refugees in Cairo. Sudanese refugees have been relocating to Egypt for almost two decades (during the nineteen-year civil war in Sudan). Media reports describe large numbers of Sudanese refugees who have been living in exile in Cairo and demonstrating for the right to resettle elsewhere than Egypt and Sudan. Egypt opposes any integration of refugees into Egypt and considers Sudanese and other refugees to be temporarily located within its borders. On 30 December 2005, hundreds of Sudanese were attacked by Egyptian police after protesting for months that the UNHCR had refused to hear their cases for third country resettlement. They do not want to return to Sudan where they believe that they will face violence, poverty, or both. Sudanese make up the largest refugee group in Egypt. The UNHCR regards Sudan as being in a post-conflict situation, is encouraging refugees to return, and had stopped processing Sudanese for resettlement elsewhere. Media images portray Sudanese refugees standing defiantly in their makeshift urban protest camp while Egyptian security troops fire water cannons on them before storming the camp, assaulting, and killing a number of refugees. In the months that followed the protest, the UNHCR agreed to open up interviews pertaining to the resettlement of Sudanese refugees.

The inability to participate fully with others as peers due to economic circumstances pertains to the dimension of redistribution. Globalization and its attendant economic relations of militarization and restructuring is a causal factor in the creation of so-called refugees (through war and other disasters) and their attendant economic status, including relations of production and reproduction, as well as class.

Fraser argues that the three orders of justice—recognition, representation, and redistribution—are interdependent in such a way that a lack of justice in any one area (e.g., misrepresentation) will reinforce and/or lead to injustice in the other two (2005: 79). For example, claims for political voice (representation) are dependant on distribution (the economic structure) and recognition (the status order). Struggles against maldistribution (as experienced by refugees unable to eke out a livelihood in exile) are dependant on recognition (work permits, the right to education, interpretation of the Convention on Refugees regarding the right to work, etc.) and representation (the right of refugees to occupy public space in an open and active way, to demand coverage by protective labor legislation, etc.).

Following Fraser, who argues that it is "a tactical and a strategic decision" as to which of the three orders of justice should be emphasized in overcoming injustice, this essay underscores redistribution. Refugee research and policy have focused largely on recognition and representation. This and the fact of long-term refugee situations warrant more attention to economic and class perspectives. As well, the complex case of Afghan refugees in Iran presents an ideal problematic for the examination of economic injustice.

Afghans as Refugees and Workers in Iran

The literature concerning Afghans in Iran points to several migration "streams": religious exiles, "other" refugees, and seasonal workers. Late twentieth- and early twenty-first-century migrations to Iran from Afghanistan are the result of a number of sociopolitical and economic circumstances ranging from the Russian invasion in 1979, the Afghan civil wars of the late 1980s and early 1990s, the repressive Taliban regime from the mid 1990s to 2001, and the effects of the more recent Western wars on "terror."[7] Mohammad Jalal Abbasi-Shavazi et al. describe in detail these more recent historical streams of migration to Iran from Afghanistan to which I refer briefly here.[8] First, those who fled the Soviet invasion after 1979 were welcomed in Iran as *mohajerin*. *Mohajer/mohajerin* is an Arab word that translates as "refugee/s" and pertains to exile for religious reasons; in particular, being barred from freely practicing Islam. This is an honorable descriptive and these refugees were issued "blue cards" with permission to remain in Iran indefinitely (until 1995 they had access to subsidized health care, food, and primary and secondary education, but were limited to employment as manual laborers; Abbasi-Shavazi et al. 2005a: 16). A second category of migrant is *panahandegan* which refers to an impoverished refugee. This group fled to Iran as a result of civil war and includes many urban, educated, middle-class Afghans (8, 14). Abbasi-Shavazi et al. describe this category as having "a pejorative nuance" resulting from the non-religious motivation for their exile. The third category of Afghans in Iran are mainly seasonal labor migrants, most of whom have moved back and forth between Afghanistan and Iran since at least the nineteenth century (13). There are presently about half a million single (mostly male) Afghan labor migrants in Iran who work mainly in construction and agriculture (7–8). These various categories of migrant streams and their histories demonstrate the class complexities of forced migration that resist an easy alignment of a homogenized victim discourse with a specific class identity. Ascribed class definitions may change considerably as a result of forced migration.

Afghans have been allowed to work in Iran in only certain areas (e.g., construction, brick kilns, tile making, tanneries, poultry farms) without work permits.[9] However, since 2000 employment has been restricted to those who have been able to obtain work permits. Since 2001 the Iranian government has not been registering asylum seekers and undocumented migrant workers, except for some vulnerable groups such as separated children, the elderly, those in need of medical treatment, and female household heads (Ashrafi 2007: 3).

Similar to most other countries of first refuge, the Iranian government has said that it will not consider the permanent integration of refugees. A high unemployment rate in Iran, resulting partly from a massive population growth is deemed by some as creating a situation that is no longer conducive to hosting large numbers of refugees. It has recently been argued that Iran must now formulate migration policy (which is essentially labor migration policy), not refugee policy (Nakanishi 2005: 8).[10] Jobs and status are generally uncertain for all Afghans in Iran.

Less than 5 percent of Afghan refugees in Iran live in eighty unregulated settlements on the edge of cities or in one of the seven government-regulated settlements.[11] The UNHCR has responsibility for this group of refugees (Nakanishi 2005: viii, 8), but UN access to refugee camps is under the control of the Iranian state. The majority of the Afghan refugees do not live in refugee camps, but work and live alongside Iranians (men work in construction, public services, or agriculture). Some male refugees who live in regulated camps are involved in construction work or seasonal work outside the camps during the summer. Most women refugees do not have access to employment outside the camps (WFP 2002a: 4–5). Those *mohajerin* who were issued "blue cards" that entitled them to work and live in Iran, as well as benefit from various social services, lost this status in the mid 1990s when government policy toward refugees in Iran altered with the economic downturn in the country.[12] After 1992 the Iranian government confiscated identification cards from Afghans in Khorassan province (near the border with Afghanistan) and stopped issuing "refugee cards" (Squire and Gerami 1998: 19). Without any identification cards, Afghans in Iran are considered illegal. Afghans who sought refuge in Iran after 1993 were not considered to be "religious migrants," but "emigrants" (Abbasi-Shavazi et al. 2005a: 8). A new Iranian refugee law adopted in 2001 requires all foreign nationals without a work permit to leave the country unless they confront "physical threats" in their home country (WFP 2002a: 6). Not welcome in Iran, it is strategic for Afghans to be mobile workers whenever possible (i.e., when security and employment possibilities permit), sustaining multi-directional movements across national boundaries, and also participating in regional and transnational social networks (Turton and Marsden and Monsutti in Abbasi-Shavazi et al. 2005a: 5, 6).

Processes and Politics of Production

Afghan refugee men are not generally able to support their families solely on their own wages and thus women and children are expected to contribute to the household income (Squire and Gerami 1998: 20). However, Afghan refugee women have little access to work. Many women are illiterate, undocumented, and confront opposition from their husbands regarding engagement in paid work outside the household. Those who live in refugee camps can make some money by shelling pistachios, cleaning wool, making brooms, cleaning saffron, making chains, and weaving (20). Women we interviewed who lived in cities believed that there were more opportunities for work in Iran than Afghanistan, especially in home-based work such as tailoring, private tutoring, etc. (Ashrafi 2007: 19).[13] When asked, Afghan women expressed their top priority for themselves as education, including literacy and skills training (Squire and Gerami 1998: 21). According to Catherine Squire and Negar Gerami (21), many of the Afghan women they interviewed in the late 1990s understandably regard their futures as bleak. Abbasi-Shavazi et al. describe Afghan female-headed households as confronting "extreme economic vulnerability . . . with monthly expenditure on average 35.5% less than other households" in Iran (2005a: 2).

There is general agreement among those we interviewed that despite the restrictions confronted by refugees in Iran, including the lack of work permits, it is possible to find a job that can at least minimally support one's household (Ashrafi 2007: 19) and the prospects for employment were considered better in Iran than Afghanistan. As well, Iranian national and international organizations have developed training programs, some of which have been specifically directed at Afghan women, i.e., reproductive health, teachers' training, income generation, and skills training programs (Ashrafi 2007: 24).

Another issue is the large number of undocumented Afghan children (ages 6–15) in Iran (up to 500,000; Nakanishi 2005: 1). Afghan refugee children in Iran start work at an early age—some as young as 5 (1). They may attend school run by Afghans for four hours a day and work between four and ten hours a day (1). International and local NGOs have provided some limited support for Afghan schools in Iran as the Iranian government made it difficult for refugee children to attend state run schools in recent years. This was ostensibly to discourage Afghan refugees from remaining in Iran. These Afghan schools provide education for the children of parents who fear exposing themselves to authorities by registering their children in Iranian state schools. However, all those we interviewed in Iran felt that, when it is accessible to them, the educational system in Iran is superior to that of Afghanistan, with qualified teachers, better resources, and more security. Although some also pointed out that the school fees and other expenses, such as books and uniforms, restricted access to Iranian schools (Ashrafi 2007: 15).

The lives of Afghans in Iran demonstrate the complexity of those caught up in a forced migration. Extreme and lengthy types of dislocation are politically and economically immobilizing and demoralizing for those defined as refugees, who need/want to work, as well as those dependent household members who are too young or old to work, or not permitted to work outside the home due to gender or other restrictions. Two case studies below demonstrate the importance of understanding livelihood, class, and mobility to fully comprehend the process of forced migration and its consequences.

H and her husband arrived in Tehran with three children in 1996 from Kabul via Pakistan. Both attended Kabul University—she has a BA in theology and her husband has a BA in law. H's first husband who was a journalist was killed during the Taliban regime. Since her remarriage she and her two eldest daughters from her first marriage have received death threats from the family of her first husband who are living in Afghanistan. These threats intensified the family's sense of general insecurity in Afghanistan and led them to seek exile in Iran. They have three teenage daughters in high school and a younger daughter in elementary school in Tehran. The family members are registered refugees, but this does not mean that they have official access to schools, medical services, or jobs. They have siblings in Australia, Austria, and Bulgaria, but similar to other Afghan refugees in Iran, remittance support from extended family members is scarce, and generally non-existent. H is presently unemployed, but in the past worked for an NGO and an INGO in Tehran assisting vulnerable Afghan refugee families. Her husband who worked for a government ministry in Afghanistan now works for a trucking company where he oversees the weight load of trucks and makes about USD $150 per month. Their children try to hide their Afghan background at school in order to avoid racial slurs and insults. The family also tries to avoid interaction with other Afghans in Iran due to ethnic hostilities. H and her family do not think that Afghanistan will be a safe and livable country for several generations to come, and they would like to find resettlement outside of Iran, but have been unsuccessful so far.

S and her husband both have high school diplomas from Afghanistan and are in their late forties. S's husband was a member of the Mojahedin, an Afghan resistance movement formed after the Soviet invasion of Afghanistan in 1979.[14] The family fled to the safety of Iran in 1984 where they lived for ten years, before returning to Afghanistan in 1994 when they thought the country was once again safe for them. By 1998 they were on the run again—this time from the Taliban. They eventually resettled in Tehran. In Afghanistan S was a government employee until the Taliban fired her. In Tehran she does tailoring at home and makes about USD $8.7 per month. Her husband sold fruit in Afghanistan and has had a series of jobs in Iran, including construction, painting, and work in a transport company; he now sews jute bags in a workshop. His monthly salary in this most recent job is about USD$28 per month. Their two teenage sons and a 20-year-old daughter had to leave high school early in Iran because their parents could not afford the tuition fees. The daughter, a hairdresser, and the eldest son are unemployed because they cannot access work permits in Tehran. At 15, the youngest son helps his father in the workshop. Their eldest son attends a religious school in Pakistan. Two nephews in Germany and two brothers in Hungary send the equivalent of USD $700 annually to the family. S appreciates the safety of living in Iran, and says that "human life has no value in Afghanistan, especially women's lives." However, the family barely ekes out a living in Tehran, and it is unlikely they will be accepted for resettlement elsewhere, due to their political background and education.

Despite educational and financial differences, what stands out in both cases is the lack of economic and physical mobility that permeates the lives of the parents and the children. The income of both families is far below the GDP per capita for Iran. Both families seemed locked into their current status: unable to return to Afghanistan (possibly ever), or create a decent livelihood in Iran, or relocate to a third country. Iranian policy toward refugees has been characterized by "asylum fatigue" since the 1990s, due to deteriorating economic conditions in Iran, a high rate of inflation, and widespread unemployment (Ashrafi 2007: 1–2). This is the period during which both families arrived in Iran (S and her family for the second time). The racialization of Afghans in Iran underscores these policies. However, the geopolitics of the situation have played a major role in Iran's frustration, first of all in seeing no end to the war and the insecurity in Afghanistan and second in the decreasing international support (Ashrafi 2007: 2) for one of the largest forced migrations and exile situations in the world today. Caught up in a local-global geopolitics that has resulted in limited access to employment or admittance to employment under precarious and vulnerable conditions, Afghan refugees are subjected not only to the geopolitics of international warfare, but also to the economic upward and downward turns of their own country and the country of exile's economy. However, the one thing that Afghan refugees state repeatedly is that despite the racism that they experience, they regard Iran as a safe place.

Returning to Fraser's methodology concerning the three orders of justice, we see that the misrecognition of Afghan refugees (e.g., their subordinate racialized status) reflects their misrepresentation (i.e., their inability to access a political voice concerning their status) and both of the aforementioned result in and are exacerbated by maldistribution (e.g., the extreme difficulty they confront in accessing an adequate livelihood). This vicious circle inhabits and controls the space in which forced migrants are located in exile and can only be understood in its entirety.

Capitalizing on Strangers

I am making an argument in this paper for breaking down the boundaries that define forced migrants as passive refugees rather than workers who are actively involved in livelihood strategies, struggling against the immobility imposed by national refugee regulations and external international refugee definitions. Michael Burawoy's (2001) ideas about "global ethnography" that lay the groundwork for an analysis of class relations in studies of refugees by illuminating the production process, no matter its location, refugee camp or beyond, and declaring it to be a *contested* political process and space are powerful methodological tools. In such a space we see forced migrants as active participants in a global political process rather than as passive and faceless masses located elsewhere. Burawoy reminds us that the local has a relationship to other scales, including the global, and cannot be otherwise understood. He cautions that we must not lose sight of the global in our ethnographic research. His "grounded globalization" relates the "experience of globalization" to its production in "specific localities," as well as to contested politics (Burawoy 2001: 158). Likewise, in chapter 10 of this volume Labrecque argues that the exploitation of workers in the Yucatán and Chihuahua takes different forms in the context of a global economy. She explores the linkages between the mobility (migration) of workers and political mobilization and the differences between workers' experiences of exploitation in both sites. Similar to Afghan workers in Iran, these groups are highly oppressed, eking out bare existences on very low salaries and with little or no recourse to unionized protection. Fraser's work on social justice claims: recognition, representation, and redistribution, and the emphasis in this chapter on the latter, benefits from and connects well to Buroway's politics of production and the location of this process in the global, and to Labrecque's analysis of how capital adjusts to "the socio-historical specificities of different places," whether in the free-market transnational space of Mexico or the transitional economic space of Iran.

The same workers who are defined as migrant workers in one era become defined as refugees in another and share the same types of work in all times (i.e., since most/all Afghans in Iran are limited to manual labor, their education, skills, and class prior to arrival have little to do with choice of livelihood). While on the one hand most Afghans in Iran are presently defined as refugees, on the other they have been and presently are also part of a labor force—albeit a surplus labor force—that has been crucial in the long term to the economy of Iran. This is similar to other countries of first exile. And as an underclass without citizenship status in Iran some livelihoods become transnational or transborder, in order to ensure the survival of their households or family.

Finally, one of the dangers in refugee discourse is its perception of refugees as passive "victims of globalization"[15] rather than "as subjects of transnational or national networks of knowledge production" (Grewal 2005: 177). Grewal's approach counters a "victim" approach and also raises new questions about class and refugees, some of which are related to Burawoy's approach to the "politics of production." Grewal argues that "the construction of the refugee subject" was "a means to create technologies of transnational governmentality" and that those defined as refugees "indexed the crisis of the nation-state in particular ways" (162). It is "attention to those who fail to make a successful refugee claim of asylum" that will tell us "a great deal about the nature of migrant networks and of the specificities of gendered, racialized, and classed subjectivities in relation to the nation and the state" (163). This is all about representation and the "misframing" of questions of justice—as per Fraser—thereby excluding some people from "first-order justice claims" wherein "they become non-persons with respect to justice" (Fraser 2005: 77). But this approach is also associated with maldistribution (e.g., the lack of access to economic resources) as well as misrecognition (e.g., status or identity) that can impede people in achieving a successful refugee claim and thus justice. It is the interrelationship of these phenomena that we need to understand better, particularly in a world in which new "zones of protection" are being established to further reduce the mobility of those who must leave their countries of origin and to assuage those parts of the world wracked by wealth and fear.

Notes

Earlier versions of this paper were presented at the following conferences: the Canadian Anthropology Society, Montreal, and the International Association of Forced Migration, Toronto. I would like to thank the following people for their helpful critiques: Pauline Barber, Jennifer Hyndman, Doreen Indra, and Winnie Lem. Thanks to the Social Science and Humanities Research Council of Canada for their generous support of research related to this paper and to Jennifer Hyndman who was Co-investigator for our SSHRC Grant: "The Globalization of Homelessness in Long-Term Refugee Camps".

1. Definitions of globalization refer to "the intensification of world-wide social relations which link distant localities in such a way that local happenings are shaped by events occurring many miles away" (Giddens 1990: 64); as "time-space compression" (Harvey 1989: 147); and as "the stretching out of the geography of social relations" (Massey 1997: 7) (in Szeman n.d.).

2. Despite the fact that internally displaced persons (IDPs) are not protected by the 1951 Refugee Convention, the UNHCR "is now embarking on its biggest operation to help displaced people since 1945" (Campbell 2006).

3. The UNHCR describes a "protracted" refugee situation as "one in which refugees find themselves in a long-lasting and intractable state of limbo" (2004: 1). What was once initially a protective space becomes over the years and decades a site where refugees "progressively waste [their] lives" (3). One of the problems with this descriptive is that it tends to essentialize refugees as victims. The process of living for a long time in a refugee camp has also been referred to as "refugee warehousing" (Smith 2004: 38).

4. Development-induced displacement has been defined as "the process of forcing communities to evacuate land needed for development projects" (El Jack 2008: chap 1)

5. GDP per capita in Iran is $8,900—ranking eighty-ninth in comparison to other countries in the world (http://www.indexmundi.com/g/r.aspx?c=ir&v=67, accessed 11 June 2007).

6. Excluding the West Bank and Gaza

7. Most of the Afghans in Iran are either Shi'a Persian-speaking Hazaris or Sunni Pashto-speaking Pashtuns. The latter form the dominant ethnic/linguistic community in Afghanistan. For geopolitical reasons, Shi'a Afghans form the majority of Afghan refugees in Iran (i.e., Iran is principally Shi'a). Another shared ethnic tie across borders is Balucj ethnicity. These ethnic bonds are described as much stronger than ties of national Iranian or Afghan citizenship (Abbasi-Shavazi et al. 2005: 10).

8. Mohammad Jalal Abbasi-Shavazi and his colleagues at the University of Tehran are engaged in extensive research on the situation of Afghan refugees in Iran. Much of their research is carried out under the auspices of the Afghanistan Research and Evaluation Unit (AREU; e.g., Abbasi-Shavazi et al. 2005a, 2005b, 2005c).

9. In 1976 when the Iranian government signed the 1951 Convention Relating to the Status of Refugees and the 1967 Protocol, they did not agree to article 17 (the right to wage earning employment; article 23 (access to public relief), article 24 (access to labor legislation and social security, and article 26 (freedom of movement; Ashrafi 2007: 2).

10. Migration policy, which selects based on skill sets, is more restrictive than the more open-ended humanitarianism of refugee policy. As well, it likely makes more sense to the Iranian state to consider Afghans as labor immigrants/migrants to Iran, as this is what they have been for centuries.

11. Presently, only about 26,000 Afghans live in refugee camps in Iran. These refugees mainly come from rural backgrounds and they choose to remain in the camps because they cannot afford the high cost of living outside the camps (Ashrafi 2007: 1).
12. The population has doubled since the Iranian revolution of 1979, resulting in serious unemployment.
13. Interviews were conducted in Iran in 2006–2007 for our (Wenona Giles and Jennifer Hyndman) Social Science and Humanities Research Council of Canada–funded project entitled "The Globalization of Homelessness in Long Term Refugee Camps."
14. The Mojahedin fought with the Soviets until their withdrawal from Afghanistan in 1989. They then tried to maintain power in Afghanistan, but the country broke into civil war, which gave way to the rise of the Taliban in 1993.
15. Hyndman and I refer to this as the "feminization of asylum" (forthcoming 2010).

References

Abbasi-Shavazi, Mohammad Jalal, et al., eds. 2005a. *Return to Afghanistan? A Study of Afghans Living in Zahedan, Islamic Republic of Iran.* Faculty of Social Sciences, University of Tehran, Afghanistan Research and Evaluation Unit. http://www.unhcr.org/cgi-bin/texis/vtx/home/opendoc.pdf?tbl=SUBSITES&page=SUBSITES&id=4430da902/.

———. 2005b. *Return to Afghanistan? A Study of Afghans Living in Tehran.* Faculty of Social Sciences, University of Tehran, Afghanistan Research and Evaluation Unit.

———. 2005c. *Return to Afghanistan? A Study of Afghans Living in Mashhad, Islamic Republic of Iran.* Faculty of Social Sciences, University of Tehran, Afghanistan Research and Evaluation Unit.

Ashrafi, Afsaneh. 2007. "Afghan Refugees in Iran: A Study of Protracted Refugee Situations." Unpublished report for the research project "The Globalization of Homelessness in Long Term Refugee Camps",. Wenona Giles and Jennifer Hyndman. Funded by the Social Science and Humanities Research Council of Canada (2005–2009).

Bauman, Zigmunt. 2002. "Reconnaissance Wars of the Planetary Frontierland." *Theory, Culture and Society.* 19(4):81–90.

Bauman, Zygmunt. 1998. *Globalization: The Human Consequences.* New York: Columbia University Press.

Betts, Alexander and James Milner. 2006. "The Externalisation of EU Asylum Policy: The Position of African States". Working Paper No. 36, University of Oxford. Centre on Migration, Policy and Society (COMPAS). http://www2.carleton.ca/polisci/ccms/wp-content/ccms-files/milner-wp0636-betts-millner.pdf

Burawoy, Michael. 2001. "Manufacturing the Global." *Ethnography* 2 (2): 147–159.

Campbell, Duncan. 2006. "Exiles in their Own Land." *Guardian Weekly*, 28 April–4 May: 28.

Citizenship and Immigration Canada (CIC). 2004. Facts and Figures. Immigration Overview: Permanent and Temporary Residents. http://www.cic.gc.ca/english/pub/facts2004/index.html/.

El Jack, Amani. 2008. "In the Name of Development: Displacement and Gender Transformation in Sudan." PhD diss., Women's Studies, York University.

Ellwood, Wayne. 2002. *The No Nonsense Guide to Globalization.* Between the Lines Press. Toronto.

Fraser, Nancy. 2000. "Rethinking Recognition." *New Left Review* 3 (May/June): 107–120.

———. 2005. "Reframing Justice in a Globalizing World." *New Left Review* 36 (Nov/Dec): 69–88.

Giddens, Anthony. 1990. *Consequences of Modernity.* Palo Alto: Stanford University Press.

Grewal, Inderpal. 2005. *Transnational America: Feminisms, Diasporas, Neoliberalisms.* Durham: Duke University Press.

Harvey, David. 1989. *The Condition of Postmodernity.* Cambridge: Blackwell.

Hyndman, Jennifer, and Wenona Giles. forthcoming 2010. "Waiting for What? The Feminization of Asylum in Protracted Situations". *Gender, Place and Culture.*

Hyndman, Jennifer, and Alison Mountz. 2008. "Another Brick in the Wall? *Neo-refoulement* and the Externalization of Asylum in Australia and Europe." *Government and Opposition* 43 (2).

Isin, Engin F., and Kim Rygiel. 2007. "Of Other Global Cities: Frontiers, Zones, Camps." In *Cities and Globalization: Challenges for Citizenship,* ed. H. Wimmen. London: Saqi Books.

Katz, Cindi. 2001. "On the Grounds of Globalization: A Topography for Feminist Political Engagement." *Signs: A Journal of Women in Culture and Society* 26 (4): 1213–1234.

Loescher, Gil. 2001. "Protection and Humanitarian Action in the Post–Cold War Era." In *Global Migrants, Global Refugees: Problems and Solutions,* eds. Aristide Zolberg and Peter Benda. New York and Oxford: Berghahn Books.

Loescher, Gil, and James Milner. 2005. "The Long Road Home: Protracted Refugee Situations in Africa." *Survival* 47 (2): 153–174.

Malkki, Liisa. 1995. "Purity and Exile: Violence, Memory, and National Cosmology among Hutu Refugees in Tanzania." Chicago: Chicago University Press.

Massey, Doreen. 1997. "Problems with Globalization." *Soundings* 7 (autumn).

Nakanishi, Hisae. 2005. "Afghan Refugees and Migrants in Iran: Who is Responsible for Empowering Them?" Paper presented at Peace-Building Studies 6 (spring). www.peacebuilding.org/data/dp/No6_nakanishi.pdf/.

Overbeek, Henk. 1995. "Towards a New International Migration Regime: Globalization." In *Migration and European Integration: The Dynamics of Inclusion and Exclusion,* eds. D. Thranhardt and R. Miles. Cambridge: Pinter.

Rieff, David. 2003. "Displaced Places: Where Refugees Try to Make a Home." *New York Times Magazine,* 21 September: 36–41.

Smith, Merrill. 2004. "Warehousing Refugees: A Denial of Rights, a Waste of Humanity." *World Refugee Survey* 2004, US Committee for Refugees and Immigrants: 38–56.

Squire, Catherine, and Negar Gerami. 1998. "Afghan Refugees in Iran: The Needs of Women and Children." *Forced Migration Review* 3: 19–22.

Stasiulis, Daiva K., and Abigail B. Bakan. 2005. *Negotiating Citizenship: Migrant Women in Canada and the Global System.* Toronto: University of Toronto Press.

Szeman, Imre. N.d. "Globalization." http://www.humanities.mcmaster.ca/~szeman/global.htm/.

United Nations Department of Public Information. 2002. *The Millennium Development Goals and the United Nations' Role.* http://www.un.org/millenniumgoals.

UNHCR (United Nations High Commissioner for Refugees). 2002. *Statistical Yearbook: Refugees, Asylum-Seekers and Other Persons of Concern—Trends in Displacement, Protection and Solutions.* Geneva.

———. 2004. *Protracted Refugee Situations.* Geneva. www.unhcr.org/cgi-bin/texis/vtx/home?page/.

———. 2005. Considerations Relating to Cessation on the Basis of Article 1C (5) of the 1951 Convention with Regard to Afghan Refugees and Persons Determined in Need of International Protection. http://www.unhcr.ch/cgi-bin/texis/vtx/publ/opendoc.pdf?tbl=RSDLEGAL&id=425a49e14&page=publ/.

———. 2005. *2004 Global Refugee Trends.* http://www.unhcr.org/cgi-bin/texis/vtx/statistics/.

USCRI (United States Committee for Refugees and Immigrants). 2009a. "Statistics: Warehoused Refugee Populations (as of December 31, 2008)." *World Refugee Survey 2009.* http://www.refugees.org/FTP/WRS09PDFS/WarehousingMap.pdf

————. 2009b. "Statistics:Refugee and Asylum Seekers Worldwide (as of December 31, 2008)." *World Refugee Survey 2009.*

————2009c. "Statistics: Resettlement by Country". *World Refugee Survey 2009. http://www. refugees.org/FTP/WRS09PDFS/Resettlementbycountry.pdf*

————2008. "Ratio of Refugees to Host Country Populations and Distribution of Refugees by Host Country Income". *World Refugee Survey 2008.* p.29. *http://www.refugees.org/uploadedFiles/Investigate/Publications_&_Archives/WRS_ Archives/2008/host%20countries_%20stats.pdf*

————2007. "Principal Hosts of Refugees (as of December 31, 2006): Table 8". *World Refugee Survey 2007. http://www.refugees.org/uploadedFiles/Investigate/Publications_&_Archives/ WRS_Archives/2007/table7–8.pdf*

WFP (World Food Program). 2002a. *A Report from the Office of Evaluation: Full Report of the Evaluation of IRAN PRRO 6126—Food Assistance and Support for Repatriation of Iraqi and Afghan Refugees in Iran* (25 January–19 February 2002). Rome, September 2002. Ref. OEDE/2002/16.

————. 2002b. Protracted Relief and Recovery Operation: Iran 10213.0—Food Assistance and Support to Education of Afghan and Iraqi Refugees in the Islamic Republic of Iran. Projects for Executive Approval. Executive Board, third regular session. Rome, 21–25 October 2002. www.wfp.org/operations/current_operations/countries/countryproject.

— Chapter 2 —

NEW MEXICAN MIGRANTS IN A NEW AGE: GLOBALIZATION, NETWORKS, AND GENDER IN RURAL MEXICO

Frances Abrahamer Rothstein

On 1 January 1994 the North American Free Trade Agreement (NAFTA) between Mexico, Canada, and the United States went into effect, eliminating tariffs on many products (some immediately and others over a ten-year period) and lifting investment restrictions on foreign investment. Despite the expectation, at least on the part of policymakers, that Mexican migration to the United States would be reduced by NAFTA, migration from Mexico is greater than ever before (Escobar Latapí and Martin 2006). Recent research also suggests that this growth is accompanied by a broadening and diversification of who comes, from where, and to where they go. Additionally there is some evidence that the rate of growth of migration has accelerated.[1] Until recently Mexican migrants to the US were mainly men from agricultural communities in western Mexico. Migrants today include more women and children and they come from urban as well as rural areas in new regions in central and southern Mexico. Furthermore, once migration from a particular community begins it grows quickly, unlike in the past when it took many years to encompass a significant proportion of the community. This chapter is part of a larger project that describes and analyzes the recent and rapid growth of international migration of men, women, and children from San Cosme Mazatecochco, a rural community in the state of Tlaxcala in central Mexico where I have been conducting anthropological research for three decades.[2] In this chapter I focus on one segment of today's new migrants, women. More specifically, I focus on how globalization and the increased proletarianization

it has brought have encouraged and facilitated women's migration to the United States.

Although a few men from San Cosme had participated in the Bracero Program in the 1940s and 1950s and many men migrated weekly to Mexico City to work in textile factories during the 1950s, 1960s, and 1970s, migration to the US from San Cosme has been very rare.[3] Today, however, as indicated above, many San Cosmeros/as have come to the US and the speed with which the migration rate has grown from a few individuals to hundreds appears to have been very rapid. Since migration from San Cosme and the state of Tlaxcala in which it is located is recent and impressionistic evidence (based on visits with migrants living in New Jersey and New York as well as conversations with people in San Cosme) indicates that it includes women and children as well as men, the community is an excellent site in which to explore new migration patterns. As David Kyle has pointed out: "New immigrant groups may share certain features with other immigrants, past and present, but their story must be told anew, explained from the ground up" (2000: 185).

There is a great deal of literature on migration, especially migration from Mexico to the United States, that documents the importance of the political economy of sending and receiving countries. There is also a large body of research that demonstrates the importance of social networks in facilitating migration (Brettell 2000; Durand and Massey 2004; Grasmuck and Pessar 1991; Massey et al. 1987; Massey, Goldring, and Durand 1994; T. Wilson 1993). In addition, during the last two decades there has been a serious effort to show the gendered dimensions of migration (Donato et al. 2006; Hondagneu-Sotelo 2000; Mahler and Pessar 2006). There is also a growing amount of research on migration, gender, and political economy (Misra, Woodring, and Merz 2006; Pyle 2006; Pyle and Ward 2003; Sassen 2003; see also Barber [7], Zontini [5], and Labrecque [10], this volume.). Along with these themes, since the 1980s a great deal of discussion about globalization—the increased and intensified flows of capital, commodities, ideas, images, and people— has taken place. This growing interconnectedness has produced a reordering of time and space that David Harvey (1989) calls "time-space compression." This chapter builds on and integrates these four bodies of knowledge on political economy and the structural causes of migration, the importance of social networks, the gendered patterns of migration, and the nature and consequences of globalization. Although some studies look at migration in relation to other global flows, such as capital mobility, little attention has been paid to the combined effects of the intensification of global flows or the effect of time-space compression on the overall pattern of international migration, its growth rates, and changing gender composition.

Anthropology, Globalization, and Migration

A number of recent discussions place contemporary migration in the context of changes in the labor markets in both sending and receiving countries. As Kyle argues, however, we need to conceptualize an overarching system that is greater than just the sending and the destination countries (2000: 48). The concept of globalization, despite some limitations, provides such a framework. Since the concept of globalization was first introduced in the early 1980s, anthropologists, along with other social scientists, have developed a number of theoretical approaches to deal with what analysts agree are profound transformations in the lives of people everywhere. Although these approaches vary on how different the present is from previous eras of capitalism, whether there is an overall pattern at all, or what the most significant aspects of the contemporary global era are, analysts agree that contemporary capitalism is different from earlier forms. Furthermore, all emphasize movement and connections—of capital, people, commodities, ideas, and images. Where analysts differ the most is on which flows are most crucial; some give causal primacy to ideas, material circumstances, production, consumption, class conflict, capital accumulation, and/or any combination of these. For Arjun Appadurai (1996), for example, the flow of ideas—through electronic media and migration—are the most crucial. For others, such as Daniel Miller (1995), the flow of commodities and consumption are given causal primacy. Others, such as Linda Basch, Nina Glick Schiller, and Cristina Szanton Blanc (1994), who stress transnationalism, focus on the movement of people and the maintenance of strong ties between migrants and their home communities. In this analysis, I rely primarily on what Harvey (1989) calls flexible accumulation. The most important characteristic of flexible accumulation is the flexible commitment of capital to particular places and workers. This flexible commitment underlies not only the acceleration of capital mobility that characterizes the global age but also lies at the center of increased labor migration. As I have argued elsewhere (Rothstein 2007), it is important to stress also that although capital has enormous power, capital is not all-powerful. Capital's paths and strategies are influenced by the struggle between capital and labor in particular places and at particular times. Although, in Harvey's approach, the struggle between labor and capital and capital accumulation have causal priority; to understand contemporary migration it is necessary also to include the increased flows of ideas and images that characterize contemporary global capitalism. Thus, this analysis argues that the flow of capital and commodities that affect labor markets and which are usually taken into account in migration studies are *not* the only global flows that have intensified and increased in the last two decades. Discussions of globalization show also an increase and intensification of global flows of images, ideas, and people moving not only to migrate but as tourists, students, and businessmen and women. Although some studies have examined the relationship between the flows of capital and migration (Canales 2003; Sassen 1988, 2003); images and migration (Appadurai 1996; Ma 2001); and commodification, consumerism, and migration (Grimes 1998; Miller 1997; Mills 1999), few researchers have looked at the complex and cumulative ways that the intensification of all these global flows can impact the growth and diversification of migration. This chapter suggests some of the ways these intensified and interrelated flows associated with globalization have resulted in new conditions, changed social networks, and cultural capital that encourage the flow of new population segments from a broader range of communities.

The chapter is divided into three parts. In the first section I discuss how labor market changes associated with globalization have pushed Mexican women into the Mexican labor force. In the second I suggest that women's proletarianization increased and broadened their social networks, their familiarity with the United States and US work practices, equipped them with relevant cultural capital, and encouraged commodification, consumerism, and consumption-based identities. In the third section I discuss how women's job opportunities in Mexico deteriorated in the 1990s and women's proletarianization, expanded social networks, and new cultural capital, along with changing family patterns, facilitated their migration to the United States for employment. In the conclusion I suggest that migration analysts need to consider Mexican women not only as wives but also as workers actively engaged in numerous efforts to improve their lives and the lives of those around them and at home.

Globalization Begins:
The "Economic Crisis" of the 1980s

Increasingly, many contemporary migrants from Mexico come not from agricultural but urban communities and, unlike many past migrants, they are more educated and were employed in Mexico before they migrated (Kochhar 2005).[4] Migration from San Cosme follows this new trend. Until ten years ago, few San Cosmeros/as migrated to the US. But for many years, men from San Cosme migrated internally to Mexico City (sixty miles away) or to Puebla (ten miles away) for jobs in the national textile industry. In 1982, however, a combination of factors, including declining oil prices and rising interest rates on a growing debt, led Mexico to announce that it could not meet its debt payments. A bailout, involving the United States, the International Monetary Fund, and the World Bank, led to a restructuring of the Mexican economy with neoliberal policies of trade and ending import substitution and protectionism of national industry.

The liberalization of trade led to the closure of 80 percent of Mexican textile firms and the loss of more than 100,000 jobs in the national textile industry between 1982 and 1984 (Becerril 1994; Chavez M. 1995). The proportion of San Cosme men in factory work declined from almost half of the economically active men in 1980 to 29 percent in 1994 (Rothstein 2000: 4).[5] Even those who did not lose their jobs had their hours reduced and feared they would lose their jobs. At the same time, the austerity programs adopted by the Mexican government in accordance with the demands of the bailout led to cuts in government subsidies of food and gasoline, restricted wage increases, and reduced government spending on health, education, and welfare. Consequently, it became even harder for families to get along. Given these circumstances, during the 1980s a variety of new supplemental income strategies emerged—including increased employment of women and youth in *maquiladoras* (in-bond assembly plants) as street vendors or merchants, and in other informal sector activities. Whereas in 1980 only 9 percent of the women age 12 and over in San Cosme were reported as participating in the labor force or in self-employment, by 1989 the proportion had nearly doubled to 17 percent. Between 1989 and 1994 it doubled again to 34 percent and among women age 25 and under almost half (48 percent) were employed (Rothstein 1999: 582).[6] Labrecque in chapter 10 similarly notes the importance of women's labor force participation in rural communities in the Yucatan.

In the early 1980s half of the women of San Cosme who were reported as being in the labor force worked in factories, usually maquiladoras elsewhere in the state of Tlaxcala or the Federal District. But, in the late 1980s, a few families who had been vendors who bought and sold clothing began producing garments in small family *talleres* or workshops. By the mid 1990s there were hundreds of small workshops in San Cosme producing garments, and almost half of the women reported as employed were workshop workers (Rothstein 1999: table 1). Most of these workshop workers were young women still living with their natal families. Many had worked in maquiladoras before they went to work in their own or other's workshops. When asked, women who left maquiladoras to become *taller* workers said they saved money on transportation and food and they seemed to prefer the less rigid, paternalistic authority structure of the workshops.[7] Women who were owners said they liked being able to combine domestic responsibilities, especially childcare, and paid work.

Globalization Goes On: The 1990s

By 1994 nearly one out of every four households had members who were involved in small-scale clothing manufacturing as owners and/or workers. Another 19 percent of the households had one or more merchants, many of whom were selling garments produced in small manufacturing workshops. By that time also, there were a number of workshops that appeared to be doing quite well. The owners of these workshops had built impressive houses and purchased vans and weaving machines to make their own fabric. People pointed to their success and their "coches del ano" (new cars every year). A preference began to emerge for owning a workshop over professional employment and there was a decline in the proportion of young people who went on to higher education and professional employment (Rothstein 1999).

During the early 1990s, in addition to income from their own workshops or from family members employed in the workshops, most families relied on their own corn production to supplement their cash earnings. In many households, even those with their own workshops, one or more family members continued to be employed elsewhere. But workshop earnings were low, there were no benefits, and the very volatile apparel market meant that the work was very uneven and insecure.

As more and more people opened workshops, competition grew, including competition from workshops within the community that subcontracted to smaller workshops. Competition also increased from the growth of workshops in other communities and more cheap goods coming into Mexico from China. At the same time, women and men who had continued working in maquiladoras or other formal sector jobs found that their factories were, like the textile factories before them, also closing to be moved elsewhere in Mexico, such as Chiapas and the Yucatan (see Labrecque, chapter 10) or China, where production costs were lower. Whether new maquiladoras move to more agricultural and poorer areas of Mexico, leave the country completely, or hire only more qualified workers as has occurred more recently (Mongelluzzo 2006), many of the former workers, including many women, are left adversely affected by neoliberalism, without jobs or with only poorer-paying jobs. San Cosme's professionals (most of whom had always been women who were nurses or teachers) also experienced declining opportunities as government cutbacks in health and education continued to impact their main sources of professional employment.

As more and more people in San Cosme and else elsewhere in Mexico began looking to the small-scale garment industry as an alternative, competition increased. Consequently, the small-scale garment industry in San Cosme began to lose its appeal. Increasingly, the workshops that managed to survive were those involved in contracting out to smaller workshops. Only those who had the resources for trucks and to rent a stall at a regional market and sufficient capital to pay for more materials for larger quantities of goods could afford to subcontract to others. These merchants benefited from the flexibility involved in hiring others when the market demanded them but not having to pay workers if the market was down. Even larger owners were in a precarious position. Owners of small- and mid-sized workshops, especially those dependent on producing for contractors, were vulnerable to the temporary fluctuations of an extremely volatile garment market. Those who did not have the capital to become contractors found themselves producing more and more for those who did. Some contractors did not pay the producers until the garments had been sold at the regional markets. Since small and mid-sized workshops absorbed the slow times for the contractors, their profits declined. As one woman whose two-person workshop (herself and her husband) did machine embroidery for others said, "When times are bad, we eat just corn." When times are good and the garment market is up, these producers are expected to work long hours until the job is completed.

Additionally, as the young workers matured and moved into the next stage of the life cycle, and as families became more dependent on purchased goods, garment workers and small owners found that their earnings, which had never supported even themselves, could not support their families. Even with two members of the household employed, many families found their earnings inadequate.

By 2001, although new workshops continued to open and new workers continued to enter the workshops, workshop owners frequently commented on the growing competition, and some workshops were closing. Workers and small owner-workers were also talking about poor wages and the low earnings derived from working for a contractor. Owners were also looking to poorer communities for new workers because experienced workers in San Cosme wanted higher wages.

In 2001 San Cosmeros/as began talking about a few people who had migrated to the United States, usually New York or Connecticut. But still only a few had done so. By 2004 many people had migrated and communities of hundreds of San Cosmeros/as had developed in New Jersey and in Connecticut. Many had been small owners who had been subcontractors for the larger owners and/or workers in others' workshops. At the same time that workshops had become less and less profitable, and more people were working for wages and therefore unavailable for subsistence cultivation, NAFTA provisions had gone into effect allowing subsidized US corn to be sold in Mexico. This led to a large drop in the price of corn; the low price for US-subsidized corn made it impractical for many Mexican cultivators to continue to grow corn. Consequently, many families stopped growing their own corn and their own production no longer subsidized garment production. Buying even cheap US-subsidized corn, however, requires cash expenditures.

Meanwhile, the increasing demand for service workers in the US, especially in flexible services such as domestic work for women and landscaping and construction for men, provided attractive alternatives. Remittances from those who had already migrated helped to make up for reduced income from other sources (Canales 2003; Otero 2004). These earlier migrants also facilitate more migration.

Women's Proletarianization and Social Networks, Cultural Capital, and Globalization

Previous research on Mexican migration to the United States as well as migration research elsewhere has found that as more people from the same community migrate to the United States, there is what Douglas Massey and his colleagues call a "cumulative causation of migration" (Massey, Goldring, and Durand 1994: 1498). Although structural factors influence the first trip that a migrant makes, "the progression from one trip to the next is determined by variables connected to the migrant experience itself" (Massey et al. 1987: 301). In this process changes occur for the individual and for the community from which the migrant comes that make further migration more likely. Massey et al. further suggest that although migration from Mexican communities usually begins with "target migration" in which the migrant plans a temporary visit to earn enough to pay the trip's costs and to return with a predetermined amount, the experience of migration develops new wants and expectations for the migrant that encourage him to migrate again.[8] Having migrated once, the migrant now has the experience and resources to make subsequent trips more easily. These first migrants also become a resource for other members of the community. Their knowledge of jobs, housing, and so forth make the trips of later migrants less difficult. As Massey, Luin Goldring, and Jorge Durand suggest, "With these lowered costs and risks, additional people are induced to migrate for the first time, which further expands the set of people with ties abroad" (1994: 1500).

Although numerous studies have documented the significance of such a cumulative process and show how the prevalence of migration within a community increases over time from a few to many migrants, most of these studies have focused on male migration in the 1960s and 1970s from agricultural communities in western Mexico. Little research has been done on the new sending communities including urban areas and communities in central and southern Mexico. Even less research has been done on women as migrants. To the extent that research has been done on women migrants, the emphasis has been on women already in the United States. Other than a few important exceptions (Arias 1995; Crummett 2001; Hirsch 2002; Stephen 2005; Wilson 1999), most of the research that has been done on women in sending communities has concentrated on the impact on women of male migration.

Research in San Cosme points to two important themes that relate to both the acceleration of migration overall and the increasing migration of women. Both of these themes stem from the large increase in wage labor or proletarianization of the Mexican population, including women, in the last two decades of the twentieth century, which, we should note, has generally been ignored in the migration literature.[9] First, these jobs often involve internal labor migration (Cohen 2002; Kyle 2000) and thus contribute to expanded social networks and new cultural capital, including new consumer and class identities, which encourage and facilitate migration.[10] Massey, Goldring, and Durand (1994) have suggested that international migration leads to the development of new wants and expectations that encourage more migration. That is true also of internal migration. Then, and this is the second theme, when women's jobs disappear or earnings decline, as we saw happening in San Cosme in the 1990s and as has happened in Mexico in general in the last ten years, the contacts and knowledge accumulated in the previous years may ease the way for migration to the United States.

Although surveys in San Cosme show that the highest proportion of employed women working in factories at any one point in time (1989) was only 28 percent, many more women were employed in maquiladoras and other factories for at least a period of time. Almost all of women's factory employment (except for two local enterprises) involve commuting or migrating daily, or for those who worked in Mexico City as did a number of San Cosmeras who worked in a Cannon Mills factory in the 1980s, weekly. As studies elsewhere have shown, it is often through the contacts people make through an earlier economic activity that social ties that form the basis of a new activity are formed (Kyle 2000: 93). Kyle suggests further that for the Ecuadorian migrants he studied, "weak ties to others within regional networks . . . [were] the first prerequisite for joining the [US] migration flow" (2000: 93). Women, like San Cosme's male textile factory workers since the 1940s, developed such ties through their work in regional factories in Santa Ana (a town twenty minutes away, with a population of approximately 60,000), Panzacola (a neighboring community), and the cities of Tlaxcala and Puebla, as well as Mexico City. In one case, for example, a young woman worked in a maquiladora in the city of Tlaxcala for a few years. There she became friends with a man who became the union leader in a new factory that opened in San Cosme a few years later. [11] She soon switched to that factory. Her new job not only eliminated the daily commute of almost an hour but also paid significantly more. A few years later she quit that job and she and her husband eventually became very successful *taller* owners. Although they do not need to consider labor migration, competition was encouraging them to begin exploring how, through their social networks, including the visiting anthropologist, they might reduce their costs by getting fabric directly from the United States.

Globalization has not only affected the opening and closing of factories and the social networks of women workers; it has also affected the cultural capital that potential migrants can acquire even before the first migrant from their own hometown leaves for the US. Some researchers have suggested that export-manufacturing is migration-inducing (Fernández-Kelly 1983; Sassen 1984) because workers are socialized for industrial work (Pessar 2003). Additionally, women who work in multinational corporations become familiar with US work practices and expectations. As Saskia Sassen (1984: 1151) pointed out many years ago, "the strong presence of foreign firms [in export manufacturing] facilitates access to information and a sense of familiarity." At the same time, globalization of marketing and media means that women, like men, are bombarded with messages about "modern" consumer items ranging from personal care products to branded clothing. One local *farmacia* in San Cosme sells not only US products such as Colgate toothpaste, Dove soap, and Kleenex, but in 2001, before 9/11, along with music boxes and other gifts they were selling replicas of the Statue of Liberty and the Twin Towers. Much of the research on consumption has focused on consumption for identity among young people. These young people, such as the *taller* or maquiladora workers of San Cosme, usually live with their families and although they may give some of what they earn to help support their households, most have some control over their earnings. Since they are subsidized by their families (and by the subsistence cultivation that was practiced until recently), they can afford to buy the CDs, clothes, and personal care products (these are typically US brands or knockoffs) on which they become increasingly dependent for their consuming identities. It should also be noted that at the same time that young workers are so bombarded with messages promoting the construction of identities, through consumption, they are also discouraged from developing identities as workers (Rothstein 2007).

Even before the *talleres* of San Cosme started experiencing difficulties, *taller* workers found that when they started to form their own families, their low wages meant they could no longer afford the consumer items they had come to desire and, more importantly, their workshop wages were inadequate to support a family. For a while, as indicated above, there was a great deal of optimism about the workshops and workers expressed high hopes of eventually having their own profitable workshops. Also, as indicated above, workshops and their workers and small-workshop owners were often further supported not only by subsistence corn production but also often by the formal sector employment of someone else in their households. Many of the original workshops were started with the severance pay that textile factory workers received when their factories closed and are subsidized by the pensions that many of those workers now get. Today, however, more and more people are feeling the squeeze. Workshop wages remain low and the increase in subcontracting has made work even less stable. Small owners are increasingly finding it difficult to survive, much less achieve success. And, the formal sector employment that offered alternative employment as well as subsidizing workshops and workshop employment has shrunk. And increasingly, formal sector employment growth is exclusive to men and for workers with more education than what San Cosmeros/as usually have (Mongelluzzo 2006).

Conclusion:
New Migrants Need New Approaches

But farther north, there are jobs! There are few people in San Cosme today that do not know someone in the US or someone who knows someone in the US. And while everyone knows how difficult it is to get across the border and they are aware of the many hurdles that must be faced, they know also that in the US they can find jobs and dollars. In the past, jobs and dollars in the US were available for men but less so for women. And in the past, Mexican women were much less likely to have been wage workers before they migrated. Today, however, most Mexican women, like Mexican men, work when they come to the US (Cerrutti and Massey 2001: 188; Kochhar 2005). More than a third of the Mexican labor force is female (World Bank 2007) and the labor force participation rate of urban Mexican women rose from 33 to 45 percent between 1990 and 2002 (Abramo and Valenzuela 2005). But most of the research on women migrants from Mexico says little about women's employment *before* they moved North. Furthermore, in many studies there is a tendency to treat Mexican communities as culturally stagnant (Gutmann 2004). There is often an implicit and sometimes explicit assumption that any recent changes in gender relations, including women's employment, even before they migrate, are the consequences of male migration to the US. Durand and Massey (2004: 8), for example, mention women's employment only as a consequence of the increased autonomy women experience when their husbands migrate. Similarly, women's migration is usually discussed primarily in relation to family migration. Although many women do migrate as wives or daughters, many men also migrate as sons. Furthermore, there are numerous hints that along with an increase in women's migration, there is also an increase in women migrating independently. Jeffrey Cohen (2002: 41) found that in the Oaxacan communities he studied, 60 percent of women migrants had a male household member across the border. Although he does not mention it, it would seem that 40 percent did not. Shawn Malia Kanaiaupuni (2000) notes that women without spouses were more likely to migrate than were those with spouses. She suggests also that prior employment may affect the probability of migration but "unfortunately," she writes, in their study they "could not control for the individual condition of employment at the moment at which the risk of migration began" (8). Sara Curran and Estela Rivero-Fuentes (2003: 14) similarly say that they could not control for employment before migration and, like Kanaiaupuni, they used community levels of male and female employment.

There is also some evidence that single motherhood has increased in Mexico in the last few decades (Abramo and Valenzuela 2005: 3; Chant 2002; Rothstein 1995) and qualitative research suggests that Mexican single mothers may migrate to support their children (Hondagneu-Sotelo and Avila 1997). Kanaiaupuni found that unmarried women with children were more likely to migrate than were married women (2000: 1337). She also found that previously conjugal women were more likely than others to migrate (1334). Additionally, according to Jeffrey Passel and Robert Suro (2005), one half of undocumented male adults migrate solo. Although fewer women do so, one in five women also migrate alone. Finally, among San Cosmeras in the US, even women who migrate as wives were usually also workers before they migrated and almost all work after they migrate.

Mexican men do migrate more, especially if one looks at undocumented migration. And they more often migrate independently. But women are migrating more today than in the past and what they do is not only a consequence of a subordinate relationship with men or of male migration.

Matthew Gutmann (2004) has recently criticized a somewhat common pattern of associating any change in gender relations in Mexico with migration to *el norte*. A related pattern in much of the migration literature is viewing women only as migrants' wives. More than twenty years ago, Sassen (1984: 1161) noted that "the study of women migrants has typically focused on their family situation and responsibilities." She went on to suggest that "the more fundamental processes are the ones promoting the formation of a supply of women migrants and a demand for this type of labor" (1161). An interesting and related pattern, discussed by Zontini in chapter 6, is Filipino women who use migration to achieve independence and get away from unhappy marriages. But, as recently as 2001, Marcela Cerrutti and Massey could note only that support for women's migration for reasons other than family motives is still only "fragmented" (2001). A primary reason for women's invisibility in many migration studies, according to Kanaiaupuni, may be that "they are commonly perceived as 'associational' migrants who follow spouses" (2000: 1335). She notes also that we still lack an adequate theoretical analysis for women's migration.

Based on a longitudinal perspective that examines women's increased employment in rural Mexico, this chapter suggests that globalization (and all that it has involved) may provide such a theoretical framework. Mexican women, like women elsewhere, do frequently find themselves in patriarchal contexts that encourage marriage and following their men. But the marriage trap of Mexican women is also being perpetuated by scholars who continue to focus exclusively on women migrants as wives.[12] Mexico's new migrants need new approaches that incorporate the changing gender and class dynamics that characterize contemporary Mexico's women migrants.

Notes

1. Following Binford (1998: 2), I define accelerated migration as "a migratory process that develops over a short period of time and incorporates a significant portion of the local adult pop. Roughly . . . migration assumes accelerated form when 30 percent or more of the adult population acquired international migratory experience in ten or fewer years."

2. Fieldwork was conducted in San Cosme from June 1971 to June 1972, from May 1974 to August 1974, from July 1980 to September 1980, from June 1984 to August 1984, August 1989, intermittently from August 1994 to December 1994, in January 1997, and from September through December 2001. Short visits, ranging from one day to two weeks have also been made to San Cosme, most recently in August 2004 and July 2005, and with migrants in New Jersey and New York.

3. The Bracero Program was a contract labor program that brought temporary Mexican workers to the United States from 1942–1964.

4. Researchers use a variety of values to indicate urban status ranging from 2,500 (used by the Mexican national statistical institute) to 20,000 (Flores, Hernández-Leon, and Massey 2004: 185).

5. Unless otherwise specified, statistical data are taken from the author's household surveys done in 1971, 1980, 1984, 1989, 1994, and 2001. In 1971 every fourth household was surveyed yielding one hundred and fifty households. In 1980 those same households plus an additional fifty and replacements for those households no longer occupied were randomly selected to give a total of two hundred. In 1984 one fourth of the households from 1980 were surveyed. In 1989 and 1994 the two hundred households (with random replacements) from 1980 were again surveyed. In 2001 two hundred households were surveyed. Approximately one hundred of these were in dwellings previously surveyed; one hundred were households in newer houses (that is, not there before the 1980s).

6. Although much of the increase in women's employment was for economic reasons, it is important to stress that women in Mexico, like elsewhere, were also increasingly entering the labor market to gain more independence and autonomy.

7. Lee (1998) distinguishes two different regimes of labor control: familial hegemony and localistic despotism and notes similar advantages and disadvantages. Wilson (1999: 342) also suggests that putting-out systems and family-based workshops offered women in western-central Mexico benefits that the formal sector, while paying better, did not.

8. Research by Massey, Goldring, and Durand (1994: 1498), as well as that of many others, has found that target migrants were usually men.

9. A common tendency in the migration literature is to focus on rural versus urban origins rather than non-waged versus waged labor status before migration. Consequently, the growth of wage work and the class implications of proletarianization have been neglected in much of the literature on migration.

10. Although the migration literature, with its avoidance of class, does not often address the relationship between labor migration, social networks, and class consciousness, studies focusing on labor organization, such as those by Collins (2003), Mills (2004), Zamudio (2002), and also Giles in chapter 1, have found diverse forms of activism based on workplace and community ties.

11. The union involved here, the FROC-CROC, is one of two "government" or *charro* unions that have been important in San Cosme since WWII and which have helped to bring about some individual social and geographical mobility, as in this case, but have not pursued collective goals that challenge the status quo (Rothstein 1979). Labrecque in chapter 10 also notes the effect of *charro* unions in the Yucatan.

12. Giles in chapter 1 similarly suggests that class and the fact that refugees are workers needs also to be addressed in the literature.

References

Abramo, Lois, and Maria Elena Valenzuela. 2005. "Women's Labor Force Participation Rates in Latin America." *International Labour Review* 144 (4): 369–400.

Appadurai, Arjun. 1996. *Modernity at Large: Cultural Dimensions of Globalization.* Minneapolis: University of Minnesota Press.

Arias, Patricia. 1995. "La migrácion feminina en dos modelos de desarrollo: 1940–1970 y 1980–1992." In *Relaciones de género y transformaciones agrarias*, eds. Soledad González Montes and Vania Salles, 223–253. Mexico City: El Colegio de Mexico.

Basch, Linda, Nina Glick Schiller, and Cristina Szanton Blanc. 1994. *Nations Unbound: Transnational Projects, Postcolonial Predicaments, and Deterriorialized Nation-States*. Langhorne: Gordon and Breach.

Becerril, Andrea. 1994. "Cerraron más de 80% de empresas textiles en los dos últimos sexenio." *La Jornada*, 6 November: 48.

Binford, Leigh. 1998. "Accelerated Migration from Puebla." Paper presented at conference, Mexicans in New York and Mexico: New Analytical Perspectives on Migration, Transnationalization and Immigrant Incorporation. Barnard College and the New School for Social Research, New York, October.

Brettell, Caroline. 2000 "Theorizing Migration in Anthropology: The Social Construction of Networks, Identities, Communities and Global Scapes." In *Migration Theory: Talking Across Disciplines*, eds. Caroline Brettell and James Hollyfield, 97–135. New York: Routledge.

Canales, Alejandro. 2003. "Mexican Labour Migration to the United States in the Age of Globalization." *Journal of Ethnic and Migration Studies* 29 (4): 741–761.

Cerrutti, Marcela, and Douglas Massey. 2001. "On the Auspices of Female Migration from Mexico to the United States." *Demography* 38 (2): 187–200.

Chant, Sylvia. 2002. "Researching Gender, Families and Households in Latin America: From the 20th into the 21st century." *Bulletin of Latin American Research* 21 (4): 545–575.

Chavez M., Marcos. 1995. "Sufre la manufactura su peor crisis de los ultimos 15 años." *El Financiero*, 24 April: 40.

Cohen, Jeffrey. 2002. *The Culture of Migration*. Austin: University of Texas Press.

Collins, Jane. 2003. *Threads: Gender, Labor and Power in the Global Apparel Industry*. Chicago: University of Chicago Press.

Crummett, Maria De Los Angeles. 2001. "A Gendered Economic History of Rural Households: Calvillo, Aguascalientes, Mexico, 1982–1991." *Frontiers* 22 (1): 105–125.

Curran, Sara, and Estela Rivero-Fuentes. 2003. "Engendering Migrant Networks: The Case of Mexican Migrants." *Demography* 40 (2): 289–307.

Donato, Katharine, et al. 2006. "A Glass Half Full? Gender in Migration Studies." *International Migration Review* 40 (1): 1–26.

Durand, Jorge, and Douglas Massey. 2004. "What We Learned from the Mexican Migration Project." In *Crossing the Border: Research from the Mexican Migration Project*, eds. Jorge Durand and Douglas Massey, 1–16. New York: Russell Sage Foundation.

Escobar Latapí, Agustín, and Susan Martin. 2006. "Mexico-U.S. Migration Management: A Binational Approach." The William and Flora Hewlett Foundation. http://hewlett/org Programs/GlobalAffairs/Publications/usmexicomigration.ht (accessed 6 December 2006).

Fernández-Kelly, Mária. 1983. *For We are Sold, I and My People: Women and Industry in Mexico's Frontier*. Albany: State University of New York Press.

Flores, Nadia, Rubén Hernández-Leon, and Douglas Massey. 2004. "Social Capital and Migration from Rural and Urban Communities." In *Crossing the Border: Research from the Mexican Migration Project*, eds. Jorge Durand and Douglas Massey, 184–200. New York: Russell Sage Foundation.

Freeman, Carla. 2001. "Is Local: Global as Feminine: Masculine? Rethinking the Gender of Globalization." *Signs: Journal of Women, Culture and Society* 26 (4): 1007–1037.

Grasmuck, Sherri, and Patricia Pessar. 1991. *Between Two Islands: Dominican International Migration*. Berkeley: University of California Press.

Grimes, Kimberly. 1998. *Crossing Borders: Changing Social Identities in Southern Mexico*. Tucson: University of Arizona Press.

Gutmann, Matthew. 2004. "Dystopian Travels in Gringolandia: Engendering Ethnicity Among Mexican Migrants to the United States." *Ethnicities* 4 (4): 477–500.

Harvey, David. 1989. *The Condition of Postmodernity*. Cambridge, MA: Blackwell.

Hirsch, Jennifer. 2002 "Que pues, con el pinche NAFTA? Gender, Power and Migration Between Western Mexico and Atlanta." *Urban Anthropology* 31 (3–4): 351–387.

Hondagneu-Sotelo, Pierrette. 2000. "Gender and Immigration: A Retrospective and Introduction." In *Gender and U.S. Immigration: Contemporary Trends*, ed. Pierrette Hondagneu-Sotelo, 3–19. Los Angeles: University of California Press.

Hondagneu-Sotelo, Pierrette, and Ernestine Avila. 1997. "'I'm Here, But I'm There': The Meanings of Latina Transnational Motherhood." *Gender and Society* 11 (5): 548–571.

Kanaiaupuni, Shawn Malia. 2000. "Reframing the Migration Question: An Analysis of Men, Women, and Gender in Mexico." *Social Forces* 78 (4): 1311–1347.

Kochhar, Rakesh. 2005. *Survey of Mexican Migrants: The Economic Transition to America*. The Pew Hispanic Center, December.

Kyle, David. 2000. *Transnational Peasants: Migration, Networks, and Ethnicities in Andean Ecuador*. Baltimore: Johns Hopkins University Press.

Lee, Ching Kwan. 1998. *Gender and the South China Miracle: Two Worlds of Factory Women*. Berkeley: University of California Press.

Ma, Eric Kit-Wai. 2001. "Consuming Satellite Modernities." *Cultural Studies* 15 (3): 444–463.

Mahler, Sara, and Patricia Pessar. 2006. "Gender Matters: Ethnographers Bring Gender from the Periphery Toward the Core of Migration Studies." *International Migration Review* 40 (1): 27–63.

Massey, Douglas, et al. 1987. *Return to Aztlan: The Social Process of International Migration from Western Mexico*. Berkeley: University of California Press.

Massey, Douglas, Luin Goldring, and Jorge Durand. 1994. "Continuities in Transnational Migration: An Analysis of Nineteen Mexican Communities." *American Sociological Review* 99: 1492–1533.

Miller, Daniel. 1995. "Consumption and Commodities." *Annual Review of Anthropology* 24: 141–161.

———. 1997. *Capitalism: An Ethnographic Account*. Oxford: Berg.

Mills, Mary Beth. 1999. *Thai Women in the Global Labor Force: Consuming Desires, Contested Selves*. New Brunswick: Rutgers University Press.

———. 2004. "From mobile fingers to raised fists: Women and labor activism in globalizing Thailand." *Signs* 31(1):117–144.

Misra, Joya, Jonathan Woordring, and Sabine Merz. 2006. "The Globalization of Carework: Immigration, Economic Restructuring, and the World-System." *Globalizations* 3 (3): 317–333.

Mongelluzzo. 2006. "Maquiladoras get New Lease on Life." *Commonwealth Business Media*, 13 March. http://web.lexisnexis.com.proxytu.researchport.umd.edu/universe/print/doc.

Otero, Gerardo, ed. 2004. *Mexico in Transition: Neoliberal Globalism, the State and Civil Society*. London: Zed Books.

Passel, Jeffrey, and Robert Suro. 2005. "Rise and Peak and Decline in U.S. Immigration, 1992–2004." Pew Hispanic Center.

Pessar, Patricia. 2003. "Engendering Migration Studies: The Case of New Immigrants in the United States." In *Gender and U.S. Immigration: Contemporary Trends*, ed. Pierrette Hondagneu-Sotelo, 20–42. Berkeley: University of California Press.

Pyle, Jean. 2006. "Globalization and the Increase in Transnational Care Work: An Introduction." *Globalizations* 3 (4): 283–295.

Pyle, Jean, and Kathryn Ward. 2003. "Recasting our Understanding of Gender and Work During Global Restructuring." *International Sociology* 18 (3): 461–489.

Rothstein. Frances. 1979. "The Class Basis of Patron-Client Relations." *Latin American Perspectives* 6: 25–35.

————. 1995. "Gender and Multiple Income Strategies in Rural Mexico: A Twenty-Year Perspective." In *Women in the Development Process in Latin America: From Structural Subordination to Empowerment*, eds. Edna Acosta-Belen and Christine Bose, 167–193. Philadelphia: Temple University Press.

————. 1996. "Flexible Accumulation, Youth Labor, and Schooling in a Rural Community in Mexico." *Critique of Anthropology* 16: 361.

————. 1999. "Declining Odds: Kinship, Women's Employment and Political Economy in Rural Mexico." *American Anthropologist* 101 (3): 579–593.

————. 2000. "Flexible Work and Post-Modern Culture: The Impact of Globalization on Work and Culture in Rural Mexico." *Anthropology of Work Review* 11 (1): 3–7.

————. 2007. *Globalization in Rural Mexico: Three Decades of Change*. Austin: University of Texas Press.

Sassen, Saskia [as Sassen-Koob]. 1984. "Notes on the Incorporation of Third World Women into Wage-Labor through Immigration and Off-shore Production." *International Migration Review* 18 (4): 1144–1168.

————. 1988. *The Mobility of Labor and Capital: A Study of International Investment and Labor Flow*. Cambridge: Cambridge University Press.

————. 2003. "Strategic Instantiations of Gendering in the Global Economy." In *Gender and U.S. Immigration: Contemporary Trends*, ed. Pierrette Hondagneu-Sotelo, 43–60. Berkeley: University of California Press.

Stephen, Lynn. 2005. *Zapotec Women*. Durham: Duke University.

Wilson, Fiona. 1999. "Gendered Histories: Garment Production and Migration in Mexico." *Environment and Planning* 31 (2): 327–343.

Wilson, Tamar. 1993. "Theoretical Approaches to Mexican Wage Labor Migration." *Latin American Perspectives* 20 (3): 98–129.

World Bank. 2007. Summary Gender Profile (Mexico). http://devdata.worldbank.org/genderstats/genderRpt.asp?rpt=profile&cty=MEX (accessed 21 January 2008).

Zamudio, Margaret. 2002. "Segmentation, Conflict, Community and Coalitions: Lessons from the New Labor Movement." In *Transnational Latina/o Communities: Political Processes and Cultures*, eds. Carlos Velez-Ibanez and Anna Sampaio, 205–224. Lanham: Rowman and Littlefield.

— *Chapter 3* —

THE STATE AND MOBILE PEOPLE AT THE US-MEXICO BORDER

Josiah Heyman

Migration has long played a central role in the assembling of labor forces, both proletarian and slaves/indentured servants. Through the twentieth and into the twenty-first century, increasingly complex and closely enforced rules of movement and residence have produced an important series of subdivisions among working people, between citizen, legal migrant, guest worker, and unauthorized migrant. How do these relationships to the state affect class relations? It is useful to approach this question from two ends, comparing the effects on class of favored status, citizenship, and highly disfavored status, illegality (following Heyman 1998; DeGenova 2002). Much like Giles in chapter 1, who asks how the immobility of refugee status affects class, this chapter asks how the unequal governance over and practice of movement affects class relations, specifically in a border zone where state surveillance and policing is extensive but not omniscient and omnipresent? Lem and Barber challenge us, in the book's introduction, to link migration and class, in both its objective and subjective moments, as mutually constitutive processes; I respond by focusing on a central process, the enforcement of immigration laws and the delineation of bounded national spaces, in terms of how it both helps constitute and may be challenged by class relations and mobilizations.

Risk has been a central discourse and practice in contemporary mobility control and national security (see Ackleson 2005). The chapter thus begins with theories of risk and society from Anthony Giddens, Ulrich Beck, Dorothy Nelkin, and Mary Douglas. They vary in how much attention they pay to power and the unequal distribution and interpretation of risk, but with the exception of Douglas, they do not address the construction of particular social groups *as risks* and recursively the risks that the state presents to such groups. Likewise, they attend only to risk and not trust, or when considering trust (Giddens), do not view it as unequally allocated among social groups. By rethinking risk theories in terms of inequality and power, we help uncover, examine, challenge, and deepen the use of risk and trust in immigration and border debates around the world.

The chapter surveys the history of US immigration politics, looking at various constructions of undocumented migrants, leading up to the post-9/11 constitution of immigrants as potential threats to the existence of state and civil society, the "securitisation" of immigration. It turns next to the border police-military zone, surveying its tactical geography of efforts to detect and apprehend undocumented immigrants, especially while on the move. It also considers the inverse, the construction of trusted social groups and how such trusted groups bypass or speed through risk points in this geography. The chapter then looks at the presence of enforcement in the lived experience of the undocumented and citizens, examining how citizenship/immigration differences in risk and trust connect to class inequality through the mediation of household economies, age and gender relations, public goods, movement, and other elements of the production and reproduction of differentiated labor. It offers some observations on how risk labels and practices affect class consciousness, and closes by reflecting on the use of risk and trust to study inequalities in mobility (Pallitto and Heyman 2008).

Risk Theories

Ulrich Beck and Anthony Giddens see risk and trust as shared existential conditions facing all people within modernity, rather than as wedges that divide segments of people. Giddens (1990) argues that risk characterizes modernity, as does a particular version of trust. Modern societies create risks that transcend direct individual recognition and control. Trust in pre-modern societies was deployed in immediate relationships, but in modern societies, distant experts and systems mitigate inherent risks.

Beck (1993, 1999) makes a similar argument. Initially, modernity was about rectifying shortfalls in basic needs, which could be treated as deterministic. In this process, however, modernity generated risks (his examples are mainly environmental). As one set of risks are addressed, new ones are generated. Beck is more attentive than Giddens to unequal distributions of risks and their consequences. But his favored approach to risk solution is through cosmopolitan alliances of disparate places and people who come together when they share such issues. Such cosmopolitan alliances are, in a fundamental way, exactly the opposite of the risk-based divisions between citizen-insiders and migrant-outsiders discussed in this chapter.

Dorothy Nelkin (1985), by contrast, emphasizes inequalities of risks in the field of political and social power. Her interests include both unequal impacts of risky processes and differential perceptions of those risks. The risks she focuses on are workplace and environmental health hazards, and like Giddens and Beck, she does not explore riskiness and trustworthiness as labels for social groups as such.

Mary Douglas (1992; Douglas and Wildavsky 1982) also largely addresses environmental and safety hazards, but her framework offers insight into construing social groups as risks. Risk arguments are not statements about objective probabilities of harm, but statements based on and addressing social order. Thus, risk constructions of a particular group, such as undocumented border crossers, might take this form: this is a group outside the normal social order, constituting a danger, and to blame for disorders and risks. She calls these blame-making propositions the "forensic" theory of risk.

Douglas also points out that the term risk conflates two different meanings: that of probabilistic statements of any sort, good or bad, as opposed to deterministic ones, and the negative meaning of risk as danger and blame for it. This chapter uses both meanings of risk. US border enforcement agencies only probabilistically encounter undocumented migrants, meaning that migrants can and do take chances without inevitably being arrested.

This discussion widens the relevance and power of risk theory. Risk certainly includes health, safety, and the environment, but it also includes statements about social groups themselves as the carriers or recipients of risk. Risk sometimes does involve shared existential hazards, but it also involves constructions that move in the opposite way from "sharing," such as seeing some sets of people as the recipients of safety and others as the sources of danger. Addressing inequalities of risk construction, in turn, connects risk theory to the making and reproduction of classes. Likewise, along with risk constructions come trustworthiness constructions, again possibly aligned with class, building on Giddens's notion of trust but with greater awareness of how trust relates to power and privilege in society.

Risk Constructions of Mexican Migrants in the United States

Northward labor migration from Mexico, which dates to the 1880s, has been construed and regulated in various ways over the years, with two key trends: the increasing role of formal legal definitions of citizens versus non-citizens (and concomitantly the decline but not disappearance of explicit racism), and intensifying construction of migrants as a "danger."

The US-Mexico border was set in place through war and treaty in 1848 and 1853, with substantial Mexican populations finding themselves abruptly included as "citizens" (with few real rights) in the United States. The United States allowed relatively free entry from Mexico through the 1920s, although some regulations came into place in the 1910s and 1920s. The Border Patrol began operations in 1924, but its first target was Chinese immigrants, who were already seen as a "danger" to US society. The Border Patrol then shifted in the late 1920s and the 1930s toward Mexicans who had entered the US without inspection, in violation of the minimal visa laws of the era (they often were avoiding fees required for the visas). Mexicans became the predilect target of US immigration policing, which continues to the present day (Lytle Hernández 2002; Ngai 2004). From the 1880s to the 1950s (and in many cases long after) people of Mexican origin were segregated and paid lower wages. They were constructed as outsiders to the US social order as a race, and statements about risk were above all pseudo biological. Because this population was seen as an indelible Mexican race, the issue was not just movement across borders but their very being as inherent outsiders within the territory of the United States.

From 1942 through 1965 there was a large-scale legal temporary worker program (the Bracero Program) between Mexico and the United States. From 1942 to 1954 there was alongside the legal program considerable undocumented border crossing, which came to an end through intensified enforcement and contracting after 1954 (Calavita 1992). When the Bracero Program ended in 1965, undocumented migration returned, and indeed grew substantially, because of increasing structural demand for migrant workers in many regions and labor markets in the United States. It has maintained a high level since then, with some fluctuations (one rough estimator of the annual flow, albeit with serious limitations, is border arrests of approximately 1 to 1.5 million undocumented entrants).

For the entire post-1880 period, except in the Great Depression, the borderlands have seen continuing, substantial permanent legal immigration flows from Mexico, so that large numbers of people of Mexican origin are legal immigrants or US citizens by birth or naturalization. The legal framework for most US immigration was changed in 1965, opening up diverse global legal migration; Mexico was integrated in this framework by 1976. Throughout the US-side borderlands, the vast majority of the population are of Mexican origin, of many different legal standings and generational depths, including millions of citizens and permanent residents with strong social and legal claims to legitimacy in the nation.

The social bounding of Mexicans as a unitary, alien race declined across the course of the twentieth century because of vigorous civil rights and social justice struggles lead by these Mexican-origin immigrant and citizen populations. But racial prejudice has transmuted into the current spate of anti-immigration politics that obsesses about the Mexican border as a source of peril. Hence, there are three different distinctions—white/ Mexican, citizen/non-citizen, and illegal/legal—that do not overlap neatly, but do combine in construing Mexican undocumented immigrants as a profound source of risk. Risk concepts include invasion of people, with a particular fear of being outnumbered and overwhelmed or swamped. Fears include the number of people, the presence of fecund women and the birth of children, and the use of public services. Also, undocumented immigrants, and especially unauthorized border crossing, raises strong concerns about violations of law, especially with law seen as a pure expression of order (Chavez 2001; DeGenova 2002; Nevins 2002; Santa Ana 2002).

US border enforcement was at low ebb in the 1960s and early 1970s, only gradually responding to the surge of cross-border undocumented migration after the end of the Bracero Program. By the late 1970s and the 1980s the border became more heavily policed, with a fluctuating level of resources and attention through 1993. Late in that year a new tactic was introduced, placing the Border Patrol directly on the front line of main urban crossing areas, such as San Diego county and El Paso. This displaced undocumented migrant flows to remote desert areas of the border, where they continued to be successful in entering the US, although increasingly employing smugglers and worsening risks of death. Since 1993 there has been a sustained intensification of border enforcement, including advanced motion sensors, lights, walls, helicopters, military support, and most tellingly, a quadrupling of the Border Patrol from four thousand to sixteen thousand officers, most of them deployed at the southern border (Andreas 2001; Fuentes et al. 2007; Massey, Durand, and Malone 2002; Nevins 2002).

The horrific attacks of 9/11 focused the United States populace on the risk of international terrorism. At first, the emphasis was on men from Islamic countries. Several thousand were arrested and deported because of various immigration violations, including visa overstays and minor violations of immigration laws, such as not reporting changes of address by legal residents. There were some expressions of fear about the porous Mexican border, but it was not a central concern. A number of separate government agencies that regulated and policed borders merged into the Department of Homeland Security in 2003. Interviews by the author after 9/11 with Customs and Border Protection officers (a unit of Homeland Security) expressed a strong commitment to preventing terrorism and a day-to-day emphasis on interdicting illegal drugs (see also Meyers 2005).

It was only in 2005 that the homeland security risk agenda focused on unauthorized border immigration and the 6 to 7 million undocumented Mexican residents (of approximately 10 to 12 million total undocumented). Although it was difficult to make a terrorism case directly against Mexican labor migrants,[1] the implicit risk construction—borders equal security—was forged through the identification of the boundary control mission of the state as one of fundamental homeland security. Thus, unauthorized labor migration was securitized, a term that refers to the application of the frameworks and agencies of protection against fundamental, existential threats to the existence of state and civil society (Ackleson 2003a, 2003b; Buzan, Wæver, and de Wilde 1998; Huysmans 1995; Wæver 1995). Securitization is the most profound risk construction possible; it encompasses but also transcends the other immigration risk concepts discussed earlier.

In the current United States, then, there are three main constructions of immigrants and particularly of undocumented immigrants. One is that they are human beings, above and beyond legal status within a given nation-state, a construction associated with labor organizing, religious, community, and human rights policy approaches. The second is that immigration can be considered a cost-benefit matter like other issues of public policy (e.g., serving as usable and disposable workers), but not that immigrants are seen as fundamental sources of risk and danger. In the final framework immigrants (especially those unauthorized by law) pose fundamental risks to society. It is the latter construction that dominates border policies.

US public opinion has fractured among these positions, and cannot be described even as coherent among them. Certainly, most citizens if asked directly would not admit to viewing undocumented Mexicans as fundamental existential threats. However, the de facto drift of US policies and practices is in this direction, the securitization of migration control through the border-obsessed mission expansion of the Department of Homeland Security. An important illustration is the initiation in 2007 of a $2.5 billion (at least) advanced surveillance and interdiction system, Smart Border Initiative, with the Boeing Corporation as general contractor, as well as 370 miles of a $4 million-a-mile border wall. Certainly this is corporate and bureaucratic aggrandizement on the part of the homeland security industrial complex, and perhaps also a diversion of attention from the bloody morass of the Iraq War. More speculatively, the public policy debate's combination of much stronger surveillance and interdiction with amplified guest-worker program and more distinctly privileged legal travel might signal important reworkings of citizenship and labor flows in the future, for which reason it is important to examine current conditions and trends at the border.

The Border as Risk Zone: State Practices

The basic patterns of border law enforcement shows how risk is constructed from the perspective of the state: that is, as a coherent policing response to a risk assessment of who and where immigration laws are being violated (and also contraband goods, which overlaps considerably with immigration enforcement). These state practices unequally allocate trustworthiness and untrustworthiness among the populations moving around in the US borderlands.

The US border with Mexico is not just a defended line but an enforcement zone in depth. Contained within this zone are substantial population centers, from small towns to metropolitan areas with millions of people; the inhabitants include US citizens, legal residents, and undocumented residents, sometimes combined in mixed-status families, as well as transient undocumented migrants moving north. To describe this enforcement zone, let us begin with legal crossing points from Mexico, ports of entry, where some unknown number (tens to hundreds of thousands, perhaps) of fraudulent entrants (those with false claims to citizenship, fraudulent documents, or false declarations of intention in visiting the United States) mix in with 250 million legitimate entries.

At ports, there is a trade-off between speed of inspections, resulting in clearing out traffic, and intensity of inspections of persons, documents, and vehicles. The government has devised two responses. One is use of Dedicated Commuter Lanes, where radio frequency transmitter-bearing cars swiftly move through inspections (an average of twelve seconds in primary [the initial go/no-go decision]). Behind this is an application process, a background check, and a $400 fee, most of which goes to the Mexican government. These well-referenced and prosperous people are officially designated as "trusted" (low risk) by the US government, though a small number are interdicted for immigration and customs violations. The other approach is to divide rapidly the main body of crossers into trusted and risky subgroups. Their unmarked entry lanes are not treated as high risk per se. Crossings average thirty seconds in primary. However, 21 percent of pedestrians and vehicles undergo much longer questioning (median of seventy seconds). About 2 percent go to secondary inspections, a sustained examination and interrogation that can lead to arrest or seizure of documents and goods (data from Villegas et al. 2006). I have described the inspections routine at ports elsewhere (Heyman 2001a, 2004); it suffices here to say that people receive extra scrutiny based on a complex construction of their putative risks for unauthorized migration and goods smuggling based on visual and documentary cues. An example is Mexican residents appearing by their clothing and vehicles to be working class, and thus potentially seeking unauthorized employment in the US. Those who do not receive this extra scrutiny are trusted on their verbal declarations and a rapid visual scan of their documents. It is common practice at the land border not to enter the document into watch lists on computer databases (United States Government Accountability Office 2003, 2006).

The choice to identify risks versus non-risks is highly variable among inspectors (Dudley Ward et al. 2008) and appears to have subjective and arbitrary components. Non-Mexicans, in particular Middle Easterners and South Asians entering from Mexico (such as students and visitors) are subject to prolonged scrutiny because of the recent terrorism construct. Since summer 2006, during the recent Mexican immigration panic, a requirement for direct visual inspection of documents of Mexicans entering the US was introduced at the port of El Paso, where I do my research. This was previously not required and not always done by inspectors. Clearly, the high-risk category has widened somewhat.

It is illegal to cross the boundary in between the legitimate ports of entry. The Border Patrol polices these spaces. In the urban areas of the border, the Border Patrol operates a relatively dense, static line of four-wheel drive vehicles, as well as fences and iron walls, all designed to deter entry. As we have seen, this displaces illegal entry to small rural settlements, farms, ranches, and remote desert and mountain areas. There, the Border Patrol operates in depth, using vehicle-based officers, observation towers, night-vision units, motion sensors, and ground-level radar.

Officers assume that individuals witnessed in or tracked from entries directly at the boundary are unauthorized, but people walking or driving in farms and settled areas near the border require the officer to perform an assessment of possible legal status, involving their behavior, clothing, and apparent race as a clue, importantly incomplete, to nationality. Settled residents, including both authorized and unauthorized people, and especially people who look like they are of Mexican origin, are always at risk of Border Patrol questioning and detention in the heavily policed zone near the border, including both cities and dispersed rural settlements. Anglo Americans and African Americans are nearly always trusted, while people of visible Mexican origin are always viewed as possibilities, but may either be targeted or removed from interest by many other clues.

Approximately twenty five to one hundred miles from the boundary, on all major highways leading away from the border area, the Border Patrol operates fixed checkpoints. This creates an interior boundary to the heavily policed border zone. Interior checkpoints face the same challenge as the ports of entry—the trade-off between speed of traffic clearance and intensity of inspections. Observations at and interviews about checkpoints indicate similar risk/trust evaluations as described above for ports of entry; for example, a Mexican American Border Patrol officer explicitly told me that he profiled cars from Mexico and US border states containing Latino-appearing people at highway stops but apologetically excused away not stopping "Europeans," to use his phrasing (Heyman 2002: 489).

In addition, the Border Patrol constantly stations officers at transportation points such as airports and bus stations, with the power to pull aside, question, and detain would-be travelers. Men using Mexican passports are regularly pulled aside at airports, including US legal residents, for extra questioning and physical inspection by the Transportation Security Administration (observation and interviews, 2007). Border Patrol officers also observe entrants at security lines in airports and pull aside those with social cues (e.g., apparent race and class) suggesting possible unauthorized migration. There are, of course, other security pull-asides in mass transportation settings, but it is interesting that in the border region people of Mexican citizenship or even just Mexican appearance are classified as categorical risks as contrasted with non-risk categorized, normally inspected travellers.

Between the border and the checkpoints is a twenty-five to one hundred–mile wide strip through which Border Patrol and other immigration enforcement units are constantly in motion, both on the surface and in the air.[2] This is not to say that every moment, every place is under surveillance—just that it is an everyday presence. People on sidewalks, in parks, in yards, at workplaces (especially visible ones), on farms, outside of schools and hospitals, and so forth, are all exposed to a sporadic immigration law enforcement presence. Bicycle patrols regularly pass by my building at the university, for example. In addition to the Border Patrol, an agency called Immigration and Customs Enforcement (ICE) conducts investigations in this region, as in the interior of the United States, including employment-document inspection raids on workplaces.

Policing the border zone is important to immigration law enforcement because it contains numerous staging areas and safe houses for smugglers to hold undocumented migrants while waiting for arrangements to move them north, through or around checkpoints. At the same time, this constant presence in and potential interaction with border society means that officers constantly have to assess people in everyday forms of movement to decide if they are trustworthy or constitute risks.

Immigration law enforcement is a federal responsibility in the United States, but a variety of other border region entities become involved in it. Local law enforcement sometimes but not always participates in de facto immigration law enforcement. For example, the El Paso County Sheriff conducts roadblocks in outlying regions of the county, ostensibly to enforce traffic laws, but whose main effect is to interrogate, identify, and turn over undocumented migrants to the Border Patrol. The El Paso City Police Department, by contrast, does not conduct such operations. Local government agencies in the El Paso area, such as the public hospital, the public schools, the Housing Agency, etc., do not seek to identify immigration status. The state of Texas does, however, for drivers' licenses. However, immigrants using public health and housing services (but not schools) are at risk of creating a documentary record of being "likely to become a public charge," a ground for their exclusion from legal permanent immigration to the United States and the denial of petitions for the immigration of relatives. A main risk of being detected comes from contact with the federal authorities who handle applications for legal immigration and other immigration benefits, since a person may incidentally make it known that they are in the territory of the United States without authorization. There are many governmental authorities in the region, and they vary considerably in the rules they follow, the attitudes they take, the benefits they potentially provide, and the risks they pose. The trust in a particular segment of government and that branch's trust of a given person or family, then, is a matter of great variability and uncertainty.

In summary, the way the state operates in the border zone is roughly to divide the population into trusted and distrusted populations, but the allocation process is complex and probabilistic rather than clear and certain. Officers encounter a substantial public, usually well over half (and often upwards of 90 percent) of Mexican origin, and they must make specific risk judgements, often in very short periods of time. Within the general concept of trust, there are layers, such as the privileged trusted population with Dedicated Commuter passes or phenotypically white people, as well as those with more egalitarian trusted status, such as all US citizens. Outside the trusted population are those without appropriate documents, who may sometimes escape scrutiny but who are always at risk.

The Border as Risk Zone: The Undocumented Immigrant Perspective

Despite dense policing in the border area, being apprehended by the US government is only a possibility and not a certainty for undocumented migrants. Jezmin Fuentes et al. (2007: 66) report that less than a quarter of former unauthorized entrants interviewed in Mexico report having been caught crossing the border on a recent trip. Immigration policing is largely circumvented through the use of smugglers to get into the US and past interior checkpoints and, among the resident undocumented population, by great caution in movement and through assistance networks, often involving citizens and legal residents.[3] The undocumented population is thus significantly constrained but they do have the ability to act on their perceived resources, needs, and understandings, for example making illegal entries coming and going from Mexico to visit elderly relatives or crossing checkpoints to seek work in other parts of the United States. Rather than categorical oppression and control, the border policing zone thus represents a set of risks that have both subjective and objective dimensions. Everyday, people experience a range of feelings from anxiety to reassurance, and practically they constantly weigh goals, options, costs, barriers, and perils.

To understand the issues faced by the undocumented, it is worth surveying exactly where and how they are at risk. They face the highest level of risk in movement. Many of the control systems described above focus on inspection points in the transportation system (coming and going from Mexico, checkpoints leaving the border zone, etc.). Movement also involves being visible and open to observation and questioning in public spaces. Movement, then, has to be weighed against the goal to be obtained and through the resources for moving—is it for earning money, visiting kin, going to school, seeking health care, and is it through walking, public transportation, a ride from a trusted neighbor, or a private car (but without a driver's license, since one is not to be had without legal status)? Thus, the pattern of perils in mobility affects a wider range of crucial resources and relationships.

Being in place is not as risky as movement, but there are degrees of risks associated with specific places, public or private, such as a hospital or a workplace. Certain places are inherently public, such as the state institutions discussed in the next paragraph. Others mix public and private, such as stores. Generally, immigration law enforcement does not arrest people in public settings (there are some exceptions) because of the disruption and controversy that could occur. Workplaces, however, are more vulnerable. Since 1986 it has been illegal to employ unauthorized immigrants, and workplaces were subject to inspection of records and workers. These laws were weakly enforced, with inspections starting out low and declining over time, but since the immigration panic of 2005 the tempo of workplace inspections has grown, though they are still infrequent compared to the number of sites where undocumented people are employed. Homes and similar spaces are assumed by the undocumented to be safe, and generally this is true, but the Border Patrol and ICE do sometimes lurk outside such structures, and on some occasions they do knock on doors, asking to enter premises (or even carrying warrants) because of investigations of fraudulent documents, serving orders of deportation, etc.

State institutions represent an enormous dilemma to the undocumented and their legal resident or citizen relatives. On the one hand, they provide resources they value and often desperately need. These include schooling, police services, and health services. On the other hand, such institutions are broadly part of the same official authorities as immigration agencies, and undocumented people are thus uncertain how much to trust them. Official organizations then vary in the trust accorded them. Schools are relatively trusted—US public schools do not have immigration-status tests for attendance (universities usually have residency tests, and states vary in whether they regard immigration status in residency decisions). Hospitals and clinics, on the other hand, are contradictory. They are sometimes distrusted because they sometimes report charity care to immigration authorities (see the explanation of the risk of being likely to be a public charge, above), but on the other hand, they are often the only place for the uninsured to access health care, especially in emergencies. The vast majority of the undocumented have no private health insurance and none have access to governmental health insurance; emergency services and some basic public health services are provided without insurance, however, and there are some free and low-cost community clinics that do not check for legal status. Local police have much the same ambiguous position as do official health services.

Trust forms an essential counterpart, both practical and psychological, to risk. Workplaces, for example, contain intricate networks of trust and distrust among employers, contractors, supervisors, and workers, heightened by the fact that work is a central motivation for coming to the United States but also in these cases an illegal act. Trust thus also involves the potential of betrayal, and the possibility of leveraging debts for assistance or even just for non-exposure into exploitation. Trust within the undocumented community is, in important ways, the inverse of official risks assessment: if risk inheres in public spaces, trustworthy spaces are often private and enclosed. If the central government poses the greatest risks, then the most trustworthy relations are the most private and personal ones—friends, kin, and neighbors—and local components of the state are positioned in-between. Public spaces and anonymous market spaces always contain risks—they may need to be entered, but cautiously and as infrequently as possible. The world of risk and trust, then, departs from the world of legally confident people, people who can move about and enter interactions and spaces on an open, "normal" basis. Such people may not give up trust in private spheres or fully embrace all public settings, but they can approach them in a less risk-aware fashion. Such observations show how the allocation of risk and trust relative to state and market power shape both outsider *and* normal life-worlds.

State-Society Relations:
Effects of Risk and Trust on Class Processes

When the state treats people as trusted, individuals and households have two advantages. Their legal status does not impact negatively their power in market relations, although they may be advantaged or disadvantaged in other ways. Also, they are not cautious about accessing state-distributed resources and services, and have more ample rights to them. When the state construes people as risks, and when in turn they experience the state as a creator of risks to them, this risk status reinforces other disadvantages in labor markets (Mexican race, low education, financial need), and also impedes access to some state goods. From this starting point, then, let us take up the question of what effects undocumented life in a covert world has on class relations. However, this covert experience is not absolute exploitation and control by evil traffickers or monster employers, but rather a probabilistic set of negative outcomes emerging from a complex set of relations and interactions, as undocumented people address various life needs, avoid state risk, deal cautiously with other governmental entities, secure movement (including smuggling), obtain and keep jobs, and develop places of safety and networks of trust. Such people have to face difficult choices under imbalanced circumstances, but are not completely frozen in terms of their capacity to act.

My approach here draws on the Marxist-feminist rethinking of class, which seeks to widen the male-biased focus on paid work outside the household, in a fashion quite similar to Rothstein's analysis of San Cosme gender and migration to the United States (see chapter 2). The wage labor relation basic to capitalism involves not just the employer and employee, but a whole network of processes that create, provision, and reproduce labor. These processes circulate through workplace interactions, control and disposal of income, public goods, unpaid work inside and outside households, and complicated relations of age, gender, and social network power (Rapp 1983). The state-society relationship inflects various points in this entire web of relations to make available to the capitalist market labor with various degrees of necessity and vulnerability to exploitation. In this way, risk and trust complexly translate into proletarian and privileged.

For the at-risk, the pattern of those risks, the caution about taking risks, and the incomplete trust in state institutions means that such individuals and households utilize few state resources, although they do use some, notably for their children. They encounter comparable issues in bureaucratized consumer markets that rely in part on official state identification, the absence of which results in poor or no credit ratings, exploitative check cashing and lending services, bad purchasing and leasing terms, etc. The role of formal institutions in stabilizing households against risk is diminished (e.g., lack of insurance against high medical costs). Finally, they have low levels of information, because of constraints on their ability to move around physically and because they are unusually dependent, even by immigrant standards, on interpersonal networks rather than formal channels of communication.

Facing low levels of support and stabilization by the state and related institutions, such households then send out workers with a strong sense of necessity, shaping both the kinds of jobs they take and the performance of their job. Their interpersonal networks shape entry into and pay and hour arrangements within specific low-wage labor markets (Griffith 1987). Households with undocumented members are similarly vulnerable in consumption, when landlords and others take advantage of their immediate needs and lack of societal subsidies. The undocumented and those closely connected to them thus transfer high levels of surplus in many different ways to the overall capitalist economy.

With respect to workplace relations, considerable evidence shows that the undocumented are relatively more vulnerable and exploitable than plain proletarians, though certainly capable of unionization and sustained struggles for social and economic justice (Thomas 1985; Zlolniski 2006). Several analyses (not mutually exclusive) have been offered for this situation (Heyman 2001b). I have proposed (Heyman 1998) that undocumented immigrants enter into manipulable relationships of obligation and trust (with smugglers, money lenders, labor contractors, supervisors, hometown mates, etc.) in order to circumvent intensive border law enforcement. Christian Zlolniski (2003, 2006) accepts this analysis, but adds that workers are also directly affected by immigration law enforcement actions in and near workplaces, resulting in their behaving cautiously and unassertively, and pulling back from publicly visible struggles for justice.

It is worth commenting at this point that risk is borne inequitably between employers and undocumented people. The vast majority of the risk occurs in movement, mostly through the border zone. Employment site apprehensions are less than 1 percent of US immigration arrests. And most of these are of workers, not employers. Most importantly, apprehensions while in movement near the border make up over 90 percent of all immigration arrests. Workers supply themselves to employers by moving across and near the border, while employers face no legal effect at all if potential workers are interdicted on their way to supply labor. In exchange for the perils they face, undocumented workers take some of the worst jobs in the US; for example having much lower rates of health insurance coverage than citizens and legal residents, which is a good measure of low-end employment in this country. One can reasonably argue that their individual decision making vis-à-vis risk is rational; for all the perils they face, undocumented Mexicans receive more income in the United States than they would get in Mexico. But in a wider view—the overall distribution of risk in the combined US-Mexico social system—unauthorized border crossers face horrific possibilities of death, injury, economic coercion, arrest, and imprisonment, largely through the concentration of law enforcement at the boundary. They live lives filled with risks: harsh economic risks, like the ones described by Rothstein and Labrecque (see chapters 2 and 10, respectively) or harsh physical and legal risks, like the ones described here. Meanwhile, the direct and indirect beneficiaries, US employers and consumers, take on few real risks.[4]

Contrasting At-Risk and Trusted Households: Two Cases

Ida Sánchez (a pseudonym), a single mother with four children, works a night shift in a dairy in southern New Mexico, in the border region. When visited by the anthropologist Guillermina Gina Núñez, she was also giving shelter to seven undocumented travellers from her hometown in Mexico, because of a strong moral sense of obligation to her family back home; doing this added to her legal risk of arrest for harboring undocumented people. She expressed extreme anxiety but also unavoidable necessity about her actions. The migrant guests (a family group) were trapped because their smuggler was concerned about heavy immigration enforcement at checkpoints on the highway leading away from the border. To help pay the smuggler's fees, some of the migrants began to work locally, picking chillies, using a document of uncertain legality and pooling all of their labor into the one paycheck of the employee with the "document." They were in an unusually disadvantageous relationship with local farmers, and accepted a distinctly exploitative arrangement. Even with their modest added income, the members of this already marginalized household had cut back on expenditures to the most inexpensive diet possible (tortillas and beans), and of course the small dwelling now housed twelve rather than five people. Thus, in response to their at-risk situation, one made more extreme by the side effects of law enforcement against unauthorized mobility, the Sánchez household intensified its output of proletarian labor and spread its sparse consumption pool over a much larger number of people (summarized from Núñez and Heyman 2007: 359–360; see parallel non-border cases in Zlolniski 2006: 106–144).

By contrast, the Wise family (a pseudonym) stands in a relationship of trust with both the US and Mexican states, as befits their prosperous household economy and their functional role in global capitalism (ethnography by Josiah Heyman). William Wise, originally from the interior of the United States, came to the borderlands as an engineer in a global assembly plant (maquiladora) in Ciudad Juárez, Mexico. He later became an equal part owner and manager of a small maquiladora, doing small runs of anything it is contracted to assemble, largely for US corporations. In Juárez he met his wife Magdalena, an educated office employee in the plant. After their marriage, she legally immigrated to the US side of the border, where she is an educator (sometimes for little compensation, which they can afford because of William's income). William commutes on a daily basis using a Dedicated Commuter Lane identity, which requires pre-clearance from both nations, as well as a $400 annual fee. They are also able to make social visits to family in both nations without legal risk. The Wise household might as much be transnational migrants as the Sánchez household, but they have important differences in the way state-regulated mobility interlocks with their class position (following Ong 2006).

Risk, Trust, and Mobilization

Following Però (see chapter 4), we need to be attentive to the political agency of immigrants, before assuming that they are dominated by their immigrant or ethnic statuses. Christian Zlolniski's (2006) rich ethnography in northern California shows that unauthorized migrants mobilize in labor frameworks (e.g., the successful campaign to organize janitors by the Service Employees International Union) and residential community frameworks (e.g., governance over local schools). However, in my own participatory ethnography[5] with the Border Network for Human Rights (BNHR, a social movement organization with a strong base in and directed by immigrants), the legal risk frame, and the issues that extend from it, dominate all other issues and frames. For example, BNHR has identified thirteeen core issues through a bottom-up consultative process, including labor rights, dignified housing, community health, access to education, and so forth—many of them issues identified through a Marxist-feminist analysis of production linked to quotidian reproduction.

However, protecting community members from border policing abuses and pushing for legalization of unauthorized migrants overwhelms other issues in BNHR's practice. The most recent public mobilizations have pressed local law enforcement agencies to desist from de facto immigration law enforcement in ways described earlier in the paper (e.g., traffic checkpoints leading to identification requests and then turnovers to federal immigration authorities). In the intensely policed borderlands, then, it is hardly surprising that the mobilization ends up focusing on the state-society relation (immigration status), rather than other issues that form the complex of class relations. While we cannot assume that immigrants' consciousness and agency follows from their legal status, the risk structure intensifies the salience of that frame. On the other hand, little is known ethnographically about how the "trustworthy" frame shapes political mobilization. One might venture a guess that it is an invisible privilege (Kimmel and Ferber 2003), one that may divide citizens from immigrants, but at the same time it does provide security for people to mobilize in immigrant-supporting as well as immigrant-criticising fashions. Much is still to be discovered on this question.

Risk, Trust, Mobility, and Class: Lessons Learned

The concept of risk provides a useful way of understanding connections between state-populace relations, households, and class. Tracing these connections, however, requires rethinking aspects of major risk theories. Such theories, first of all, should consider the construction of social groups *as risks*, as well as biases in the distribution and perception of biophysical risks. This helps in understanding current tendencies toward the securitization of various issues and populations, and consequent surveillance and regulation of mobility of labor within and across borders. Also, it is helpful to contrast the risk or danger labels with an explicit or implicit trustworthy label. Trustworthiness constructions, in turn, can be subdivided into unmarked normalness in access to movement and formal institutions, and marked, privileged standings in movement and institutional access, again helpful in understanding the mobility of privileged classes.

Borderlands show in dramatic fashion the effects of state-populace relations on class relations. The study of differential risk in movement at borders, both local and long-distance, helps us understand an important feature of contemporary societies, the distinctions and connections between substantial illegalized migrant "classes," legal immigrant, and more prosperous citizen "classes," allowing for the great variability and complexity of those categories. Borders and immigration law enforcement, however, do not simply lock people in place, nor do law, surveillance, or governmentality omnisciently sort people into definitive social categories (Heyman 2001b). Rather, the practices of law, especially the unequal governance of movement, derive from and inflect wider webs of relationships. To delineate these connections, we need carefully to specify the characteristics and effects of various state activities, including border entry control points, border surveillance and interdiction, roadway checkpoints, mass transportation checkpoints, and an overall policing zone that cuts perpendicularly across movement corridors. Likewise, we must explore the risk-coping and -avoiding actions of unauthorized migrants (and those with whom they are related), as well as the trust-utilizing activities of privileged and "normal" travellers. We can then build toward understanding ramifying connections of risk and trust to reproduction and sustenance, public spaces and activities, workplaces, markets, and so forth—in general, to include movement in a context of household (gender and age), state, and class relations. In this fashion, we can deepen our understanding of just how and why legality, illegality, and mobility matter to social inequality.

Notes

* I would like to thank the Prion Disease and Social Research Lab of the University of Calgary for supporting the presentation of an earlier version of this chapter, and the department of anthropology, Josephine Smart, Alan Smart, and the audience at that talk for their discussion of my work. This chapter draws on three parallel projects with Robert Pallitto, Guillermina Gina Núñez, and Patrick Gurian. The present work is my own, but I gladly acknowledge the contributions my collaborators have made to my thinking. Data and descriptions were current as of 2007, the time of writing.

1. There was no connection between Latin American immigration or the Mexican border and 9/11, nor has any other connection to terrorism surfaced in public since then (Leiken and Brooke 2006). Failures in the US visa and entry inspections systems contributed to 9/11, and some, though not all, of the hijackers, who entered via airports (and not land borders), overstayed non-immigrant visas. The Mexican border is unquestionably porous, and smuggling organizations have demonstrated a remarkable ability to defeat the US state. Nevertheless, there is little demonstrable connection between protecting civilians from political terrorism and policing against unauthorized labor migration, especially from Mexico and Central America (Ewing 2007). This gives the lie to post-2005 conflation of mass immigration and homeland security agendas.

2. Some of these enforcement processes also occur in the US interior. Enforcement in the border zone is much denser and interactions or potential interactions between immigration officers and the border population more common, from which follows greater importance of sorting into "trusted" and "risky" by officers.

3. The undocumented population is not an isolated entity, but rather includes mixed status households (citizens, legal residents, and undocumented living together), networks, and communities.
4. Although effects rather than design of border policy is the focus of this chapter, readers may wonder about the extent to which US immigration and border policy is a systematic mechanism for producing an exploitable workforce for US capitalism. Please see Heyman (1998: 160–162, 1999; and also Purcell and Nevins 2005); a more recent essay on this subject can be obtained from the author at <jmheyman@utep.edu>.
5. I am on the BNHR board of directors, participate in some activities, and work quite extensively in a closely related public policy coalition, the Border and Immigration Task Force.

References

Ackleson, Jason. 2003a. "Securing Through Technology? 'Smart Borders' after September 11th." *Knowledge, Technology, & Policy* 16: 56–74.
——— . 2003b. "Directions in Border Security Research." *The Social Science Journal* 40: 573–581.
———. 2005. "Border Security in Risk Society." *Journal of Borderlands Studies* 20: 1–22.
Andreas, Peter. 2001. *Border Games: Policing the U.S.-Mexico Divide*. Ithaca: Cornell University Press.
Beck, Ulrich. 1993. *Risk Society: Towards a New Modernity*. Translated by Mark Ritter. Thousand Oaks: Sage.
———. 1999. *World Risk Society*. Cambridge: Polity Press.
Buzan, Barry, Ole Wæver, and Jaap de Wilde. 1998. *Security: A New Framework for Analysis*. Boulder: Lynne Rienner.
Calavita, Kitty. 1992. *Inside the State: The Bracero Program, Immigration, and the I.N.S.* New York and London: Routledge.
Chavez, Leo R. 2001. *Covering Immigration: Popular Images and the Politics of the Nation*. Berkeley: University of California Press.
DeGenova, Nicholas P. 2002. "Migrant 'Illegality' and Deportability in Everyday Life." *Annual Review of Anthropology* 31: 419–447.
Douglas, Mary. 1992. *Risk and Blame: Essays in Cultural Theory*. London and New York: Routledge.
Douglas, Mary, and Aaron Wildavsky. 1982. *Risk and Culture*. Berkeley: University of California Press.
Dudley Ward, Nicholas, et al. 2008. "Observed and Perceived Inconsistencies in U.S. Border Inspections." *Journal of Homeland Security and Emergency Management* 5(1) Article 17. http://www.bepress.com/jhsem/vol5/iss1/17
Ewing, Walter. 2007. "Beyond Border Enforcement: Enhancing National Security Through Immigration Reform." *Georgetown Journal of Law and Public Policy* 5: 427–446.
Fuentes, Jezmin, et al. 2007. "Impacts of U.S.-Immigration Policies on Migration Behavior." In *Impacts of Border Enforcement on Mexican Migration: The View from Sending Communities*, eds. Wayne A. Cornelius and Jessa M. Lewis, 53–74. La Jolla: Center for Comparative Immigration Studies.
Giddens, Anthony. 1990. *The Consequences of Modernity*. Stanford: Stanford University Press.

Griffith, David. 1987. "Nonmarket Labor Processes in an Advanced Capitalist Economy." *American Anthropologist* 89: 838–852.

Heyman, Josiah McC. 1998. "State Effects on Labor Exploitation: The INS and Undocumented Immigrants at the Mexico-United States Border." *Critique of Anthropology* 18: 157–180.

————. 1999. "Why Interdiction? Immigration Law Enforcement at the United States-Mexico Border." *Regional Studies* 33: 619–630.

————. 2001a. "United States Ports of Entry on the Mexican Border." *Journal of the Southwest* 43: 681–700.

————. 2001b. "Class and Classification on the U.S.-Mexico Border." *Human Organization* 60: 128–140.

————. 2002. "U.S. Immigration Officers of Mexican Ancestry as Mexican Americans, Citizens, and Immigration Police." *Current Anthropology* 43: 479–507.

————. 2004. "Ports of Entry as Nodes in the World System." *Identities: Global Studies in Culture and Power* 11: 303–327.

Huysmans, Jef. 1995. "Migrants as a Security Problem: Dangers of 'Securitizing' Societal Issues." In *Migration and European Integration: The Dynamics of Inclusion and Exclusion*, eds. Robert Miles and Dietrich Thränhardt, 53–72. London: Pinter.

Kimmel, Michael, and Abby Ferber. 2003. *Privilege: A Reader*. Boulder: Westview Press.

Leiken, Robert S., and Steven Brooke. 2006. "The Quantitative Analysis of Terrorism and Immigration: An Initial Exploration." *Terrorism and Political Violence* 18: 503–521.

Lytle Hernández, Kathleen Anne. 2002. "Entangling Bodies and Borders: Racial Profiling and the U.S. Border Patrol, 1924–1955." PhD dissertation. Los Angeles: UCLA Department of History.

Massey, Douglas S., Jorge Durand, and Nolan J. Malone. 2002. *Beyond Smoke and Mirrors: Mexican Immigration in an Era of Economic Integration*. New York: Russell Sage Foundation.

Meyers, Deborah Waller. 2005. *One Face at the Border: Behind the Slogan*. Washington, DC: Migration Policy Institute.

Nelkin, Dorothy. 1985. "Introduction: Analyzing Risk." In *The Language of Risk: Conflicting Perspectives on Occupational Health*, ed. Dorothy Nelkin, 11–24. Beverly Hills: Sage.

Nevins, Joseph. 2002. *Operation Gatekeeper: The Rise of the "Illegal Alien" and the Making of the U.S.-Mexico Boundary*. New York and London: Routledge.

Ngai, Mae M. 2004. *Impossible Subjects: Illegal Aliens and the Making of Modern America*. Princeton: Princeton University Press.

Núñez, Guillermina Gina, and Josiah McC. Heyman. 2007. "Entrapment Processes and Immigrant Communities in a Time of Heightened Border Vigilance." *Human Organization* 66: 354–365.

Ong, Aihwa. 2006. *Neoliberalism as Exception: Mutations in Citizenship and Sovereignty*. Durham: Duke University Press.

Pallitto, Robert, and Josiah McC. Heyman. 2008. "Theorizing Cross-Border Mobility: Surveillance, Security and Identity." *Surveillance & Society* 5: 315–333. http://www.surveillance-and-society.org/articles5(3)/mobility.pdf.

Purcell, Mark, and Joseph Nevins. 2005. "Pushing the Boundary: State Restructuring, State Theory, and the Case of U.S.-Mexico Border Enforcement in the 1990s." *Political Geography* 24: 211–235.

Rapp, Rayna. 1983. "Peasants into Proletarians from the Household Out: An Analysis from the Intersection of Anthropology and Social History." In *Social Anthropology of Peasantry*, ed. Joan P. Mencher, 32–47. Bombay: Somaiya Publications.

Santa Ana, Otto. 2002. *Brown Tide Rising: Metaphors of Latinos in Contemporary American Public Discourse*. Austin: University of Texas Press.

Thomas, Robert J. 1985. *Citizenship, Gender, and Work: Social Organization of Industrial Agriculture*. Berkeley: University of California Press.

United States Government Accountability Office. 2003. "Weaknesses In Screening Entrants Into the United States." Report GAO-03-438T. Washington, DC: Government Printing Office.

———. 2006. "Border Security: Continued Weaknesses in Screening Entrants into the United States." Report GAO-06-976T. Washington, DC: Government Printing Office.

Villegas, Hilma, et al. 2006. "Tradeoffs between Security and Traffic Flow: Policy Options for Land Border Ports of Entry." *Transportation Research Record* 1942: 16–22.

Wæver, Ole. 1995. "Securitization and Desecuritization." In *On Security*, ed. Ronnie Lipschutz, 46–86. New York: Columbia University Press.

Zlolniski, Christian. 2003. "Labor Control and Resistance of Mexican Immigrant Janitors in Silicon Valley." *Human Organization* 62: 39–49.

———. 2006. *Janitors, Street Vendors, and Activists: The Lives of Mexican Immigrants in Silicon Valley*. Berkeley: University of California Press.

Part II

Migrants and Mobilization

— *Chapter 4* —

POLITICAL ENGAGEMENT AND LATIN AMERICANS IN THE UK

Davide Però

Drawing on fieldwork conducted among Latin American migrants in London in 2005 and 2006, this chapter seeks to respond to recent calls from within anthropology for a greater disciplinary engagement with collective action and social movements (Escobar 1992; Edelman 2001; Gibb 2001; Nash 2005), a topic that, in relation to migrants, has received very little attention (Però 2005a).[1] This response is here articulated not so much by engaging with the prevailing social theories on the collective action of migrants, something I have done elsewhere (Però 2007a), but by juxtaposing migrants' needs and mobilization to the ongoing British and, to an extent, European public debate on their integration. Starting on the assumption that migrants should have a say about their own integration in society, the article explores the extent to which public debate is sensitive to migrants' own collective concerns.

This chapter also offers a grounded account of the political strategies of a new migrant group that has so far largely been ignored in studies of migrants and ethnic minorities in the UK. In doing so the chapter helps to rebalance the prevailing trend that treats migrants as objects of policies rather than subjects of politics acting upon their disadvantageous condition (Hargreaves and Wihtol de Wenden 1993; Kofman et al. 2000; and Zontini 2002; see also below). The chapter also offers a corrective to recently emerged "alternatives" that focus on migrants' involvement in transnational cultural politics and in sustaining long-distance diasporic communities as well as in "homeland" politics, and which tend to privilege identity politics in isolation from the practices of citizenship migrants deploy to confront the conditions encountered in the receiving context.

Since the early 1990s the UK has been experiencing a new immigration flow from a large number of non-Commonwealth countries. This flow contrasts with that of the post-WWII years when migrants—now settled minorities—came predominantly from Britain's former colonies. As pointed out by Steven Vertovec (2006), the UK is increasingly characterized by: a sizeable migrant population from poor countries with no direct colonial link to the UK (alongside those of Commonwealth and Western origins); a greater linguistic diversity; a proliferation of smaller groups (e.g., Latin Americans, Romanians, Ghanaians, Kurds, Afghans) alongside large and longstanding "ethnic communities"; a more fluid duration and greater variety of legal statuses; and greater transnational connections "from below" (social, religious, political).

This emerging scenario suggests that it is no longer appropriate to think of the UK as a "post-immigration" country—i.e., a country merely characterized by the presence of long-standing ethnic minorities—as much research and policy-making activity has been doing. In this respect the UK is also a country of new immigrations—as are, for example, Italy or Spain—but with one very important difference. In the UK the new immigrations have not taken place in a situation of relative ethnocultural homogeneity—as in the above countries—but in one of high ethnocultural heterogeneity. This specificity of the British case has been recognized by Vertovec, who has branded it "super-diversity" (2006).

Changes in the British Debate on Integration and Research Strategy

Parallel but only partly connected to the new immigrations are the transformations in the British public and policy debate on integration in the most recent years. These transformations are characterized by the emergence of a "neo-assimilationist" wave which has put "multiculturalism"—the prevailing public and policy attitude in the last decades—on the defensive. Multiculturalism is a kind of integration that characterized British society between 1960–2000 and which Ralph Grillo has summarized as follows:

> By and large there was a consistent policy . . . which on the one hand sought to control and regulate immigration, but on the other accepted that the bulk of immigrants and their families were actually here to stay. Secondly, there was a widespread desire to address issues of racial discrimination and racism, and inequalities and disparities of achievement. . . . Thirdly, there was a recognition of the legitimacy of cultural difference and a willingness to allow the expression of such difference, within certain limits, in the private sphere, and to some degree in the public sphere too. (2005: 6)

Since the early–mid 2000s it has been increasingly common in public discussions of ethnocultural diversity to hear dismissive statements on multiculturalism like the following one by the right-of-center *Daily Mail* columnist Melanie Phillips in a radio interview on BBC radio on 1 June 2006:

> My view is that multiculturalism . . . has been quite lethal in fact to our culture. . . . It is actually an engine to destroy national identity, it's an attack on British identity because it says that . . . any attempt to impose or assert majority values—i.e., the values of the nation—is racist, so it's an attack on the majority as racist. And this has many disastrous consequences not the least of which is that we are thus unable to integrate our minorities because in order to integrate minorities you've got to have something to integrate them into. In the past we used to integrate them into something called British National Identity. Now we say we don't believe in that any more and instead it's everyone for himself.

This "backlash against diversity" (Grillo 2005) has not only come from the mainstream Right, but also from important sectors of the Left[2] who are now arguing that: the UK is too diverse; diversity undermines cohesion and solidarity; multiculturalism leads to separatism; and a stronger subscription to British national values and way of living is to be expected of minorities and migrants.[3] One example of neo-assimilationist thinking in its progressive inflection is offered by David Goodhart's article "Too Diverse?" in the February 2004 issue of the political magazine *Prospect*:

> Britain in the 1950s was a country stratified by class and region. But in most of its cities, suburbs, towns, and villages there was a good chance of predicting the attitudes, even the behaviour of the people living in your immediate neighborhood. In many parts of Britain today that is no longer true. . . . We now not only live among stranger citizens but we must *share* with them. We share public services and parts of our income in the welfare state, we share public spaces in town and cities where we are squashed together on buses, trains, and tubes, and we share in a democratic conversation—filtered by the media—about the collective choices we wish to make. All such acts of sharing are more smoothly and generously negotiated if we can take for granted a limited set of common values and assumptions. But as Britain becomes more diverse that common culture is being eroded. And therein lies one of the central dilemmas of political life in developed societies: sharing and solidarity can conflict with diversity. . . . The Left's recent love affair with diversity may come at the expense of the values and even the people that it once championed.

At governmental/policy level this "neo-assimilationist" turn can be seen in the statements of leading Labour politicians ranging from David Blunkett who—when home secretary—began to demand from migrants and minorities greater conformity to British norms and values (see interview in *The Independent on Sunday*, 9 December 2001), to Gordon Brown who—when still chancellor of the exchequer—explicitly subscribed to both Phillips's and Goodhart's positions (*The Guardian*, 7 July 2004) and who—once prime minister—talked about "British jobs for British workers" (speech to Trade Union Congress, 10 September 2007). It can also be seen in the general disappearance in the most recent years of the word *multiculturalism* from the policy documents of Tony Blair's Labour government and in the increasingly negative connotation being attached to "multiculturalism," now sometimes ironically referred to in informal conversations of academics, policy makers, and activists as the "the *m*-word."

This shift in left-wing thinking about diversity is to be seen as part and parcel of the wider transformation that the political Left has undergone in recent years, which consists of a historical rupture with its redistributive history and identity. As eloquently pointed out by Gerassimos Moschonas (2002: 293), the contemporary mainstream Left has undergone a major qualitative transformation consisting of a "break" with its past and rupture in its identity, one which entails the abandonment of any even moderate attempt to redress social injustice and promote equality in favor of a mild endorsement of neoliberalism with its inherent inequalities.

In particular, the neo-assimilationist turn of the mainstream Left constitutes one of the latest forms in which its recent endorsement of neoliberalism is manifesting itself: multiculturalism is costly, increasingly unpopular and unrewarding in terms of votes, and dysfunctional to the creation of a homogeneous citizenry easy to govern. In other words, multiculturalism is seen as running against the efforts that late-modern governmental forces are making to reinvent themselves as powerful actors (with power over the people) at a time when they have lost much of their economic power to global capital (powerless over the economy). On the contrary, neo-assimilationism articulated in a nationalist-patriotic rhetoric of the type illustrated above is seen as functional to facilitating such efforts.

In addition to the neo-assimilationist turn with its populist scapegoating of minorities and migrants for the shortcomings of complex social transformations and its nostalgic sense of "loss" for a mythical cohesive past, the British debate on integration seems also characterized by a general treatment of migrants and minorities as *objects of policy* rather than also political agents. This point is underscored by Zontini (chapter 5) and Lem (chapter 8) in their discussions of politics of migrants in Europe, as well as by Giles (chapter 1) in her discussion of official attitudes toward forced migrants. As Lem has noted, the debate is essentially centered on the nation-state, which has embraced the philosophy of "governance" and the dismantling of its welfare structures.[4] Furthermore, such debate at best includes voices from ethnic minorities, but not those of new migrants.

Unlike the prevailing public, policy, and academic discourse on integration, this chapter prioritizes the perspectives of the new migrants, focusing on the latter's collective action to improve their living conditions in the UK. It thereby addresses the question of what concerns new migrants have in the receiving society that make them mobilize. The new migrants' perspectives thus form the background against which I, in concluding, assess the British, and to an extent European, public debate on integration.

Migrants and the Study of Collective Action

As anticipated, the treatment of migrants as objects rather than subjects of politics has not only been characterizing policy makers who act on behalf of the neoliberal state, but also many scholars who often uncritically embrace the perspective of the nation-state (see Wimmer and Glick Schiller 2003), developing their research within the dominant policy frame, not least in order to maximize their chances of funding from governmental bodies that are increasingly demanding policy-relevant research (see Smith 2002). Scholars addressing issues of migrants and politics tend to do so at the macro level, often in the abstract and in isolation from the lived experiences and practices of citizenship of the migrants themselves. For example, they do so by: abstractedly counterpoising integration models (e.g., assimilationism versus multiculturalism); by focusing on the effects of migration on the politics and policies of the receiving state and on the electoral patterns of the "host" population; by addressing the politics and policies of "homeland" governments and diplomacies toward their expatriates; or by considering migrants in connection to the rise of the extreme Right or in terms of security threats to maneuverable electoral blocs (for an overview of existing work on the subject see Castles and Miller 2003).

Migrants have "existed" as political actors only when they are entitled to vote or when they put themselves forward as political candidates. Of course, this narrow understanding of political engagement (often accompanied by an interest in migrants' compliance to the norms of the host society) cannot account for the political practices of migrants in the many countries in which they do not enjoy formal political entitlements. Nor can it account for the practices of those migrant residents that are not from "special" areas of emigration—as the commonwealth or the EU in the case of the UK—and that as a result enjoy no formal political rights.

Moreover, for the most part the limited literature on migrants' mobilization has been concerned with explaining the emergence of migrants' political behavior in terms of "political opportunity structure" (or POS).[5] This largely theoretical concern with the ultimate "origin" of migrant collective action has, however, favored the neglect of the objects of migrants' contention as well as promoted a "detached" and "neutral" rather than "engaged" and "committed" model of research on the topic. For example, research on migrants' collective action has scarcely been connected to the critical analysis of the hegemonic debate about the integration that contemporary migrants encounter in "Fortress Europe," let alone to wider debates about global and social justice, citizenship, and uneven development.

To be sure, not all scholars fall into the above categories, and some— especially from anthropology and feminism—have recently developed approaches that seek to critically reconcile the micro and the macro level, the experiential and the abstract, and to be more "people-centered" and recognizant of migrants' agency and subjectivity. As Lem and Barber have noted in their introduction to this volume, this "alternative" scholarship is visible in the work of transnationalist scholars (e.g., Basch, Glick Schiller, and Szanton Blanc 1994; Smith and Guarnizo 1998; Levitt 2001; including the powerful critique of "methodological nationalism" developed by Wimmer and Glick Schiller 2003), in that of the emergent ethnographic scholarship on migrants' political agency, and—to a significant extent—in the political anthropology of migration that gave migrants a prominent position in developing critical examinations of the institutional practices of receiving societies (European examples are Grillo 1985; Grillo and Pratt 2002; Carter 1997; Cole 1997; and Però 2007b).

This chapter will contribute in particular to the development of the second of these scholarships by applying a critical, committed, and people-centered approach to the field of integration through the examination of a group of migrants' integrative efforts and practices of citizenship and their relationship with the public discourse about diversity of their "host" society.

The Significance of the Latinos

In "super-diverse" Britain, a migrant group that has received little attention despite its numerical significance is that of Latin Americans. In the UK, Latinos are for the most part a "new immigrant group" for whom there are not yet reliable official statistics.[6] As Heyman's study (chapter 3) demonstrates in the US, by contrast, the Latin American population is on the whole much more established. In my fieldwork I have repeatedly come across Latin Americans estimating their presence at approximately 500,000. This estimated figure is made up of some 250,000 Brazilians, 200,000 Colombians, and 50,000 Ecuadorians and other Latin American nationalities.[7]

Latin Americans arrive in Britain through a broad range of immigration channels and hold a variety of different statuses—for example, students, unauthorized/irregular migrants, asylum-seekers, and refugees.[8] The majority of Latin Americans migrated primarily for "economic" reasons although, as is often the case among Colombians, migration can be the result of a combination of "economic" and "political" reasons. Apart from a sizeable group of refugees, there are many people who left Colombia for the general climate of violence, fear, and instability that—with poverty—characterizes vast geographical areas of the country.[9]

In Britain, Latinos reside predominantly in London, with significant concentrations in Lambeth, Southwark, Islington, and Camden. They are heavily employed in the cleaning sector where they work for subcontracted companies (often multinationals) to clean commercial and public buildings often under very exploitative conditions.[10] They have also developed a wide range of "ethnic" commercial and cultural activities. These "self-directed" activities include: restaurants, bars, cafes, discos, food shops (e.g., groceries, butchers), *locutorios* (shops from which to phone "home" at discounted rates), *giros tiendas* (shops from which to send remittances to Latin America), doctors and dentists, barbers and hairdressers, launderettes and tailors, video rentals and music shops. Sometimes some of these activities are hosted in large multicultural/cosmopolitan shopping centers and markets, sometimes they are part of smaller "all-Latino" shopping malls.

Not being from Commonwealth countries, Latinos recognize that their linguistic competence in English at their arrival is on average rather poor and tends to improve only slowly over the years. Their voice in public discourse in the UK is largely absent—as is that of the other new migrant groups. In spite of such marginalization, the Latinos have a growing "ethnic" or "community" media in Spanish that includes several radio programs and news magazines widely and freely distributed covering developments in Latin American countries as well as in the UK. By addressing the entire Spanish-speaking Latin American collective in the UK, the Latino media are simultaneously facilitating the Latino population in the UK to imagine themselves as a "community" (Anderson 1983; Chavez 1991). Again, unlike migrants from Commonwealth countries or the EU, Latinos are not entitled to vote in any type of British elections. This however makes it all the more compelling to adopt a notion of politics that transcends the electoral focus of much political science to include a broader range of collective political initiatives.

It is important to note that the wide range of social, cultural, and economic initiatives just outlined has not only been promoting physical and virtual encounters and networks among Latino migrants from the same nationalities but also among Latinos of different nationalities. They are forging a growing sense of a common Latino identity that has recently begun to be deployed politically in initiatives articulated by people of different Latin American nationalities and branded as "Latino." It is for this reason that soon after beginning fieldwork on the collective initiatives of Colombians in the UK, I moved my focus from Colombians to Latin Americans.

Latin American Mobilization in Britain

As I argue elsewhere in greater detail (see Però 2007a), Latin American migrants' political engagements in Britain come in two parallel ideal-typical forms: those directed at the transnational level (especially toward Latin America) and those directed at Britain.[11] Of course, in practice these types of engagements intersect and influence each other as people and organizations are often involved in "multidirectional" politics involving both homeland and transnational political practices and "integration" practices. Among Latin Americans in Britain, "integration" politics has, however, grown quite significantly in recent years, both quantitatively and qualitatively.[12] In particular, since 2004 there have arisen a number of collective initiatives that have gone beyond the previous "charitable," publicly funded, short-term oriented provision of services connected to immediate resettlement needs (basic information about health, welfare, immigration, etc.) to address the growing concern about issues of long-term integration such as exploitation, marginalization, lack of recognition, legal status, racism, religious sectarianism, drug addiction, domestic violence, and political exclusion. As one of my informants Pablo[13] said:

> We are realizing that it's time to do something about our conditions here rather than just keep thinking about Colombia, as here we are having many problems like marginalization, lack of opportunities, education, religion [with the "Christian" sects], drug-addiction . . . and it's not just the society here that is the cause of the problems but the mentality of the Latinos too. . . . We are realizing that a new way to approach politics in this country is necessary. . . . Rather than supporting the Labour Party automatically we

are realizing that we need to become more demanding and become aware also of our political and electoral weight for using it as a bargaining tool.

Below I examine the two important new "integrative" political initiatives, namely the Latin Front (LF) and the Latin American Workers Association / T&G.

The Latin Front

Arguably the most ambitious political initiative of the Latinos in Britain to date, the Latin Front came into being in the second half of 2004 on the initiative of two liberal, middle-class Colombian women. The intent was to politically represent the interests of Latin Americans in the UK and the Front's official goals included: creating a sense of community; achieving recognition as an ethnic group; lobbying British and European Institutions to promote the rights of Latin American residents, including the regularization of those with an irregular status, working rights, social security rights, voting rights, health and education, and citizenship for Latinos' children being born in the UK; and quantifying the potential Latino political "weight" in political bargaining.

In the first year of its existence the LF successfully intercepted and expressed the growing concern among Latin Americans for recognition as an ethnic minority and for the improvement of their living conditions in a long-term perspective, as well as for the regularization of many of its members whose irregular/unauthorized status had confined them to a situation of great precariousness, insecurity, vulnerability, and marginality. With a loose organizational structure and a great deal of entrepreneurship, the LF started off as an umbrella organization with the ambition to federate Latino civic organizations, create a strong unitary and representative "community voice," and lobby British political institutions. As, in the words of one of its founders, "the Latin Front is a political but not party political group," the possibility of acquiring a "charity" status was discarded.

The political background of the LF activists is quite heterogeneous.[14] The two founders have a liberal, centrist identity. One of them has been simultaneously active with the Liberal Democrats in Britain, where she stood as candidate councilor at the local 2006 elections, and with liberals in her country of origin where, taking advantage of changes in the electoral law, she tried to be appointed candidate MP for one of the foreign constituencies.[15] The majority of the activists involved, however, had left-of-center orientations. Among these, officially recognized refugees and others who had fled political violence in their country of origin were prominent. Some also had taken part in political, civic, and community initiatives in Britain. On the whole the LF was, initially at least, a collective and inclusionary initiative by people of diverse political socialization, sensitivity, and identity.

The main arena in which the LF operates is that of party politics. Lobbying all the main British political parties and institutions has characterized the Latin Front from the outset. In its first year, it organized three major public events with such parties and a meeting with the home secretary, all held in the hall of one of the main Latino shopping malls in London and arranged so as to present the Latin Front and the wider Latin American collective as authoritative and powerful. As figure 5.1 illustrates, two long desks were placed in an "L" shape with the side facing the floor sitting the British Politicians and an LF moderator and the other sitting journalist from the Latino media observing the event to report to the wider community. An amplified lecture podium was placed next to the politicians' table and a lot of care went into presentational details and arrangements. A program was distributed, all speakers and journalists wore badges, and all had a signpost with the logo of their organization. A professional cameraman filmed the entire event and professional photographers took pictures of the Latino leaders and British politicians throughout the event. A large printed banner reading "Frente Latino" was placed over the invited politicians' table.

Figure 4.1   The Latin Front meets British politicians, Spring 2005. Photo Davide Però.

The substantive politics of the LF has been directed primarily at gaining recognition. It mobilized to make Latin Americans visible and recognized as an "ethnic minority," not least in the political arena where it aspired to politically represent the entire Latin American collective residing in Britain. It also mobilized for the regularization of unauthorized Latin Americans living and working in Britain and of their children, especially those born in the UK, for whom they asked citizenship.

The strategy of appealing to British political institutions followed a pattern of deliberately ambiguous and flexible positioning. This involved avoiding alliance to only one political party and engaging instead in relationships and negotiations with all of them simultaneously so as to try and set them in competition with each other for the support of the LF and of the Latin American population it claimed to represent. The LF's political visibility was achieved through the political networks and capital that one of its founders had built through her activism at the borough level. From the outset the LF also dealt carefully with Latin American diplomatic institutions and personnel. In order to retain full autonomy, a courteous distance was deliberately kept to prevent powerful and skilled diplomats from interfering with their respective national and home-country agendas.

In trying to widen its support basis and project a powerful image of itself vis-à-vis British institutions, the LF deployed a shrewd identity politics based on the strategic use of the "Latino" category. This category, which becomes salient outside Latin America to indicate a shared distinct ethnocultural background, had until then circulated spontaneously in the everyday social arena in London but had not yet been deployed contentiously. Other community organizations had used the term to appeal to potential users or members, but not yet for purposes of explicit, large-scale political claim making. The LF is thus the most ambitious and grand-scale attempt to date to introduce "Latino" as a category of contention in the British political arena by capitalizing on existing Latino identity, networks, and resources. By clustering together all Latin American, and even southern European, nationalities this strategy has asserted the existence of a large and politically organized collective comparable to those of the established ethnic minorities and therefore deserving similar attention from British institutions. It is a strategy that reflects the multicultural setup of the UK and its encouragement to organize around ethnicity.

However, this organization around ethnicity was not just based on narrow ethnic interests. It also derived from a genuine belief—at least on the part of some—that organizing as Latinos is an intermediate stage necessary to create a larger and confederated movement to protect migrants' general interests. As my informant, Ubaldo put it: "we must learn to organize politically among Latinos and then begin to collaborate with other immigrant communities. If we can't unite among ourselves, how can we unite at a wider level?!"

The LF has taken every major opportunity to become active and visible. Most emblematic of this responsiveness were perhaps the LF's attempts to strengthen the links with the Brazilian community following the killing of an innocent Brazilian immigrant, Jean Charles de Menezes, by the police, who had mistaken him for an Islamist terrorist. The LF organized ad hoc events—including meetings with the police—for the occasion and provided support and solidarity to Brazilian protests and initiatives, in so doing enhancing its visibility and links with both the Brazilian and British public institutions.[16]

The identity politics of the Latin Front extends not only horizontally across ethnic/nationality lines but also vertically across class lines. Hardly identifiable along a Left-Right continuum and in a somewhat populist and ambiguous fashion, the LF has turned political transversalism and ecumenism into its political flag. Its leadership conceives of Left/Right divisions as unhelpful to the goal of creating a united and strong Latino voice in Britain. As one of the LF founders once said in a meeting, "All the efforts of the Latin American organizations must converge in a broad and strong bloc."

Many Latinos, also those not actively involved in the LF, moreover appreciate this transversal character of the LF, arguing that Latinos ultimately experience similar difficulties in the UK, no matter what political affiliation they have. Juana, for example, said "there exists a common interest among many Latinos to have one voice representing us . . . for example many work and pay taxes and would like to be regularized or that there were an amnesty."

Criticism and achievements

Despite the popularity achieved during its first year and the general support from Latino media, not everybody within the Latino "community" subscribed to the idea of confederating under the overarching framework and leadership of the Latin Front. In fact, the majority from the civic and political Latino organizations steered away from the LF invitation to join in. Their reasons included reservations about the LF's ambiguous political nature and the personal agenda and political affiliation of part of its leadership, including in relation to their home country. Many Leftist Latin Americans also rejected the idea of a transversal and interclassist organization organized around ethnicity and some saw the leadership of the LF as too involved in "politicking" and "vote exchange," both in Britain and in Colombia.[17]

One way in which LF activists explained the lack of support from Latino community organizations was "jealousy," competition, and fear of losing the visibility, status, and benefits acquired by having carved out a niche for themselves. They also pointed to the obsolete participatory model subscribed to by most existing community organizations, which entailed specialization in the provision of advice and assistance on short-term issues of immigration, housing, and access to welfare, but failed to respond to emerging preoccupations around issues of long-term integration such as education and voting rights.

The initiatives of the LF have nevertheless made Latin American migrants more visible to local and national British politicians and administrators. The LF has also conveyed the impression of having certain organizational and mobilization skills and resources, even if these are not considered adequate by some local authorities.

Finally, after the LF initiatives of 2005, some of its leaders have become part of mainstream public committees, such as the Refugee & Asylum Seekers Listening Group (which features the London Metropolitan Police). Even if such "recruitment" may have had a cooptative dimension it still denotes a degree of recognition on the part of the British institutions and represents an institutional forum for voicing concerns and demands. The LF has also created a feeling of empowerment among Latin American migrants themselves, especially through the public meetings it arranged. It raised awareness and boosted the confidence that Latinos possess the resources and skills that can turn them into a collective capable of positively influencing its own integration in the UK.

The Latin American Workers Association and the Transport and General Workers Union

The Latin American Workers Association (or LAWA) was set up by three Colombian and one Chilean male trade unionists as part of the British Transport and General Workers Union (or T&G) in the second half of 2004, after they had existed in a more informal way for several months.[18] Forming LAWA was seen as a necessary step to more effectively support the large number of Latin American workers experiencing super-exploitation and abuses of various types at the work place. Until the creation of LAWA, employment had been a crucial aspect of life that was left "uncovered" by the existing Latino community organizations. In the words of one of LAWA's founders:

> The LAWA is the product of a necessity, which has emerged progressively after many Latinos had solved their immigration, housing, and benefits problems. . . .

Besides addressing some of the exploitative aspects experienced by Latino workers in Britain, LAWA struggles for helping the Latino workers coming out of their invisibility with dignity, not by "asking" (*pedir*) but by "demanding" (*exigir*). Together with other workers' organizations—the Portuguese, the Turkish, the African—we share the same class need (*necesidad de clase*).

LAWA started out of the desires of Marcelo and Arturo, two of the founders, to combat the many abuses experienced by Latin Americans at work. They worked with others such as Fernando and Pedro, to look for support in the British trade union movement in order to do that more effectively. The view that needs play a key role in the emergence of LAWA emerged also in an interview with another activist, Irene: "It is out of necessity that people get organized: 'they are stealing my salary, they are underpaying me, they are sacking me without a justification, they are violating my rights.' This is why people get organized. If people had it all they wouldn't organize."

The kind of problems that Latin Americans experience and the nature of LAWA's activity are illustrated by Ines in her comments to me during an interview.

Sexual harassment, psychological maltreatment . . . abuses concerning working time, verbal abuses and discrimination of all sorts. Essentially all that happens because one doesn't know the [British] laws . . . and people [employers and managers] take advantage of that and abuse the power they've got. . . . I myself had a case and after solving that, I stayed on working with them [LAWA] as a volunteer. I was abused verbally and psychologically by my managers. . . . It happened in a clothes shop for which I worked.

Indeed, Ines saw her decision to mobilize with LAWA as being connected to her working conditions but also to her civic and political identity and formation.

Yes . . . it was like a means of protecting myself, because not only was I getting affiliated to protect myself in this case but also in future situations. It is a way of protecting oneself here as a worker, as an individual, and as a human being. . . . I also always wanted to work together with my community. . . . It's not possible that this [exploitation/abuse] is happening in a developed country and people just ignore it. . . . So I said: "My community needs it [trade union work], the volunteers are few and also I am passionate about this kind of work.". . . I've always had the urge to help people politically, since high school. . . . My mother always told me that I was "the lawyer of the poor," that I always went out to defend this and that.

Although support in the field of employment was, in principle, available to Latino workers through the existing British trade unions, such support was not, in practice, accessible to them for reasons of communication and language, trust, lack of relationships or links between the T&G and the Latin collective, and lack of adequate efforts on the part of the union to reach out to migrant workers.

An important concern when setting up LAWA was the preservation of its autonomy. LAWA founders had always been determined to form a political rather than a civic or community "charitable" organization. They wanted to avoid relying on public funding because this would entail economic dependence on the state (an institution that they did not see as promoting the interests of working people and in particular of migrant workers) and political restrictions (for receiving public funding and a "charitable" status). In the end, the four founders' guess about the need for LAWA proved right and the organization "boomed" straight away (and with it Latino affiliations to the T&G) to the extent that after a few months of activity LAWA already struggled to keep up with the demand for assistance.

In terms of background, political socialization, and experience the four founders all had previous experience in trade union activism in their country of origin, which was also connected to why they had left their country. The other members of the directive committee also had a past of activism in their home country, although not necessarily, strictly speaking, in the trade union movement. LAWA has also begun to recruit activists among young people with more limited political experience (if only for their younger age), as in the case of Ines.

Before joining LAWA, all its activists had been involved in other Latino civic organization. Some became immediately active once in the UK, while others took longer as they went through a period of withdrawal, partly connected to the discouraging social environment (made of kin and acquaintances) in which they arrived and partly due to their contingent psychological situation.

As these organizers did not know each other in Latin America, it was their participation in the Latino civic and political circuit that brought them in contact with each other and that they now, through LAWA, are in turn making more comprehensive and stronger. This relationship of symbiosis with the Latino associative circuit is sustained by LAWA's members participating in other Latino organizations which, in turn, contribute to LAWA's growth by referring to them people with work-related problems.

The field of political initiative in which LAWA operates can be described as "sociopolitical." LAWA is neither interested in party politics nor in lobbying national and local politicians and officials. They privilege political initiative in the socioeconomic sphere around issues of workers' rights, and more generally, material justice. In addition to the protection of Latin American workers in the UK, they are connected to the initiatives of social forums and of the global justice movement. For example, in 2004 they participated in the European Social Forum in London. They have also been developing direct international/transnational links with trade unions in Latin America.[19]

In terms of "identity politics," LAWA articulates a particular blend of class and ethnicity. Like the Latin Front, they are promoting greater ethnocultural recognition of Latin Americans at a "continental" rather than "national" level, but unlike the former LAWA is doing that within the class framework of the trade union movement. Overall, LAWA values being fully part of a large and organized British trade union, but feels there are ethnocultural specificities that require a "customized" treatment, hence their organization as Latinos within the T&G. However, as Fernando said, "the objective and the essence of the struggle, as well as what unites us with other immigrant groups, is a question of class." The attitudes that LAWA members have toward unauthorized migrant workers further help us to form an idea of LAWA's political vision. In Irene's own words, "Work is a right that all human beings have, if they are illegal or not is not something that makes any difference to us . . . and this is why we also fight for [the regularization of] illegal immigrants."

In addition to the cases attended at their office, LAWA has been involved in several initiatives for workers' welfare in London that ranged from supporting the strike and protest of the cleaners of the British House of Commons to organizing trainings on working rights for its membership.

Latin Americans are increasingly also becoming active directly through the "mainstream" Transport and General Workers Union. For many of them this involvement developed as a result of the "Justice for Cleaners" campaign and other such recent large-scale efforts on the part of the T&G to organize workers in the cleaning sector, who are almost all migrants and subject to severe exploitation. Although not centered around ethnicity, the trade union is a growing form of engagement among Latinos that is not only important in itself but also crucial to recognize if we want to avoid ethnicist or culturalist reductionism and be able to achieve a more comprehensive and complete understanding of Latino migrants' mobilization. In fact, at present there is a diffused tendency within migration and minorities studies to consider migrants and minorities as merely ethnocultural subjects, overlooking all their other political identities, relationships, and engagements, like those hinging around gender or, as in this case, class.

In terms of politics, this mobilization represents a rather typical form of class initiative, i.e., one in which the socioeconomic component is paramount and the ethnocultural is complementary but still significant. This is also a politics that targets all workers independently of their ethnocultural background, though in the cleaning sector workers happen to be essentially migrants. Alongside Justice for Cleaners, the T&G has also recently started to strengthen its pro-migrant stand by campaigning (together with other organizations) for the regularization of irregular migrants as it recognizes that their immigration status renders them vulnerable to super-exploitation and abuses and condemns them to exclusion and marginality. As in LAWA, the prevailing attitude within the T&G toward unauthorized migrants is inclusionary; they tend to be seen as workers regardless of the legal status attached to them by the state.

Through Justice for Cleaners, the "mainstream" T&G has been adopting an "organizing" strategy/model which has been explained to me as consisting of reaching out to migrant cleaners at the workplace, creating self-reliant trade union outposts. From then on the newly "organized" workers will collectively and directly deal with the cleaning company that employs them without, except in extraordinary circumstances, resorting to trade union officials from the central headquarters. The "organizing" approach is different from the "service" approach, which by and large tends to characterize LAWA and which consists of providing support to migrant workers' needs on an individual basis in LAWA's headquarters.

The typical sequence of T&G action can be summarized as follows. First, the T&G approaches the cleaning subcontractors (e.g., hired by a Bank or Transport Authority) exploiting (migrant) labor to demand better conditions for the cleaners (e.g., living wage, sick pay, holiday pay, pension contributions) and the recognition of the trade union at the work place. Simultaneously, it starts to unionize the cleaners and inform them about their rights and possibilities for improvements. The cleaning company usually rejects T&G's initial demands. T&G then starts to simultaneously build up pressure from above and outside as well as from below and inside. From above and outside, the union approaches the contracting company asking them to demand ethical and lawful practices from their subcontractors. This is done by progressively attracting media and public attention on what goes on in the premises of these contractors in terms of exploitation and malpractices, which can be damaging to the reputation of such contractors. From below and inside, the newly unionized cleaners will start demanding the application of the law and regulations where this does not happen and the improvement of their employment conditions. Caught between these two forces, in the end the cleaning company gives in to the requests of the union and its cleaners.

Figure 4.2. A T&G's organized demonstration outside an international bank hiring an exploitative cleaning subcontractor. Photo Davide Però.

Criticism and achievements

While on the whole, the T&G and LAWA are characterized by collaboration and broadly similar attitudes toward migrant workers, some differences and sometimes frictions exist—as is common in any large organization. Though it goes beyond the scope of this essay to discuss them in detail, one concerns the previously described "organizing versus service" approach. For example, Justice for Cleaners is criticized for focusing on the big cleaning corporations and neglecting workers employed in smaller ones, who need individual attention. Yet, the organizing model is revealing itself to be successful to the extent of enabling a reinvigoration of the trade union movement in many advanced economies. Other differences concern (over-)bureaucratization, moderation, and dirigisme.

In terms of achievements, LAWA and the T&G have unionized a remarkable number of Latin American workers (about one thousand). This process has happened in a relatively short period of time and by overcoming a number of fears and prejudices such as that of deportation (recurrent and yet unjustified among unauthorized migrants). The second achievement is the operationalization of the Latino workers protection, which both LAWA and the T&G have performed. Thirdly, they have also gained a greater visibility and popularity in the eyes of the Latin American collective and among employers who are becoming aware that there is an increasing chance to face the trade unions if they abuse migrant workers. Finally, on balance, all this activity seems to have strengthened the overall integration of Latin American migrants into British society, particularly in the sociopolitical sphere.

Conclusions

By focusing on Latin American migrants' mobilizations in London, this chapter has responded to recent calls from within anthropology to engage more with the study of social movements and from within migration studies to rebalance the prevailing trend identified by Lem and Barber (see Introduction) of considering migrants as objects of policy by looking at them as political actors. By examining Latino's "integration politics from below," this chapter has also offered a corrective to recent alternative approaches to the above that have focused on the constitution of transnational communities and networks and that have conceived migrants' political practices as merely sustaining long-distance diasporic communities.

At a case study level the chapter has shown how Latino migrants' collective initiatives have recently broadened to include political mobilization around issues of long-term integration and policy change in the UK. In particular, it has illustrated how Latino migrants have intensified their collective efforts directed at combating the several forms of super-exploitation that so often affect them as workers: demanding political rights; claiming citizenship for their children born in Britain; calling for the regularization of the many thousands of Latinos whose undocumented or irregular status forces them to live in fear and under conditions of vulnerability and marginality; demanding recognition as an "ethnic community"; and providing support to other (multi-ethnic) initiatives concerned with the achievement of dignified living standards for the London working classes.

This illustration has been provided by examining two different collective initiatives: the Latin Front, which operates mainly in the "formal" political field, and the Latin American Workers Association / T&G, which operates mainly in the "sociopolitical" field and as part of the wider trade union movement. The article also showed how these collective initiatives have made an unprecedented politicization and strategic deployment of "Latino" as a category of contention in the UK. Moreover, the article has shown how these mobilizations are not only concerned with issues of cultural recognition (i.e., as an ethnic minority), but also with those of social recognition (i.e., in terms of residence and citizenship), as well as with material justice and inclusion (i.e., against exploitation and for dignified working and living conditions). In other words, the material presented has given a sense of *what* Latin American migrants in the UK mobilize about—namely, their increased visibility as well as the improvement of their working and living conditions—and *how* they do so, through a range of collective initiatives taking place broadly outside the formal political system and hinging around different combinations of ethnicity and class.

These collective efforts for recognition and dignified working conditions that Latin Americans have recently begun to make (in absence of voting rights) denote active political engagement on their part. In fact, if, as Marco Martiniello (2005) has recently outlined, the main indicators of "non-conventional" migrant political participation in the receiving country are "presence in the trade unions" and the "creation of collective actors," then the instances of Latino collective initiatives presented here show that this is a migrant group with significant political vitality.

These ethnographic findings enable the formulation of theoretical inferences in relation to British society at two levels: the actually existing British multiculturalism and the public discourse on integration. The examination of Latinos' mobilization reveals significant limitations of current multiculturalism in relation to the new migrants. Despite its rhetoric of appreciation of ethnic diversity, multicultural Britain is de facto revealing difficulties in recognizing the Latinos, both as an ethnocultural minority and as citizens (see also Giles's discussion in chapter 1 of recognition). More generally, British multiculturalism, as a set of practices, is showing problems in acknowledging the presence of the new migrants and adjusting to the situation of "super-diversity" that has been developing in recent years. The recent neo-assimilationist wave—with its demand for homogeneity and conformism—is not encouraging a public debate on how a multiculturalism tailored around long-standing ethnic minorities should develop to recognize more effectively the new migrants and adjust to a situation of super-diversity.

The experience of the Latinos presented also reveals some strong limitations in the practice of multiculturalism regarding exploitation. British society is multicultural in the sense that it may be more tolerant and recognizant than others in Europe but it is also characterized by the diffused and structural exploitation of migrant workers.[20] This situation of marked material injustice that new migrant groups—like the Latinos—experience is an issue that is broadly neglected in the public debate on integration by both multiculturalists and neo-assimilationists. When preoccupations with people's welfare are being expressed, these concern the defense of the shrinking welfare of those of "our own kind" (to use Goodhart's words) against the erosive attacks not of the capital but of migrants and minorities. The silence over issues of material justice and welfare of migrants that we encounter on both sides of the debate on integration in Britain reminds us of the important similarities that exist between multiculturalists and neo-assimilationists, such as the similar posture vis-à-vis neoliberalism, one which has abdicated the promotion of equality in favor of the moderate but substantial acceptance of an increasingly unequal and exploitative system.

Notes

Earlier version of this essay were presented at the CASCA conference (Montreal), in the seminar series of the School of Sociology and Social Policy of the University of Nottingham and at the B6 workshop of the International Migration, Integration, and Social Cohesion network (Warsaw). I wish to thank Pauline Gardiner Barber, Rainer Baubock, Winnie Lem, Jake Lagnado, Elisabetta Zontini and the two anonymous referees for their helpful comments.

1. A reason for this seems to be the relatively late engagement of the discipline with the study of migrants and migrations more generally (see Brettell 2000; Foner 2003). Concerned with the study of "cultures" as territorialized and bounded units (Brettell 2000) and informed by a "sedentaristic metaphysics" (Malkki 1997), anthropologists tended to focus on people who stayed put and to ignore migrants.

2. For an anthropological examination of the trajectory followed by the Left in relation to the integration of migrants see Però (2007b).

3. For a critical discussion of neo-assimilationism see Grillo (2005), but also Back et al. (2002), and Cheong et al. (2005).

4. For an anthropological discussion of "governance" see Però (2005b, 2005c).

5. As pointed out elsewhere (Però 2007a), the suggestion here that migrants mobilize as a result of the favorable opportunities provided by the institutional context of the receiving society is problematic, for it tends to provide a mono-causal explanation of migrants' mobilization that is based on a rigid and nation-state centered notion of political opportunities structure that overlooks the role of other factors, such as migrants' political socialization and background, the exploitative and marginalizing conditions they experience, and their own networks.

6. Though in the US, *Latin American* and *Latino* refer to recently arrived and established migrants respectively, in Britain this distinction does not apply.

7. At least for the Colombians, these estimates are consistent with those reported in Bermudez Torres (2003) and Macilwaine (2005), although somewhat exaggerated as pointed out by Guarnizo (2006). The number of people with a Latino background in the UK is likely to grow further also because of their high birth rates (Lewenstein 2006: 2).

8. For the Colombian case, see Guarnizo (2006).

9. See Macilwane (2005). This "political" violence is paralleled by a "common" violence that is particularly present in deprived urban areas.
10. For an analysis of Latin Americans' involvement in the contract cleaning sector, see Lagnado (2004).
11. For an examination of the political transnationalism of Colombian migrants in the UK, see Bermudez Torres (2006).
12. For an overview of the broad and heterogeneous range of both "transnational" and "integrative" engagements of Latin American migrants in Britain, see Però (2007a).
13. Pablo is a pseudonym and I have used fictitious first names for all informants.
14. Heterogeneity characterized also the work activity of its main activists, including journalists and media professionals, students, teachers, cleaners, doctors, shop owners, and law advisors.
15. This reveals that "host" and "home"-country politics can be articulated not only simultaneously but also in synergy.
16. This initiative also represented a genuine anxiety on the part of the Latino migrants about being subjected to intensified anti-terrorist checks for having "olive-color skin."
17. In addition, after about a year of activity, several key Latin Front activists abandoned the project due to the realization of the impossibility of transforming it into an open and participatory umbrella organization and due to the feeling of having been "used" to confer the LF greater authority and representative character.
18. During the "pre-T&G" period much of LAWA's activity was conducted in coffee shops, fast food restaurants, and private homes.
19. The development of such links shows how, in the context of politics, transnational and integration practices do not constitute a "zero sum game," as they often intersect and are articulated simultaneously by the same social actors.
20. These exploitative conditions have been legitimized and even encouraged by New Labour's "managed migration" policy approach, which while arguing in favor of migrant workers has been simultaneously stripping them of many substantial rights (see Flynn 2006).

References

Anderson Benedict. 1983. *Imagined Communities*. London: Verso.
Back, Les, et al. 2002. "New Labour's White Heart: Politics, Multiculturalism and the Return of Assimilationism." *The Political Quarterly* 74 (4): 445–454.
Basch Linda, Nina Glick Schiller, and Christina Szanton Blanc. 1994. *Nations Unbound: Transnational Projects, Postcolonial Predicaments, and Deterritorialized Nation-States*. New York and London: Routledge.
Bermudez Torres, Anastasia. 2003. *ICAR Navigation Guide: Refugee Populations in the UK, Colombians*. London: Information Centre for Asylum and Refugees.
———. 2006. *Colombian Migration to Europe: Political Transnationalism in the Middle of Conflict*. COMPAS Working Paper No. 39. Oxford: Centre on Migration Policy and Society.
Brettell, Caroline. 2000. "Theorizing Migration in Anthropology." In *Migration Theory: Talking Across Disciplines*, eds. Caroline Brettell and James Hollifield, 97–136. New York and London: Routledge.
Carter, Donald. 1997. *States of Grace: Senegalese in Italy and the New European Immigration*. Minneapolis: University of Minnesota Press.

Castles, Stephen, and Mark Miller. 2003. *The Age of Migration*. 3rd edition. Houndmills: Palgrave.

Chavez, Leo. 1991. "Outside the Imagined Community: Undocumented Settlers and the Experiences of Incorporation." *American Ethnologist* 18: 257–278.

Cheong, Pauline, et al. 2005. "Immigration, Social Cohesion and Social Capital: A Critical Review." Paper presented at the "Whither Social Capital?" conference. London, 7 April.

Cole, Jeffrey. 1997. *The New Racism in Europe: A Sicilian Ethnography*. Cambridge: Cambridge University Press.

Edelman, Marc. 2001. "Social Movements: Changing Paradigms and Forms of Politics." *Annual Review of Anthropology* 30: 285–317.

Escobar, Arturo. 1992. "Culture, Practice and Politics: Anthropology and the Study of Social Movements." *Critique of Anthropology* 12: 395–432.

Flynn, Don. 2006 *Migrant Voices and Migrant Rights: Can Migrant Community Organizations Change the Immigration Debate in Britain Today?* London: The Migrant Rights Network and Barrow Cadbury.

Foner, Nancy. 2003. "Anthropology and the Study of Immigration." In *Immigration Research for a New Century*, eds. Nancy Foner et al. New York: Russell Sage Foundation.

Gibb, Robert. 2001. "Toward an Anthropology of Social Movements." *Journal des Anthropologues* 85/86: 233–253.

Grillo, Ralph. 1985. *Ideologies and Institutions in Urban France*. Cambridge: Cambridge University Press.

———. 2005. *Backlash Against Diversity? Identity and Cultural Politics in European Cities*. COMPAS Working Paper No. 14. Oxford: Centre on Migration Policy and Society.

Grillo, Ralph, and Jeff Pratt, eds. 2002. *The Politics of Recognizing Difference: Multiculturalism Italian Style*. Aldershot: Ashgate.

Guarnizo, Luis E. 2006. *Londres latina: La presencia colombiana en la capital britanica*. Unpublished manuscript.

Hargreaves, Alec, and C. Wihtol de Wenden. 1993. "Guest Editors Introduction." *New Community* 20 (1).

Kofman, Eleonore, et al. 2000. *Gender and International Migration in Europe: Employment, Welfare and Politics*. London and New York: Routledge.

Lagnado, Jacob. 2004. *The London Service Sector and Migrant Labour in the 1990s: Colombians in Contract Cleaning*. Unpublished MSc dissertation. Milton Keynes: Open University.

Levitt, Peggy. 2001. *The Transnational Villagers*. Berkeley: University of California Press.

Lewenstein, Dan. 2006. *The Invisible Community: Counting London's Latin Americans and Responding to their Needs*. London: Indoamerican Refugee and Migrant Organization.

Macilwaine, Cathy. 2005. *Coping Practices Among Colombian Migrants in London*. London: Queen Mary, University of London.

Malkki Liisa. 1997. "National Geographic: The Rooting of Peoples and the Territorialization of National Identity Among Scholars and Refugees." In *Culture, Power, Place: Explorations in Critical Anthropology*, eds. Akhil Gupta and James Ferguson, 52–74. Durham and London: Duke University Press.

Martiniello, Marco. 2005. "The Political Participation, Mobilization and Representation of Immigrants and their Offspring in Europe." In *Migration and Citizenship: Legal Status, Rights, and Political Participation*, ed. Rainer Bauböck, 52–64. Amsterdam: IMISCOE.

Moschonas, Gerassimos. 2002. *In the Name of Social Democracy: The Great Transformation, 1945 to the Present*. London: Verso.

Nash, June. 2005. "Introduction: Social Movements and Global Processes." In *Social Movements: An Anthropological Reader*, ed. June Nash, 1–26. Oxford: Blackwell.

Però, Davide. 2005a. "Engaging Power: Recent Approaches to the Study of Political Practices." *Social Anthropology* 13 (3): 331–338.

———. 2005b. *Immigrants and the Politics of Governance in Barcelona.* COMPAS Working Paper No. 19. Oxford: Centre on Migration Policy and Society.

———. 2005c. "Left-Wing Politics, Civil Society, and Immigration in Italy: The Case of Bologna." *Ethnic and Racial Studies* 28 (5): 832–858.

———. 2007a. "Migrants' Mobilizations and Anthropology: Reflections from the Experience of Latin Americans in the UK." In *Citizenship, Political Engagement and Belonging: Immigrants in Europe and the United States,* eds. D. Reed-Danahay and C. Brettell. New Brunswick: Rutgers University Press.

———. 2007b. *Inclusionary Rhetoric/Exclusionary Practices: Left-Wing Politics and Migrants in Italy.* New York and Oxford: Berghahn Books.

Smith, Gavin. 2002. "Effecting Reality: Intellectuals and Politics in the Current Conjuncture." *Focaal* 40: 165–177.

Smith, Michael, and Luis Guarnizo, eds. 1998. *Transnationalism from Below.* Edison: Transaction.

Vertovec, Steven. 2006. *The Emergence of Super-Diversity in Britain.* COMPAS Working Paper No. 25. Oxford: Centre on Migration Policy and Society.

Wimmer, Andreas, and Nina Glick Schiller. 2003. "Methodological Nationalism, the Social Sciences, and the Study of Migration: An Essay in Historical Epistemology." *International Migration Review* 37 (3): 576–610.

Zontini, Elisabetta. 2002. "Resisting Fortress Europe: The Everyday Politics of Moroccan and Filipino Women in Bologna and Barcelona." Paper presented at the 7th EASA conference. Copenhagen, 14–17 July.

— Chapter 5 —

GENDER AND RESISTING FORTRESS EUROPE IN ITALY AND SPAIN

Elisabetta Zontini

Today we are witnessing the consolidation of a "Fortress Europe" whereby stricter rules are passed in all of the member states to "protect" them from what public opinion and policymakers perceive as waves of "dangerous" third-country immigrants threatening the stability of a supposedly ethno-culturally homogeneous Europe (Stolke 1995; see also Lem, chapter 8). Whereas internal borders within the EU have been progressively lifted and previous "aliens," such as Southern Europeans, are becoming accepted in northern countries, external European borders have become tougher, separating Europe from its Third World "others" (Shore 2000). After a period of regulated immigration following the WWII, from the 1970s onward, northern European countries have started to limit the entrance of both migrants and asylum seekers. The privileges enjoyed by colonial populations have eroded and European states have moved toward harmonization and convergence (usually based on the most restrictive national legislation available), lessening the distinctiveness of different European migratory regimes (Kofman et al. 2000). Southern Europe represents a partial exception to this trend, having become, during the 1980s, a new destination of mass immigration after the sealing off of northern European borders (King 1993, 2001). Southern European governments started to recognize the need for foreign domestic labor for their transformed economies, granting permits to incoming workers in areas of labor shortage, such as agriculture, construction, industry, and domestic work. Here too, however, in spite of the continuing demand for unskilled workers, immigration policies have shifted toward control and reduction of numbers, after an initial laissez-faire period. Predictably, these policies have resulted in a growing number of undocumented workers joining an expanding informal sector rather than tighter border control (Zontini 2002).

Although the new immigrants are prevented entrance, those already living within European territory are subjected to policies aimed at fostering their "integration"[1] in the societies where they are now residents. On the one hand, the underlying discourse behind such policies appears to be one that sees immigrants as a threat to Europe, and on the other hand, one that sees them as intrinsically problematic, lacking skills and resources, and thus destined for the margins of European societies. As is discussed by Lem and Barber (introduction), Però (2007), and elsewhere in this volume, immigrants are generally depicted as objects of public policies rather than as political actors in their own rights.

Among immigrant groups residing in Europe, Muslim women are those whose agency is most often obscured in both academic and popular accounts (see De Filippo and Pugliese 2000; Magli 1999; Phillips 2006; Sartori 2000; for a critique, see Moualhi 2000). In a European climate characterized by "cultural fundamentalism" (Stolke 1995), gender relations and sexuality become central in defining boundaries between who is considered "modern" and "European" and who is assumed to be "traditional" and incapable of being included in the nation. "Religion has become the key signifier of incompatible differences. Islamic groups, regulated by patriarchal structures, are singled out as being too distinctive in their daily lives and social norms to be able to cohabit with groups whose practices are derived from Christian traditions" (Kofman et al. 2000: 37). The validity of this diagnosis for the southern European context I have studied is, unfortunately, confirmed by the ideas advanced by some Italian intellectuals. In an article in an Italian newspaper entitled "The Muslim Invasion in Italy," anthropologist Ida Magli (1999) writes: "The arrival of so many Muslim groups both from Africa and the Balkans is organized, directed, programmed from above. Women and children are sent ahead not because it is more difficult to send them away but because they are territorially and culturally more invasive since they can procreate and multiply." Muslim women, we can infer from the above quote, are considered only as passive victims, oppressed by their fundamentalist and traditionalist men, and merely concerned with giving birth to high numbers of children.

The material on which this chapter is based draws on a larger three-year doctoral project comparing the experiences of Moroccan and Filipino female immigrants in Bologna and Barcelona (Zontini 2002).[2] This chapter aims to challenge the views and perspectives previously presented and focuses instead on the active political role of immigrant women, arguing that, rather than being passive subjects, they are actively engaged in negotiating their citizenship rights and in securing a space for themselves and their families in Europe. However, in order to be able to appreciate the kinds of engagements of immigrant women, I argue that two preliminary steps are necessary. The first one is the adoption of a broad definition of *the political* that includes (as anthropologists and feminist scholars have long argued) more than the sphere of institutional politics. The second one is a shift toward a transnational focus. I will illustrate these two points in the first two parts of the chapter. The final part adopts the definition of *citizenship* as a negotiated process developed by Daiva Stasiulis and Abigail Bakan (1997) in the Canadian context and applies it to the European one. In so doing it explores the ways in which immigrant women are responding to their situation in Bologna and Barcelona and are organizing in order to gain rights and access to citizenship. Specifically, I will focus on how immigrant women negotiate their rights to entrance and settlement and how they try to improve their working conditions. Throughout the chapter different forms of female political organization—or engagements—will be explored: those built around community solidarity, associationism, and trade-union involvement of the Filipinas and those built around motherhood and gender identity as a strategy to make claims on housing and welfare deployed by Moroccan women.

Extending the Definition of the Political

Before dealing with immigrant women's political activities it is necessary to spell out what is meant by *political* in this chapter. Conventional definitions associate it mainly with electoral politics and formal institutions. These kinds of definitions are inadequate for interpreting women's citizenship politics generally (see Lister 2005) and immigrants' in particular. In fact, they generally lack voting rights at the national and, in the majority of states, even at the local level. If we were to focus on formal political processes, immigrant women would indeed appear as non-active and excluded. They, however, act and participate in other spheres that, though going beyond what is normally understood as conventional politics, are no less "political." Their activities usually take place at the interstices between the public and the private sphere. According to Ruth Lister (2005: 21), migrant women are becoming active citizens in what Nancy Fraser (1987) has called the "politics of needs interpretation," forging practices of "everyday-life citizenship."

If we take anthropology's and feminists' understanding of politics as concerning power and inequalities beyond political institutions (e.g., Lister 2005; Vincent 2002) and adopt the definition of political engagement of this edited collection, we can appreciate how migrant women are involved in a wide variety of political activities through which they aim at challenging power relations within the home, the workplace, and society at large. Eleanor Kofman et al. (2000: 163) stress the importance of migrant women's political engagement: "As the social and civil rights of migrants have been eroded . . . this has brought new forms of engagement, and migrant women frequently take the lead in this form of activity."

Apart from electoral politics, the forms of female political engagements identified by Kofman et al. involve struggles in the workplace, campaigning for immigrant rights, community political activities, and politics of the country of origin and pan-European organizations. Some recent work has started to examine in detail migrants' forms of collective action both transnationally (Østergaard-Nielsen 2003) and in the countries of settlement (Però 2007). This chapter looks specifically at women's involvement in forms of collective action, but I have chosen to extend the analysis to other forms of infrapolitics that are articulated at the individual, rather than collective, level. This is because, consistent with Barber's arguments in chapter 7, many of the most vulnerable subjects I worked with found it hard to organize collectively given their precarious legal status and their confinement to the isolation of domestic work, but were no less involved in trying to improve their families' living conditions and to confront exploitation and oppression.

The political activity of my interviewees was often rooted in their personal experiences. As Julia Sudbury (1998) has noted, black and immigrant women's struggles are often linked to their everyday lives. Her study indicates how children are often central to black women's politics. For black women, she argues, the family becomes a site of political resistance, not just to patriarchy but also to institutional racism. One example of a typically female political strategy rooted in daily experience is the "motherist movements" (Werbner 1999), whereby maternal qualities such as caring, compassion, and responsibility for the vulnerable are valorized and used for making political claims. Werbner considers these movements important because rather than being hidden (as several female resistance strategies tend to be) they are "by definition, overt; a move into the public domain which challenges the confinement of women to domesticity" (1999: 231).

Adopting a Transnational Perspective

The second step necessary to understand immigrant women's actions is the adoption of a transnational perspective (see Glick Schiller, Basch, and Szanton Blanc 1992) or, as Andreas Wimmer and Nina Glick Schiller

(2002) would put it, the abandonment of "methodological nationalism," which is the tendency, common in much migration research, to limit the focus of analysis to the receiving society and use the nation-state as the natural framework from which to assess the experiences of migrants. My research has shown how migrant women are both migrants enmeshed in transnational webs and settlers who are involved in creating long-lasting links with the local contexts of reception. Their experiences not only seem to confirm Atvar Brah's (1996) point that transnational movement and the maintenance of strong ties with more than one society are not incompatible with settlement, but show that such transnationalism is the actual way that settlement takes place.

The Filipinas I worked with, for instance, were at the center of transnational kinship and other networks: Through their work they maintained family members in the Philippines and through their contacts and the rights they acquired in Italy and Spain (e.g., nationality) they could sponsor the migration of children and parents to Italy and Spain and beyond. There had been a phase in which migrant women were sending their children away to be raised in the Philippines; now there is a new trend of "importing" grandparents to care for the immigrant's family while the woman dedicates herself totally to paid work (Zontini 2002). Moroccans in Spain also receive help, support, and information from their families and former neighbors living not only in Morocco but also in other European countries. It is through these channels that women learn about laws and entitlements in other destinations and thus can assess their situation in southern Europe and act to improve it.

This type of settlement has implications for reception policies, which at present do not seem to recognize the possibility of multiple identities and different loyalties, neither do they appreciate the primary role of women migrants in the settlement process. Both Filipinos and Moroccans live transnationally, maintaining close links and participating in social and family life in at least two countries. This is not necessarily in conflict with their desire and efforts to establish themselves in southern Europe. It may, however, be in opposition to reception policies that tend to oversimplify migrants as inevitably "excluded" and in need of "integration" in the local society.

For example, the recent rich international literature on Filipinas describes them as transnational migrants condemned to a situation of "partial citizenship" (Parreñas 2001) and "provisional diaspora" (Barber 2000). Such concepts refer to Filipinas "liminal" position both in their countries of destination as well as of origin. Filipino migrants' constant talk (and yet postponement) of return, their spending of savings on the purchase of properties in the Philippines, their prolonged feeling of obligation toward kin left behind, and their constant sending of remittances that do not seem to decrease over the years, can all be seen as evidence of such a position of liminality in host societies.

Filipinas' strong ties and commitments toward their country of origin and their ambiguous position toward return certainly emerged from my own research. However, my work also shows that Filipinas in southern Europe, rather than being liminal, are in some respects quite rooted in their immigration contexts. Their involvement in their societies of origin and their centrality in transnational links do not imply their passivity or their lack of interest or concern with their situation in the receiving context. On the contrary: They buy properties there, they develop links with local civil society, they assert their political and citizenship rights, they reunite their families there.

This difference with the situation of Filipinas in other contexts may be due to the somewhat favorable conditions they encounter in southern Europe. Here, although they are restricted to the domestic-sector niche and therefore suffer from deskilling and a lack of opportunities, they can gain among the best wages worldwide for this type of work and more than a professional earns in their own country. They can also obtain long-term residence in Italy and even privileged access to citizenship in Spain, allowing them to plan for long-term settlement. What is more, they can obtain entrance for relatives and friends more easily than in other countries. This often occurs not through policies for family reunion, whose restrictive criteria are also difficult to meet in southern Europe, especially for live-in domestic workers, but rather thanks to Filipinas' position at the top end of the hierarchy of domestic workers in the region and the very high demand for their services.

In this chapter I argue that a transnational focus is necessary in order to interpret the experiences of immigrant women. An exclusive focus on the context of arrival may lead us to depict them as an oppressed group marginalized for reasons of class, gender, and race (see also Barber, chapter 7). These women are indeed oppressed; however, such a focus obscures the agency and the personal story behind each of these women. By focusing exclusively on their oppression we do not explain why they accept these situations and often act in ways that may seem irrational from the point of view of the receiving society. Considering the commitments linking immigrant women to other members of their scattered families and their simultaneous involvement in different societies gives us clues to interpret and perhaps better comprehend some of their decisions and their migration experience in a broader sense.

For instance, the main reason given by married Filipino women for migration was the need to pay for their children's education. Women give up their qualified jobs at home in order to take manual jobs in

Europe for the well-being and futures of their children. Gender roles clearly play a part here since it is the mother who is the one who has to "sacrifice herself" for the family; her job is invariably considered more disposable than that of her husband (even if she is a professional). But married women can also use their responsibilities toward the family to their own advantage, for example, to get away from unhappy relationships without incurring the local social stigma that a separation would entail. This is the case for Maricel, who found herself having to provide alone for her five children in the Philippines because of the negligence of her alcoholic and abusive husband. When she left her job as a police officer in Manila in 1986 and paid traffickers to reach southern Europe she saw in emigration both an escape route from her unhappy marriage and a viable option for providing independently for her children. For many Moroccan widows and divorcees, low-skilled jobs in southern Europe also offer new possibilities of economic independence, ways of supporting their children and families, and an escape from their stigmatized social position (Zontini 2002).

How Migrants Negotiate Citizenship

A transnational focus does not mean that issues of citizenship lose salience for contemporary transmigrants, quite the opposite. One criticism that can be aimed at Western-European-based (especially British) feminist discussions on citizenship (Anthias and Yuval Davis 1992; Lister 1997; Lutz, Phoenix, and Yuval Davis 1995; Yuval Davis 1991, 1997; Yuval Davis and Werbner 1999) is that they tend to focus on ethnic minority women, paying scant attention to the processes of exclusion experienced by immigrant women. Although ethnic minority women and immigrant women may share a number of experiences—such as their presence in gendered and racialized labor markets—there are important differences between the two, not least the fact that the former enjoy full formal social and political rights, whereas the latter do not. The fact that many immigrants in southern Europe (including women) are undocumented enhances the relevance of this difference. Whereas feminist debates in Britain center on new notions of citizenship that can offer women *more* than formal rights, in the southern European context the issue for immigrant women is their access to basic rights such as the right to enter, reside, and work there.[3]

The case of Maricel mentioned previously illustrates this point well. As we saw earlier, emigration was her only chance to support her five children and she had to pay traffickers to access "Fortress Europe." She tried three times to emigrate until she finally succeeded in 1987. It was

Maricel's mother who helped her raise the money to leave by borrowing money and mortgaging the house. Her first attempt collapsed because the agency proved to be a fake. The "directors" of this agency collected considerable sums of money from Maricel and other Filipinos eager to leave the country, gave them false documents, and then disappeared to North America. The second time Maricel tried to leave through an agency based in Barcelona recommended to her by one of her sisters who was already working there. Again they gave her false documents and she was apprehended by the police at Barcelona's airport and sent back to the Philippines. After having lost her mother's money twice and under a lot of pressure from her family she turned again to the same Barcelona agency begging them to give her a second chance. She had to pay more money, but this time she managed to enter the country, arriving through Alicante. Maricel's problems did not end there. After having finally reached her destination she realized that she was an illegal immigrant who could potentially be arrested by the police and deported any time. She lived in this nightmare for three years, frightened that she would be forced to leave before paying back her considerable debts. Thus, she spent her first years in Barcelona working extremely hard, scared even to walk around the city.

In the debate on citizenship, an approach that seems more relevant for the situation of immigrant women in Southern Europe is the one developed by Stasiulis and Bakan (1997). Their idea is that citizenship should not be seen as static, but rather as a negotiated relationship: "Subject to change, it is acted on collectively, or among individuals existing within social, political, and economic relations of conflict that are shaped by state hierarchies that are gender, race, class, and internationally based. Citizenship is therefore negotiated on international, as well as national, levels" (113). Stasiulis and Bakan analyze how Filipino and Caribbean women negotiate their citizenship rights in Canada by "engaging" with those individuals and institutions that deny them access to basic rights. They show, on the one hand, how Western states—like Canada—try to exclude these women from citizenship rights but also how, on the other hand, such women are far from passive. In fact, they manage entry in spite of stricter border controls, they try to improve their living and working conditions in spite of regulations that tie them to live-in domestic work, and they struggle to obtain landed-immigrant status in spite of their recruitment as contract workers.

Despite their difficult positions in Southern Europe, Moroccan and Filipino women have also developed several strategies to negotiate their rights and positions in Italy and Spain. These included the ability to enter southern Europe in spite of stricter border controls,[4] get a legal status in

Bologna and Barcelona for themselves and their families, and to improve domestic workers' working conditions.

Negotiating entrance and rights to settle

Contrary to common assumptions that portray them as passive victims, migrant women often see and undertake migration with a clear emancipatory goal. For instance, in the case of the Moroccan women I have worked with, their aims were to study, earn an income, enjoy more freedom, elude social control, start a new life, and so on. Patriarchy—which comes with the assumption that fathers have primary responsibility for the welfare of their families—dictates sequential migration whereby men migrate ahead of their wives and children. It is only when their economic position in the receiving context is secure that Moroccan men feel that their families should reunite with them. In several cases men tried to delay the migration of their families, having failed to secure enough earnings to allow them to continue to remit to Morocco and support their nuclear family in southern Europe. Women, however, bargain with their husbands and their families in order to be able to join them in southern Europe, and in many cases they are successful.

Fatima, for instance, had to wait three years before being able to join her Moroccan husband in Italy in 1999. She was a young Moroccan woman from Casablanca and had been a university student but had given up her studies to work in a factory to help her family financially following the sudden death of her father. She had married Mustafà during one of his holidays to Morocco from Italy—after having turned down two other suitors who were also migrants in European countries. Her delayed arrival to Italy was partly a result of the difficulty that her husband had in meeting the requirements for family reunion, the most problematic one being adequate housing, but it was also due in part to the opposition of her in-laws. It took a lot of time for Fatima to convince her husband to take her to Italy. Her argument for coming to Italy with him was that she would be able to work in Bologna and thereby more quickly save enough money to fulfill their dream of building a house in Morocco. Migration thus became a form of political engagement itself, used to alter power inequalities within the household and the family.

For Filipinas migration tends to be more in line with their roles as dutiful daughters, sisters, and mothers who have to "sacrifice themselves" for the family well-being by working abroad. Yet, they too, even if more subtly, exercise their agency and try to fulfill personal objectives. They tend to opt for conflict-free ways of bettering their position within families and kinship groups; such strategies allow them to avoid upsetting social expectations but at the same time allow them to gain more control and independence over their lives, for instance, when they seek de facto separation from their husbands through migration.

Getting access to Europe proved difficult for most of my interviewees, who nevertheless in the end had of course managed to challenge current borders and reach their planned destinations. A great number of my interviewees arrived in Bologna and Barcelona illegally, in spite of the existence of quotas for domestic workers and laws that protect family reunion. In both groups a majority of women moved from one migrant status to another with little control over their lives. Their living situation was thus strongly characterized by precariousness. For example, they went from tourist to illegal immigrant when their visas expired, from illegal to legal immigrant after an amnesty was granted, and from legal to illegal immigrant again when the elderly person for whom the migrant was working died and the residence permit could not be renewed. Such switches occur not only because of changes in the circumstances of the individual migrant, but also because legislation can change abruptly, modifying the conditions under which a person can acquire a residence permit or taking away rights that were previously enjoyed. The latter happened with the introduction of the restrictive Spanish immigration law 8/2000 and the Italian law Bossi/Fini.[5]

Often women undertake the considerable risks involved in emigration with the citizenship rights of their children in mind. They are not only interested in immediate economic gains but often conceive their moves in order to get access to citizenship rights for themselves and above all for their children. Batul and Ilham moved from France, where they had originally migrated from Morocco, to Spain in the hope of being legalized. Once in Madrid, they both got jobs as live-in domestic helpers and with the help of their employers managed to legalize their position.

Selma said that she decided to go to Spain for the sake of her son. She was a Moroccan woman in her late forties who had migrated to Spain in the early 1990s after her husband had taken a second wife. In Barcelona she supported herself and her son by working as a domestic helper.

> When I came here it was for my son. He didn't want to study in my country, he didn't want to do anything. I was thinking of what to do and finally I thought—better that we go to Europe to look for something. Because you know we [Moroccans] have to study a lot but there isn't any work and my son didn't study a lot and so, what kind of job will he find? There isn't anything. I thought—I have family in Belgium, my brother and my sister—but I didn't want to go there. I thought—Spain is near, close to my country, it's better to go there so when we want to go to Morocco it's very near. (Interview, September 2001)

Batul, an illiterate woman from Tangier and thirty-seven years old at the time of the interview, separated from her husband a few months before her baby was due. She found herself alone in Barcelona with no economic support and a newborn. She immediately found a job and for a year spent half of her income to pay for the babysitter who looked after her daughter. Her family in Morocco had offered to take care of the baby but Batul waited a year before accepting this arrangement. She wanted to make sure that her daughter had all the right papers for acquiring Spanish nationality. Today she says that the future citizenship rights of her daughter are her main concern.

> In my family they are all asking me why I don't go back to Morocco, but I don't want to go. You know what happens is that my daughter is from here, she has got a father who has Spanish nationality and she has Spanish papers. When my daughter will grow older there will be a lot of problems, she would tell me that she doesn't like to work in Morocco, that she wants to work in Spain, a lot of problems. It's better for me to stay here, now I'm suffering but one day I'll be fine. (Interview, November 2001)

Filipino mothers also do all they can to ensure that their children have access to citizenship rights in Western countries. Vivian, for instance, a Filipino domestic worker in her thirties, left her job in Bologna and went to stay with her sister in the US in order to give birth in that country. After she achieved what she had planned (a US passport for her daughter), she returned to Bologna with the baby where she could earn more money. She explained that this passport is an investment for the future of her child, which will solve many problems for her daughter in the future.

Improving living conditions

The main area of political engagement of Moroccan women centered on accessing and extending services previously denied to migrants, especially in the sphere of housing and childcare. The Moroccan women I worked with used their maternal function as a political strategy to negotiate with local authorities, as theorized by Pnina Werbner (1999). In Bologna, Moroccan women had arrived in the early 1990s usually to reunite with their husbands, who had migrated to Italy a few years previously. Their husbands worked in local industries, whereas the women found part-time employment as cleaners in offices and sometimes as domestic workers in local households (see Zontini 2002). Most were working-class, illiterate women from rural backgrounds, but there were also some who were younger and better educated among them. All of them were confined to the cleaning and domestic sector in Bologna. These women used both their socially prescribed roles as good mothers and household manag-ers and the existence of state and international legislation protecting chil-dren's welfare to demand that the local authorities in Bologna fulfill their obligations. Not only did they protest at the Institution for Immigration Services (ISI),[6] but they also started to engage in direct action. Such actions included camping out with their children in the offices of the ISI, forcing the officers to take up their cases and through their protests publicly de-nouncing the inadequacies of the council's provisions for migrants. These women can thus be seen as political actors, attempting to alter power re-lations between public institutions and immigrant families excluded by service providers. By using their gender role to improve the situation of their families, they also challenged their position as passive receivers of social policies.

The strategy employed by Moroccan women that has received most media and public attention in Bologna is that of the illegal occupation of empty buildings. The first of such occupations occurred at the begin-ning of 1990, when about two hundred Moroccans (many of whom were women and children) occupied a former school and divided it up into a number of "flats" that became their home (Bernardotti and Mottura 2000). Saida, a Moroccan divorcee in her forties, was among the people who took part in that occupation. She went to the immigration service of the city council to see if they could help her to find accommodations to be able to reunite with her children (at the time she was living in a bedsit provided by the cooperative where she was working). They were not able to help her but it was there that she heard that some Moroccans were going to occupy an empty building and transform it into temporary housing; she decided to go along with them. "I heard about it because when I went there [at the ISI] I talked with this person and the other and they were saying: 'have you seen that there is a house, an empty house, you know.'. . . It wasn't the council that gave it to me. It was just a group of people who went there like that, you know, I wasn't the only one, there were a lot of people without a house then, without anything" (interview, February 2000). As a growing number of immigrant families, particularly those with children, did not have adequate housing, the council was forced to intervene in the early 1990s and take responsibility for the problem. When in 1993 the first re-ception center for families was opened, the first immigrants to be housed there were those who had carried out the occupations. Other female-headed initiatives followed at this center, such as the mother's campaign against drug trafficking and criminality. These unconventional forms of politics forced local authorities to approve for the first time a housing pol-icy for migrants, which was a remarkable victory for nonvoting residents. Even the Moroccan women who were against the occupations and did not participate in them were actively engaged in trying to negotiate rights for adequate housing for themselves and their children.

As documented by authors working in other geographical contexts (e.g., Hondagneu-Sotelo 1994 for Mexicans in the US; Jones-Correa 1998 for Latin Americans in the US; or Ganguly-Scrase and Julian 1998 for Hmong in Australia), as for Moroccans in southern Europe, it is the women who deal with the public services in order to obtain resources. This is one way in which women reinforce their positions within the family and consolidate the process of settlement. By so doing they also break out of domesticity and get involved in the public sphere. They are not only involved in changing power relations between migrants and local institutions, but also in altering their subordinate position within the home. By having to negotiate with local authorities, these women acquire knowledge about the receiving society, which gives them more bargaining power within the household. Some of the Moroccan women I interviewed were reluctantly granted the freedom to travel in the city unaccompanied by their husbands because the husbands recognized the crucial role their wives had in securing benefits, contacts, and goods from charities and local authorities.

Filipinas were absent from this type of engagement. They generally accepted their exclusion from council housing and were less involved than Moroccans in legalization campaigns. This can be partly explained by their different purpose in migrating. For Filipinas the primary goal of migration was economic gain and their migratory project centered on being able to sustain their transnational families, rather than settling into the new environment. They looked negatively on the possibility of relying on the state and saw this as undermining their identity as workers and providers for their distant families. Contrary to Moroccan women, the sphere of work is where Filipinas in southern Europe focus their political activity.

Improving working conditions

Most immigrant women in southern Europe are employed as domestic workers. This is a sector in which "the workplace is foreclosed as a site of political activity" (Kofman et al. 2000). Yet the women I worked with were politically engaged in trying to improve their rights as workers in a number of ways. This is particularly the case for the Filipinas. Filipinas are making a career out of domestic work and have become highly specialized in this sector. I noted how they play with the stereotype of Filipinas as being docile, hardworking, and dedicated domestics, using it to their own advantage as a kind of marketing strategy to sell their labor more expensively than other groups on the labor market for domestic services. Filipinas in both Bologna and Barcelona seem to spend a great deal of energy in preserving the good reputation of the group, since such a positive image is considered an asset for securing good working conditions and higher rates of pay.

They also try to improve their position through small steps, negotiating better working conditions each time they change employers. Filipinas normally start working as live-in maids, accepting the hardest and most demanding jobs. As they acquire skills and experience (in many cases they never did domestic work before) they move to better-paid jobs and/or jobs with better working conditions. They leave the previous occupation to the newcomers and those starting their "career." The ones with more years of experience normally work as live-out domestics with indefinite contracts and do the less demanding tasks within the household.

Some of my interviewees wanted to get out of domestic work altogether. Their options are very limited, however. A form of political engagement to which many of them have resorted has been to try and improve their work situation by checking out another market in a different country. Priscilla and Eleanor both went to try to work in the US. Their stories defy the stereotypes about the passivity of Filipino women and their submission to domestic work. Both women were working in this sector and both suffered a severe downturn through migration. Both also nevertheless tried hard to escape this market niche by using their transnational connections. Eleanor finished high school in the Philippines and trained in information technology in Barcelona, whereas Priscilla had been a teacher in the Philippines. As many of their Filipino counterparts who are also often graduates or professionals, they had to renounce more engaging, but low-paid jobs in their home country for economic security in the West. Once in Europe, the only jobs they could access were in the domestic-service sector, even though both had lived in Barcelona for nearly twenty years and had acquired Spanish citizenship.

Eleanor worked for a while as a cashier in the US. She did not dislike the job but her earnings were low due to the fact that she did not have a work permit. She stayed in Los Angeles for three months and then decided to return to Barcelona. Like Eleanor, Priscilla tried to see if she could escape the domestic-service niche by exploring working opportunities in other countries. First, she went to Japan with the help of a brother. There she worked in a factory and as a babysitter. She thought that the work possibilities were better in Japan but she finally decided to go back to Catalonia because it was where her family was. Subsequently she went to San Diego, California, to open up a business with the help of another brother who was living there. She tried to open a video rental and a Filipino food shop with the capital her brother lent her (he had the same type of business). However, she stayed only five weeks and then returned the money and went back to Barcelona because she did not manage to convince her youngest daughter to stay in the US.

In addition to informal and individual strategies, Filipinas are also getting organized (see, e.g., Anderson 1999 for the UK context). In Bologna and Barcelona some of the women who realized that changing their occupation would be unfeasible and who have achieved part of their economic goals are now reducing their working hours and engaging in voluntary and community activities. Women in both cities have become the pillars of well-organized and internationally linked Filipino associations. These bodies cover cultural/recreational activities and campaigns for the protection of worker's rights, and are active participants in and sustainers of various church groups. All women involved in such organizations talked about the personal fulfillment they got through these activities. Contrary to the experience of most other immigrant groups in southern Europe, for Filipinos the so-called "community leaders" chosen as preferential interlocutors by the local institution are usually women. They are operating in groups and associations where their activities in favor of Filipino migrants have brought them popularity and respectability among their compatriots.

In the late 1990s a group of sixteen Filipinas founded Liwanag, the association of Filipino women of Bologna, after having met the delegates from Rome of the Dutch organization CFMW (Commission for Filipino Migrant Worker's Network). The aim of Liwanag was to give support to Filipina domestic workers in the city. One of the founding members, Jenny, then got involved with the local branch of the trade union CGIL (Italian General Confederation of Labour). She worked for four years as a volunteer in the Centro Diritti (Rights Center) giving free advice to foreign domestic workers. Thanks to this activity she learned the legislation concerning domestic work and started to spread the word (*ho sparso la voce*) within the Filipino "community." From then on, several Filipinas started to visit the CGIL "to get further information." Over the years Jenny and her colleagues at the union helped several domestics to solve their work-related problems (*a mettersi a posto*). Jenny realized that several Filipino maids did not know their entitlements and this benefited their employers. At the CGIL she started giving information about things like holiday entitlements, child benefits, unemployment benefits, and maternity leave (several women did not know about this right and were going to the Philippines to give birth).

Initially Liwanag was only a loose organization sharing information among its members and organizing occasional events. In November 1999, however, they opened their own office. Their aim is to provide the same service Jenny was offering at the CGIL, but every day rather than once a week, as well as new services, such as language courses. Although Liwa-nag now has its own office, Jenny wants to remain closely linked to the CGIL because through them she can keep updated on the latest legislation concerning domestic work and immigration. For the same reason, the members of Liwanag were also planning to affiliate with RESPECT, the EU Commission for Filipino Migrant Workers International. They already have other international contacts through the Dutch CFMW (Commission for Filipino Migrant Workers; their mother organization) as well as national links through FILCAMS (Italian Federation of Commerce Tourism and Services Workers). Over the past two years delegates from Liwanag participated in several local events, in an international meeting on the conditions of domestic workers, as well as a national meeting organized by FILCAMS in Modena.

In Barcelona there are several active Filipino associations, generally headed and staffed by women. They are active both locally and internationally and lobby the Filipino national government. It was Filipino "transnational" networks that opened up a channel for me to do my fieldwork in Barcelona. I approached the president of the Association of Filipino Women in Barcelona thanks to the details of her association outlined in a publication of RESPECT given to me by members of Liwanag in Bologna. The main activities of Filipino associations in Barcelona involve providing information and training to Filipino women as well as organizing cultural activities. The Association of Filipino Workers has specialized instead in dealing with cases of labor conflicts. The president of the association in Barcelona acts as a mediator in conflicts that may arise between workers and employers, trying to impose conciliatory resolutions whenever possible and in so doing helping maintain the good reputation of the group. Open conflict is preferably avoided since it is believed to be detrimental not only to the individual worker but also to the general "community."

By networking (both locally, nationally, and internationally) Filipinas are trying to keep updated on the changing national and European legislation on domestic work and immigration. They then inform and sensitize Filipino workers in Bologna and Barcelona as to their rights and help to implement them through the trade unions. This strategy seems to be working. Many of my interviewees were aware of their rights and several cited episodes in their work histories in which they turned to the trade union to solve work-related matters. Such success is also confirmed by my interviews with staff members at job centers in Bologna who bitterly lamented that Filipinas have changed in the last few years, becoming more expensive, difficult, choosy, and aware of their rights (and insisting to have them implemented).

Although present in trade unions, Moroccan women were generally less active in workers' rights than their Filipino counterparts. The Moroccan women I worked with found it hard to accept that all their aspirations were confined to an undervalued domestic job. Rather than improving their position in this sector, many women I interviewed hoped to leave this sector altogether. They tended to consider paid work, especially unskilled and devalued domestic work, a sign of poverty and something that sets them apart from the ideal of the housewife/mother supported by a breadwinning husband. My research has shown how patriarchy may become a refuge from a marginalized role in the economic system for Moroccan women. Many Moroccan women find themselves faced with the choice between a low-paid, hard, and (for them) degrading job, or a full-time position as wives and mothers in a patriarchal household. Many have chosen the latter option after disappointing experiences in the local labor markets. Few Filipinas have this choice. They are the economic pillars of their extended families who have often incurred high debts in order to make migration possible. Often their husbands have low-paid jobs in the Philippines. Moreover, as Pauline Barber (2000) has pointed out, their autonomy and prestige increase with migration thanks to the wages they earn abroad. Their working class jobs in southern Europe help to sustain middle class status or aspirations in the Philippines.

Conclusions

My work has shown that the possibility of enjoying full citizenship rights in the immigration country does not lose importance in the age of transnationalism; quite the opposite is true. The enjoyment of social and political rights has a direct impact on an immigrant's position in the receiving society. Their often insecure legal status has important consequences for their position in the labor market and in relation to their family commitments and ability to conduct a transnational life. The lack of basic rights directly reduces the space of women's agency and conspires to render them weak and powerless subjects as sometimes portrayed in literature and as preferred by some employers. The exclusion of resident workers from a number of rights shows the irresponsibility of Western states in apparently endorsing the power of capital to super-exploit immigrant workers.

In spite of their precarious circumstances, however, migrant women are far from passive. By adopting a definition of the political derived from anthropology and feminism, this chapter has documented the ways in which seemingly powerless actors engage with power relations in a number of spheres. It has shown how Moroccan and Filipino migrant women struggled to achieve some of their entitlements, such as nationality, family reunion for all those who were potentially entitled, and legal work contracts. I have also explored how they engaged with power inequalities within their households and families.

The analysis of the experiences of Filipino and Moroccan migrant women shows that there are different strategies deployed in the migration and settlement processes that lead to different possible outcomes depending on varying circumstances in the sending and receiving contexts. Whereas Filipino immigrant women were concerned with improving their working conditions, Moroccan immigrant women focused on accessing services. In spite of all their differences, the stories I have collected have important similarities and common threads. They all develop and articulate in more than one context; they unfold in relation to people and realities beyond those of the place where the women are residing. Nation-states exert their power over these women by controlling their moves, attaching degrading labels to them, denying them rights, and facilitating their economic exploitation. Yet, these women develop skills and build connections that allow them to partly bypass nation-states.

Notes

1. "Integration" is a problematic concept. It is commonly used in academic and policy circles as the opposite of "exclusion." A generic and open definition of integration would be "the process by which immigrants become accepted into society, both as individuals and as groups" (Pennix 2003). However, many grassroots activists fear that when mainstream politicians and policy makers declare to be promoting integration they do not have in mind a two-way process requiring adaptation on the part of both newcomers and the host society (Castles et al. 2003), but rather a one-sided process of adaptation in which "immigrants are expected to give up their distinctive linguistic, cultural, or social characteristics and become indistinguishable from the majority population" (Castles and Miller 1998: 250).
2. The research involved participant observation and in-depth interviews in the two locations over a period of one year. One hundred interviews were conducted, seventy-six with migrant women from the two groups and the remaining ones with NGO representatives and policy makers.
3. Focusing exclusively on ethnic minorities is also problematic in northern European countries that (like Britain) continue to be the destination of a variety of new migrants, including considerable numbers of undocumented workers (Vertovec 2006).

4. This involved several strategies ranging from accepting demanding jobs that were linked to a work permit, to crossing borders on foot and paying so-called "traffickers."

5. The law 8/2000 restricted many rights previously guaranteed to migrants and was strongly opposed by both immigrants and a wide spectrum of civil society. Among its new provisions were important limitations on the social and political rights of immigrants. With this law "undocumented" immigrants lost the right to association and reunion as well as that of union affiliation; the right to work and to social security was also eliminated for undocumented immigrants; tighter conditions for entry were introduced; visas could now be refused without written justification; stricter rules for family reunification were introduced, eliminating the clause that allowed the reunion with "other family members" besides the spouse, parents, and children. The same process of contraction of immigrants' rights also happened in Italy, where the "center-right" government of Silvio Berlusconi passed the very restrictive Bossi-Fini law.

6. The Institution for Immigration Services (ISI) was a council-run office that centralized all the services for immigrants in the city. Its responsibilities included housing, and it was in charge of council residences for immigrants (Zontini 2002).

References

Anderson, Bridget. 1999. "Different Roots in Common Ground: Transnationalism and Migrant Domestic Workers." *Journal of Ethnic and Migraton Studies* 27 (4): 673–683.

Anthias, Floya, and Nira Yuval Davis. 1992. *Racialized Boundaries: Race, Nation, Gender, Colour, and Class in the Anti-Racist Struggle.* London: Routledge.

Barber, G. Pauline. 2000. "Agency in Philippine Women's Labour Migration and Provisional Diaspora." *Women's Studies International Forum* 23 (4): 399–411.

Bernardotti, Adriana, and Giovanni Mottura. 2000. *Il Gioco delle Tre Case: Immigrazione e politiche abitative a Bologna dal 1990 al 1999.* Turin: L'Harmattan Italia.

Brah, Avtar. 1996. *Cartographies of Diaspora.* London: Routledge.

Castles, Stephen, et al. 2003. *Mapping the Field: Integration Research in the UK.* London: Home Office.

Castles, Stephen, and Mark Miller. 1998. *The Age of Migration.* London: Macmillan.

De Filippo, Elena, and Enrico Pugliese. 2000. "Le donne nell'immigrazione in Campania." *Papers* 60: 55–66.

Fraser, Nancy. 1987. "Women, Welfare and the Politics of Needs Interpretation." *Hypatia* 2 (1): 103–119.

Ganguly-Scrase, Ruchira, and Roberta Julian. 1998. "Minority Women and the Experiences of Migration." *Women's Studies International Forum* 21 (6): 633–648.

Glick Schiller, Nina, Linda Basch, and Cristina Blanc-Szanton. 1992. *Towards a Transnational Perspective on Migration: Race, Class, Ethnicity and Nationalism Reconsidered.* Annals of the New York Academy of Sciences 645. New York: New York Academy of Sciences.

Hondagneu-Sotelo, Pierette. 1994. *Gendered Transitions: Mexican Experiences of Immigration.* Los Angeles: University of California Press.

Jones-Correa, Michael. 1998. "Different Paths: Gender, Immigration and Political Participation." *IMR* 32 (2): 326–349.

King, Russell, ed. 1993. *The New Geography of European Migrations.* London: Belhaven Press.

———. 2001. *The Mediterranean Passage: Migration and New Cultural Encounters in Southern Europe.* Liverpool: Liverpool University Press.

Kofman, Eleanor, et al. 2000. *Gender and International Migration in Europe: Employment, Welfare and Politics*. London: Routledge.

Lister, Ruth. 1997. "Citizenship: Towards a Feminist Synthesis." *Feminist Review* 57: 28–48.

———. 2005. "Feminist Citizenship Theory: An Alternative Perspective on Understading Women's Social and Political Lives." In *Women and Social Capital*, ed. J. Franklin, 19–26. Families and Social Capital ESRC Research Group Working Paper No. 12. London: London South Bank University.

Lutz, Helma, Ann Phoenix, and Nira Yuval Davis. 1995. *Crossfires: Nationalism, Racism and Gender in Europe*. London: Pluto Press.

Magli, Ida. 1999. "L'invasione dei musulmani in Italia." *Resto del Carlino*, 18 August.

Moualhi, Djaouida. 2000. "Mujeres musulmanas: Estereotipos occidentales versus realidad social." *Papers* 60: 291–304.

Østergaard-Nielsen, Eva 2003. *Transnational Politics: The Case of Turks and Kurds in Germany*. London: Routledge.

Parreñas, Rachel. 2001. "Transgressing the Nation-State: The Partial Citizenship and 'Imagined (Global) Community' of Migrant Filipina Domestic Workers." *Sign* 26 (4): 1129–1154.

Pennix Rino. 2003. *Integration: The Role of Communities, Institutions, and the State*. Migration Policy Institute. http://www.migrationinformation.org/Feature/display.cfm?ID=168/.

Però, Davide. 2007. "Anthropology and Migrants' Mobilisation: Reflections from the Experience of Latin Americans in the UK." In *Immigration and Citizenship in Europe and the United States: Anthropological Perspectives*, eds. D. Reed-Danahay and C. Brettell. New Brunswick: Rutgers University Press.

Phillips, Melanie. 2006. *Londonistan*. London: Gibson Square Books.

Sartori, Giovanni. 2000. *Pluralismo, multiculturalismo e estranei: Saggio sulla società multietnica*. Milan: Rizzoli.

Shore, Chris. 2000. *Building Europe: The Cultural Politics of European Integration*. London: Routledge.

Stasiulis, Daiva, and Abigail Bakan. 1997. "Negotiating Citizenship: The Case of Foreign Domestic Workers in Canada." *Feminist Review* 57: 112–139.

Stolke, Verena. 1995. "Talking Culture: New Boundaries, New Rhetorics of Exclusion in Europe." *Current Anthropology* 36 (1): 1–24.

Sudbury, Julia. 1998. *"Other Kinds of Dreams": Black Women's Organisations and the Politics of Transformation*. London: Routledge.

Vertovec, Steven. 2006. *The Emergence of Super-Diversity in Britain*. COMPAS Working Paper No. 25. Oxford: Centre on Migration Policy and Society.

Vincent, Joan. 2002. "Introduction." In *The Anthropology of Politics: A Reader in Ethnography, Theory and Critique*, ed. J. Vincent, 1–13. Oxford: Blackwell.

Werbner, Pnina. 1999. "Political Motherhood and the Feminisation of Citizenship: Women's Activism and the Transformation of the Public Sphere." In *Women, Citizenship and Difference*, eds. N. Yuval-Davis and P. Werbner, 221–245. London: Zed Books.

Wimmer, Andreas, and Nina Glick Schiller. 2002. "Methodological Nationalism and Beyond: Nation-State Building, Migration and the Social Sciences." *Global Networks* 2 (4): 301–334.

Yuval Davis, Nira. 1991. "The Citizenship Debate: Women, Ethnic Processes and the State." *Feminist Review* 39: 58–68.

———. 1997. "Women, Citizenship and Difference." *Feminist Review* 57: 4–27.

Yuval Davis, Nira, and Pnina Werbner, eds. 1999. *Women, Citizenship and Difference*. London: Zed Books.

Zontini, Elisabetta. 2002. *Family Formation and Gendered Migrations in Bologna and Barcelona*. PhD dissertation. Brighton: University of Sussex.

— *Chapter 6* —

Gender, History, and Political Activism in Spain

Susana Narotzky

This chapter will center on two life histories of women workers with migratory experiences during the same historical period but whose local historical and personal contexts were extremely distinct and provided different conditions of possibility for class resistance and activism. The object of the article is to show how material economic conditions and the production of coherence in personal experience explain the greater or lesser presence of political activism, and the particular form that it takes, locally.

As a theoretical framework I will be using Pierre Bourdieu's idea of "habitus" and its incorporation as durable dispositions, as it is applied to the conditioning of expectations for a better future and its tension with the power of the symbolic domain in providing the tools for envisioning the transformation of existing structures (2003). For Bourdieu, in a situation where the lack of a future becomes an expanding experience for many people, it is the relative autonomy of the symbolic order that can "provide some margin of freedom for a political action that may reopen the space of possibles. By being capable of manipulating expectations and hopes, particularly through a performative evocation more or less inspired and exciting of the future . . . symbolic power can introduce some play in the correspondence between hopes and chances opening thus a space of freedom by positing, in a more or less voluntaristic fashion, more or less improbable possibles, utopia, project, program or plan, that the pure logic of probabilities would lead to hold as practically excluded." (336–337). Political mobilization in this view hinges on the production of this "margin of freedom" through symbolic struggles. The major stake of these symbolic struggles being that "the belief that this or that future, desired or feared, is possible, probable or inevitable, may, in certain conjunctures, mobilize around it a group of people, and contribute in this form to facilitate or obstruct the coming of this future" (338). The question, however, remains of how and under which historical circumstances the creation of a margin of freedom becomes possible. An additional question is that of the connection between particular habitus, with their reproductive tendency to support a "causality of the probable," and the different forms and modes that the "more or less improbable possibles" can take in their symbolic emergence. This differentiality will in turn orient the mobilization forms available for individual subjects.

At this point I will be turning to Antonio Gramsci's concept of the organic intellectuals that have "worked out and made coherent the principles and the problems raised by the masses in their practical activity, thus constituting a cultural and social bloc" (1987: 330). In this Gramscian view, organic intellectuals of the working class are essential elements for effecting the transcendence of common sense into a philosophy of praxis enabling the production of a historical bloc and guiding the struggle for hegemony (346). From this perspective, then, there is a particular work that has to be done in order for workers' experience of exploitation to become coherent in a collective way.

The articulation of Bourdieu and Gramsci will provide me with a framework to compare two rather different situations in contemporary Spain, both dealing with the life and struggles of women trying to produce a better future. I now turn to the particular cases.

Setting 1: The Case of Catral (SE Spain)

The first area I will present is located to the southwest of Valencia, in the Vega Baja del Segura (Alicante province).[1] Some historical factors about the region are important to the understanding of particular trajectories of working class women and their attempts to control their lives.

Irrigated and interspersed with barren scrublands, this area had a historical pattern of pluriactivity and active commercial agriculture since the eighteenth century. A few large absentee landowners held most of the land and managed it through large tenants that in turn rented some small plots (less than what was needed for a family to subsist on) to subtenants. The latter were thus tied to the land and became "stable" day laborers indentured through their debt of the subtenancy. Large parts of the local population, however, were "free" day laborers. At the outbreak of the Spanish Civil War (1936–1939) more than 70 percent of the local population consisted of daily hired laborers, without access to land. The patterns of mutual responsibility that developed were very different for the "tied" and "free" laborers, the former strongly dependent on particularistic patronage links, the latter increasingly organized in terms of a homogeneous, politicized working class ideology. We have dealt elsewhere in detail with the local processes of differentiation that the unequal development of capitalism in Spain and the forms of political regulation produced for this region (Narotzky and Smith 2006). Here I want to stress how these produced differently situated groups of people in the region that had heterogeneous notions of solidarity and responsibility—toward their family, their peers, their employers or employees. As a result, strategies became available for thought and action from within different, historically construed, cultural and sociological positions.

In the late 1970s the Fordist footwear industry that had developed in the local town of Elche was restructured as a dispersed network of subcontracting small firms, workshops, sweatshops, middlemen, and home workers. In this conjuncture, the particular way in which personal responsibilities and moral obligation became entangled in the development of a "regional economy" was not homogeneous locally, and could be referred to past histories of differentiation but also past histories of producing consent and struggle, and of managing dissent. While unions became very active in the industrial town of Elche (Benton 1990) up to the late 1970s, they did not re-emerge in the rural agricultural areas. There, the pattern of social relations that became hegemonic was that of dependent links and patron-client networks of "favors." Moreover, the crisis of the footwear industry in the mid 1970s was credited by local subjects both to the international economic conjuncture and to the national political transition process (1975–1982) that legalized class unions and unleashed a period of sustained strikes. The subsequent reorganization of footwear production in a dispersed network of small—mostly informal—units of production, including large amounts of home workers, was predicated upon a discourse voiced by entrepreneurs, and shared by many workers, about the responsibility of union claims and unrest that had "caused" entrepreneurs to close down their large factories. In this conjuncture, the dispersed and informal structure of production enhanced personalized modes of dealing with structural suffering that referred to the local memories and past experience of dependent agricultural labor (Narotzky and Smith 2006), but were nevertheless often inflected by a consciousness of class dignity, as the following case illustrates. These points are also underscored by Leach (chapter 9) who stresses the centrality of particular work histories.

It is this region and its footwear production sector that was defined in the 1990s as a particularly "successful" industrial district by local actors such as union leaders, regional government agents, and entrepreneurs.

Social scientists, however, exposed mixed feelings about these "local economies," both applauding the use of social capital for industrial development while pointing to the lack of local institutional structures that would enhance its potentialities (Ybarra 2001, 2003). Writing in 2004, a group of social scientists describe the region's footwear sector as one in crisis, regionally sustained by the use of 52 percent of informal labor in its production process, thus obtaining a cut of around 15 percent in labor costs that makes it marginally competitive (Ybarra et al. 2004: 33–51).

Conchita: Multiple Migration Patterns and the Limits of Dignity

I will start with an ethnographic vignette of the struggles to earn a livelihood and retain some sense of dignity of Conchita and her husband in the Vega Baja del Segura (Alicante).

Conchita started working when she was eleven years old as a maid. When she was twenty-four she married a *jornalero* (day laborer) and started working in a canning factory in the nearby village of Dolores. When the drought years (1959–1961 and 1964–1966) came the consequences for local agriculture were dramatic (Olcina Cantos 2001; Morales Gil, Olcina Cantos, and Rico Amorós 1999; Olcina Cantos and Rico Amorós 1995). The 1966 drought was particularly significant in that it mobilized peasants in the area: many decided to migrate to the expanding industrial urban centers, while others organized to demand for water regulation policies in the face of increased demand of the agricultural irrigation system and of the expanding local urban and tourist resort areas. The government responded with the decree allowing the transfer of water from the Tajo river to the Segura river in 1968, a highly polemic waterworks project.

Conchita and her husband decided to migrate to the then expanding footwear industry in Elche. In Elche, however, her husband found it difficult adapting to the routines of factory work and felt cut off from the reciprocity networks in their hometown Catral. So they returned and she got a job at the canning factory again. Her husband began to go to France as a migrant agricultural worker in the early 1970s. He migrated to the town of Marguerittes (about 8500 inhabitants in the region of Languedoc-Roussillon, Gard department), known for wine and other horticultural produces. Many local young men were going to this particular area, sometimes seasonally for the grape harvest, while others would stay for the year, moving around with seasonal agricultural jobs or working steadily for a particular farmer. During this period Conchita's mother took care of her children and cooked for her while she went to her job at the canning factory. This arrangement seems to have worked for a couple of years but then her husband had a serious confrontation over wages with his employer in France. Conchita recounts: "My husband argued [with the boss] that he was entitled to know what he was going to get paid by the hour in order to see if it was worth it to have left his wife back home, working in Dolores, and his children . . . because if he was to die of hunger he preferred to die in his village, he wasn't going to die in a foreign country" (fieldnotes, 1995). The conflict brought him back to his village where he started to get some work in construction in the slack agricultural season.

After a few years of working as a mason in the early 1980s her husband got seriously ill with cancer. This coincided with the closing of the canning factory. Conchita was able to find home work finishing heels at piece rates in the informal footwear manufacturing network. She did this work not only to survive but to give her children better chances in life—through higher education. Conchita expresses a strong feeling that her family was caught in a frenetic cycle that was not moving them forward. Somehow her work needed to be transformed into some longer-term investment in the future; for her this becomes condensed in the idea of formal education for her children.

For Conchita and her husband, their sense of self-respect informed much of their actions and guided a particular individually confrontational way of dealing with a life of extremely constricted opportunity. While they were aware that they had to accept exploitative relations with those who had the power and the resources, they were not prepared to go beyond the threshold of self-respect. Similarly, in chapter 7 Barber discusses the muting of particular class performances. An understanding of the extension of political activism beyond formal politics is also discussed by Zontini in chapter 5.

Setting 2: The Case of Ferrol (NW Spain)

Ferrol in the region of Galicia (northwest coast of Spain, north of Portugal) is a coastal town that has been centered on the ship-building industry for more than three centuries. Ferrol was until the 1990s a town centered around the shipyards. It was also a naval garrison with military of all graduations living in special quarters with their families. However, because of the shipyards, Ferrol had a mass of specialized laborers that became strongly unionized at the turn of the twentieth century. The shipyards were a state industry and produced military and civil ships. Labor was highly specialized and was formally apprenticed at the shipyard school for four years before being admitted to the shipyard as workers. The shipyard had a tradition of strong workers' unions since the nineteenth century and work conditions and work pay defined them as privileged and with a high job security ("almost like civil servants"). Indeed, after the Spanish Civil War, even though most workers had been active on the republican side fighting against Franco, most of them went back to their jobs and were not repressed. Specialized workers were needed in the shipyard. This situation of stability and relative privilege lasted until the 1980s and was crucial in the re-emergence of a clandestine but very active class-based workers' union during the dictatorship in the early 1960s. Union activism reorganized by taking advantage of the corporatist union framework *"Sindicato vertical"* (vertical union), mostly a strategy of the communist union Comisiones Obreras (CCOO). This union became the guiding light of the entire working class in Ferrol and was very active at organizing and solidarizing shipyard workers with other local industries' workers.

After the "transition" to democracy, the first socialist government of Felipe González started a restructuring of all national state industries: unemployment and early retirement became a generalized feature in the region, as well as the closure of job opportunities in the shipyard for the younger generation. During that same period the unions became bureaucratized and part of a neo-corporatist compact (Pacto de la Moncloa) oriented toward enhancing productivity and generally the competitive aspect of Spanish economy, preparing for Spain's incorporation into the European Economic Community. This trend has continued until the present, with various moments of restructuring and job loss, ending in 2005 with the virtual privatization of the shipyard. The present-day structure of the local shipyard industry is one of medium and small enterprises located in the premises of the original public shipyard but independent from the main company, subcontracted to do the various production processes involved. Workers that had stable jobs in the "old" public shipyard are now dismissed from the main company and re-employed by some of the small subcontracted shops, with precarious, task-related contracts. Parallel to this transformation, the region has experienced the spectacular increase of small to medium enterprises (SME), mostly in the textile- and garment-production and service sectors in new industrial parks surrounding the town of Ferrol. These "new" jobs are addressed mostly to women and younger people and are highly volatile and unprotected. There is almost no unionization or collective action in this new area of employment: a stronger sense of individual strategizing and networking as the main instrument of social mobility seem to be at work. In economic terms there is a demise of the "big" traditional shipyard industry and an emergence of a "flexible" model of SME, regionally integrated in both the shipyard industry and other (textile/service) industries.

Gelines: Becoming a Union Organizer in Ferrol and Paris

Gelines's story is very different from Conchita's. In the 1960s when Gelines starts her working life at age twelve, the town is divided between
the military aristocracy who keep to themselves and the shipyard workers who are the main income earners in most working families. Auxiliary
industries subcontracted by the shipyard also give jobs to many (mostly
male) workers. Aside from the shipyard industry there is an important
processing industry related to fisheries, where mostly women work. The
1960s is historically the period when the working class starts to reorganize
after the first twenty years of Francoist repression. Ferrol and Asturias are
the two strongholds of this reorganization around the emergent (communist) union of Comisiones Obreras.[2] It is essential to note that the shipyard workers are the organizing elements in the class movement. They
are perceived by workers of other industries as their guides, not only in
a pedagogical sense but also in a strategic sense. I have dwelt elsewhere
on the role of organic intellectuals articulating the memory of republican
class struggles and organization to present-day struggles and organization (Narotzky 2004). What I want to highlight here is the centrality of the
union's restructuring of "class" as a concept to be used both in the analysis of present realities and in the active mobilization toward transforming
social relations of production.

We will see how this structures Gelines's life story in a very different
way from Conchita's. Gelines started working when she was a child of
twelve loading coal into boats of the Navy. As soon as she could legally get
an apprenticeship contract (at age fourteen) she found a job at a preserve
factory salting cod. The cod was fished in Terranova, salted in Ferrol, and
exported to Brazil. The work was very hard physically and "morally": "It
was like a whip," she says: "you unloaded trucks, you pieced the fish, you
worked in the cold-storage room at −25°C." During the first four years she
earned an apprenticeship salary although she was fully trained in a few
months. It is during this period that she was "recruited" (*captar*) by a communist neighbor, Manuel, a fisherman, who "initiated" (*iniciar*) her into a
particular understanding of social relations: those articulated around the
concept of "class." It is worth noting that this fisherman was the father of a
shipyard worker, Rafael, who was to be the main leader of the 1960s union
struggle within the shipyard.

In any case, Gelines, together with some of her male coworkers at the
factory, organizes a shop-floor section of the communist union (CCOO)
and starts claims for better working conditions. We must bear in mind
that class-based unions were banned from Francoist Spain. In 1967, a year
of strikes in the shipyard, 250 women are fired from the fish-processing

factory. Gelines, the union shop steward, is among them but refuses to accept the final settlement (*finiquito*). The police make an enquiry about the union at the factory and she is taken to the police station and later on to jail. The shipyard union workers organize a general strike in support of the fired women and against the repression of unionized workers, and as a result fourteen people are tried in Madrid by the Tribunal de Orden Público (TOP) in charge of repression. Gelines is the only woman and the only one from her factory. At the trial, only she and another worker are sentenced to more than a year in jail; the rest are acquitted. While in prison she considers moving to France, with a sister who lives there, but when she gets out she thinks she must go back to the factory, not run away.[3] She says she wanted to leave things "tied up" before leaving, she did it for her coworkers in order to show the strength of organized struggle, and also so that the bosses didn't think she had been broken and discouraged. After four months she went to France, but she left her factory union well organized.

It was 1970 by then, the moment of the great Spanish migration to France and other northern European countries. Gelines went to Paris and after working at several odd jobs she finally found a stable job as a waitress at the Lutetia Hotel in Paris, where she worked until her retirement. There she immediately entered the Confederation Generale du Travail (CGT) union and became an active shop steward and organized some strikes. In 1990 she retired and came back to Ferrol.

Different Experiences of Class

The two cases I have presented are very different in their modes of articulating migration with class and gender. Conchita's experience appears to be much more fragmented and although class seems to be clearly an operative concept in her analysis of the relations of production, it operates more as constituting the limits to self-respect than as a mobilizing element. While in the Vega Baja's agriculture industry *jornaleros* had been extremely well organized around the (socialist) UGT and (anarchist) Confederacion Nacional del Trabajo (CNT) unions during the Republic, after the Civil War the rural sections of the unions only reorganized very weakly. Although the *jornaleros* kept a memory of class that oriented their analysis, solidarity, self-respect, and cultural aspirations, they never reorganized a structure of class mobilization. In the late 1960s and early 1970s it was the massive migration to the nearby industrial town of Elche to work in the shoe factories that renewed their contact with effective structures of class mobilization (basically CCOO). This related with the general urban- and industry-oriented mobilization strategies of the unions (mostly the communist CCOO) during the 1960s and early 1970s. So there is a connection that appears in between class as a structure for mobilization through the unions and industrial and/or urban locations in this historical period. And the memory of class in the agricultural context of the Vega Baja seems to evolve more as a setting of the limits of dignity. Conchita's husband migrates to France as an agricultural worker while she stays, but then turns back because he prefers to be exploited at home. It is obvious that he does not get involved with local unions as did most of those that migrated to take industrial jobs in northern Europe. His understanding of his position as exploited labor in France leads him to individual action: return. The subsequent work history of Conchita as a homeworker for middlemen in the shoe-making subcontracting network of the Vega Baja is one that very clearly expresses this duality of class analysis and class dignity without an organized structure of class mobilization. This is a situation that leads her to invest all her energy in attaining social mobility for the next generation, through proper formal education credentials. In order to attain this she is willing to let herself be exploited, up to the outmost limit of dignity but not beyond.

The case of Gelines is entirely different. It is set in an urban context with a strong labor movement tradition centered on the shipyards.[4] Although repression during and after the Civil War was also very important here, several elements were crucial in allowing for the re-constitution of an organized labor movement. First, the need for a specialized and trained labor force restrained massive layoffs at the shipyards after the war, which enabled the generation of those who entered as apprentices in the 1950s to be trained both technically and politically by workers who had the experience of class union organization and mobilization. Second, the strategy of the communist party and its union CCOO favored the policy of *"entrismo,"* having people from the communist union participate in the official corporatist union elections in order to fight the vertical union from within. This gave voice to the workers' unions and made public their analysis in terms of class (this was true for CCOO and USO, while UGT had the opposed strategy of non-participation). And finally, there was the fact that shipyard unions' leaders acted as organic intellectuals of the local working class as a whole, and actively encouraged class solidarity in the struggles that involved the different industries in the area.

Gelines's working life is, from the start, structured by an understanding of class that is inherently tied to its organization for active mobilization and the collective struggle for economic, social, and political claims. In her case dignity is tied to an organized labor movement. It is worth noting, however, that after her migration to France it is not until she gets to work in a large firm that she can get involved in organized class struggle once more, thus hinting at the obstructive effect of small, particularized and often domestic workspaces for collective mobilization (see also Barber, chapter 7).

How do migratory experiences affect these women's forms of resistance to exploitation? How do mobility and fixity articulate with the production of a conscious experience of class? How does this relate to people's ability to imagine a different future and act to produce it?

In the case of Conchita, the various migration movements through which she and her husband try to control their miserable life expectations seem to increase their sense of insecurity and constant humiliation. In the case of Gelines, migration transforms the location of her struggles against exploitation but not the modes of action that rely on working-class collective mobilization through a union structure. For Conchita and her husband mobility appears as forced displacement—although it is freely chosen—that disrupts the solidarity patterns linked to kinship and locality, tied to personal responsibility, individual effort, and emotional care. For Gelines, on the contrary, mobility—although responding to political repression—appears as an opportunity to better economic and social conditions because solidarity patterns are based on a strong ideology and practice of collective and universal class arguments. This does not preclude the instrumental use of personal networks (she initially goes to her sister's place in France), but it orients her vision of the future differently.

It is as if the point of fixity anchoring Gelines's sense of direction in life is the concept of "class" as a collective sense of responsibility guiding action and mutual care, transcending personalized and localized links. But it is paradoxical and revealing of class movements that this very delocalized framework is strongly dependent on a local history not just of class organization and mobilization, but also of an active group of organic intellectuals forming the local working class in particular "modern" and "universalistic" socialist interpretations of reality and how to deal with it. Organic intellectuals of the working class were missing in the rural Vega Baja, due to the differential, particular, and localized patterns that Francoist repression took in Spain. This pedagogical function, then, was completely absent there and hence the point of fixity orienting people's lives became the material location in space, enabling close, face-to-face networks of personal responsibility.

Conclusion

In conclusion I would say that what seems to have affected the conditions of possibility of these women's modes of resistance to exploitation is the very material basis of the structure of production together with the strategic decisions of political institutions, including clandestine parties and unions that were often tied to an international decision-making center, such as was the case with CCOO.[5] But it was also, I think, the emergence of local organic intellectuals who often became leaders that turned the individual experience of suffering into a meaningful framework for collective action through critical analysis and education. In Ferrol, these organic intellectuals that actively sought to link a memory of class struggles to the reconstitution of class organizations and present-day struggles were crucial elements for the emergence of a philosophy of praxis that oriented action through collective mobilization (Narotzky 2004; for philosophy of praxis, see Gramsci 1987: 323–377). But the reason why these intellectuals emerged in Ferrol and did not emerge in the Vega Baja is linked to the particular structure of the shipbuilding heavy industry, its secular history of collective action and the specialized and qualified nature of labor that set a check to repression within the local workforce after the Civil War (1936–1939). In the Vega Baja, although there was a history of labor mobilization in the urban footwear factories since the early nineteenth century (Moreno Saez 1987), the less specialized nature of the work and the systematic use of rural workers as an alternative workforce in different conjunctures (economic, political), inhibited the emergence of a long-lasting strand of organic intellectuals, even more so in the rural areas where pluriactivity was the norm (Narotzky and Smith 2006). Labrecque (in chapter 10) also discusses the historical development of locally distinct production structures and their effect on worker mobilization.

I am aware that the ethnographic comparison that I present supports a very traditional perspective of what indeed favors class mobilization. Forms of resistance and mobilization against exploitation seem conditioned by the structure of expectations and objective possibilities that make workers' daily experiences. In his *Méditations pascaliennes* (2003) Bourdieu makes the point that people's practical sense of the future, their hopes of a better life, their investments in terms of continuous oriented action are attuned to the objective possibilities allowed by the social and economic framework of their existence. The habitus here is the expression of the limits that frame future expectations and therefore condition the modes of mobilization in *the* present for *a* future (see also Lem, chapter 8). Differentiation is thus structurally incorporated when future expectations and decisions about personal investments toward change take form.

But I want to stress another factor of Bourdieu's analysis: the connection between the practical ability to *make* the future—the capacity to preoccupy one's mind with it in the present—and uncertainty. If every engagement and investment toward the future is associated with uncertainty, it is always a bounded space of uncertainty, limited and regulated by a particular habitus. This is what Bourdieu terms *"la causalité du probable"* (2003: 332) where "will adjusts to possibilities" (312). However, Bourdieu points to the fact that "absolute uncertainty" destroys the capacity to produce "reasonable expectations" and is the mark of a situation where those holding power can change the rules at any moment, "manipulating fear and hope" (331) through the modification of objective chances.

Thus the ways in which people get a hold of their future through mobilization in the present is structurally tied to the limits of uncertainty that are materially produced by economic and political agents in history.

This is what our cases seem to support: the more uncertainty is produced, the less capacity to orient personal action toward a future expectation. One of the main objectives of an emancipatory action would be, then, to produce some limits to uncertainty. Gramscian "organic intellectuals" seem to have such a function, but also working class institutions, such as the unions, may serve that purpose. In a context without any of them, mobilization becomes an individual struggle for survival, through tactics that enforce resignation in the present and acceptance of exploitation, in exchange for future generations' social mobility.

Notes

I want to acknowledge research funds provided by the Ministerio de Ciencia y Tecnología (Spain), project BSO2003–06832 and project SEJ2007–66633 of the Ministerio de Ciencia e Innovación (Spain).
1. The fieldwork in this region was conducted in 1978–1979 by Gavin Smith (University of Toronto) and in 1995–1996 by Gavin Smith and myself. A monograph (Narotzky and Smith 2006) has resulted from this collaborative long-term work.
2. Other unions will contribute as well to the re-emergent class politics, mainly the UGT (socialist), and the USO (catholic) unions.
3. The firm refuses to hire her but the shipyard union again mobilizes people in solidarity and she is finally rehired.
4. The shipyard is finished by 1751 and in 1760 already has 4600 workers. The first strike is in 1795.
5. Leaders of the Comisiones Obreras (CCOO) union, attached to the communist party, were often sent to East Germany to be trained. General strategic decisions about the union's interventions (i.e., its participation in the "vertical" corporatist union during the dictatorship [1939–1975]) were a part of the communist party's orientations and were dependent on Soviet international politics.

References

Benton, Lauren. 1990. *Invisible Factories: The Informal Economy and Industrial Development in Spain*. Albany: State University of New York Press.

Bourdieu, Pierre. 2003. *Méditations pascaliennes: Édition revue et corrigée*. Paris: Seuil.

Gramsci, Antonio. 1987 [1929–1935]. *Selections from the Prison Notebooks*. New York: International Publishers.

Morales Gil, Alfredo, Jorge Olcina Cantos, and Antonio M. Rico Amorós. 1999. "Diferentes percepciones de la sequía en España: Adaptación, catastrofismo e intentos de corrección." *Anales de la Universidad de Alicante-Instituto de Geografía* 22: 5–46.

Moreno Saez, Francisco. 1987. *El movimiento obrero en Elche (1890–1931)*. Alicante: Instituto de Estudios Juan Gil-Albert.

Narotzky, Susana. 2004. "Una historia necesaria: ética, política y responsabilidad en la práctica antropológica." *Relaciones: Estudios de historia y sociedad* V.XXV (98): 107–145.

Narotzky, Susana, and Gavin Smith. 2006. *Immediate Struggles: People, Power and Place in Rural Spain*. Berkeley: University of California Press.

Olcina Cantos, Jorge. 2001. "Tipología de sequías en España." *Ería* 56: 201–227.

Olcina Cantos, Jorge, and Antonio M. Rico Amorós. 1995. "Sequías y golpes de calor en el sureste ibérico: Efectos territoriales y económicos." *Investigaciones Geográficas* 13: 47–80.

Ybarra, Josep-Antoni. 2001. "El nacionalismo económico en la era de la globalización: un ensayo de pensamiento económico nacionalista." In *Identidades: IV Semana de Filosofía de la Región de Murcia*, ed. Manuel Hernández Iglesias, 205–212. Murcia: Diego Marín Editores.

———. 2003. "Los distritos industriales: ¿Instrumento analítico de la Economía Política o instrumento práctico de Política Económica? El País Valenciano como paradigma en el debate internacional." In *La economía regional en el marco de la nueva economía*, eds. Juan José Rubert and Ana María Fuertes, 313–318. Castellón: Universitat Jaume I.

Ybarra, Josep-Antoni, et al. 2004. *El calzado en el Vinalopó, entre la continuidad y la ruptura*. Alicante: Universidad de Alicante.

— *Chapter 7* —

CELL PHONES, POLITICS, AND THE PHILIPPINE LABOR DIASPORA

Pauline Gardiner Barber

Seventy percent of the nearly one million documented labor migrants leaving the Philippines each year are women who work in service sector jobs. But in 2004 Dr. Elmer Jacinto became yet another Filipino labor migrant to make international headlines. This was not, as has often been the case for women migrants, because he was "victimized" working abroad, but because of his decision to relocate and deliberately, if temporarily, deskill his labor.[1] As the year's top-ranked medical graduate he refueled the long-standing national debates over migration politics when he declared his intention of traveling to the United States to pursue a career in nursing. Lured by particularly attractive US wages caused by a labor shortage, Jacinto justified his decision on the grounds of his family's impoverishment. Patracio N. Abinales and Donna Amoroso (2005: 301) characterize the public discussion as expressive of class ambivalence; elite voices spoke of Jacinto's betrayal of the nation, others defended the rights of migrants to seek economic improvement abroad. This type of polarization is common in Philippine migration politics, revealing both the transnational complexion of debates over national dependence upon migration and the role migration plays in class ambition. A further feature highlighted in the transnational discussions about Jacinto was the immediacy and nature of responses from Filipinos living in the diaspora. Apparently, understanding Philippine political agency calls for a transnational analysis of the multiple social fields of migrants' lives, a perspective reinforced also by Zontini in chapter 5.

Commencing with an ethnographic vignette from a more typical, feminized, migrant recruitment scenario, this chapter explores the gendered class tensions and political scenarios suggested by the Jacinto debate and

Philippine reliance on labor export. The debate also points to the role of new media, particularly cell phones in migration politics. In considering the phenomenal adaptation to cell phones and text messaging by Filipinos, including in political campaigns, I explore how cell phones both enable and deflect migrants' political mobilization. Cell phones and other new media do facilitate migrants' awareness of migration and labor politics but they also provide constant reminders of the economic desires that compel migration, basically for class mobility. This tempers critical responses to the strictures of employment.

Class tensions in the labor diaspora relate to the structuring of gendered labor subordination for women migrants in domestic service, a labor assignment reinforced by cultural ideologies about Filipina femininity and caring expertize in global labor markets. Even as migrants' awareness of the exploitative, classed, and racialized character of labor migration is heightened, economic aspirations limit critical action. Further, what appears in the Philippines to be class mobility resulting from migration—seen in increased education and consumption levels—is recast abroad as gendered class subordination. Complicity results from the manner in which gendered cultural practices are valorized throughout the migration process, by the institutional gatekeepers who manage and profit from migration, including state agents, and by the migrants themselves who "perform subordination." Migrants' compliance with gender scripts thus mitigates class tensions. In concluding I link migration politics—which reveal both complicity and militancy—to ambivalence. This lends a Janus quality to migration and class politics.[2]

Performed Subordination

Also in 2004 I met Merlina, a woman in her early thirties, at a recruitment agency in Iloilo city, in the Western Visayas. The agency specialized in hiring workers for domestic service abroad, primarily in Hong Kong, Singapore, and Taiwan. It was one of seven agencies I visited during the year's fieldwork, which also included extensive interviews with returning migrants, their families, and staff of the Philippine Overseas Employment Administration, the government office responsible for the promotion and regulation of migration. Iloilo has a flourishing migration industry and a labor export profile. The recruitment agency selected by Merlina and her friends acknowledges market competition through a subtle form of niche-marketing going beyond the usual practice of specializing in one particular region of the global labor market. The company presented itself and was represented by government officials, as having "reputable clients" (both migrants and employers contracted through a partner agency in Hong Kong), a thinly veiled allusion to the complexities of the class encounter in the domestic service labor market. The agency's owner told me: "my girls have college education," which in Hong Kong, as Nicole Constable (1997, 2004) noted, is not necessarily the case for the Chinese and expatriate women whose domestic labor the migrant workers are hired to replace. In addition to offering an explicitly classed migrant subject, the agency sought to maintain its competitive edge through the application of new media in the form of promotional videos produced on-site.

The ten women, migrants-in-waiting, I spoke with during my time at that agency were enthusiastic about the idea of video production but also apprehensive about their performances. Merlina was rehearsing for her video and said it might calm her nerves to talk with me. She explained that she had completed some university education as part of her five-year plan to locate a position abroad. The highest paying jobs overseas—whether in the regional labor market or in Europe, North America, or Australasia—are most readily available to Filipino nurses who are graduates of nursing programs certified through national board examinations. Such programs are expensive and, as in the example of Dr. Jacinto's, it is common for nursing graduates, primarily women but men also, to voluntarily accept deskilling work abroad, in feminized jobs as domestic workers and nannies.[3] Merlina's "second-best" scenario was to complete a college course in midwifery because she could not afford to study nursing. Nor could she afford to complete the unpaid practical work necessary to obtain her midwifery certificate. Symbolically, however, she anticipated that potential employers might appreciate the medical connotation of her training and conclude she was qualified to work with young children.

The video consisted of a short speech to the camera in mid shot, from the waist up. Merlina and the other recruits were instructed by the harried staff to recite their names, education levels, family status, hobbies, and any personal qualities they wished to communicate to potential employers. The women wore simple white uniforms provided by the agency. They seemed quite aware that their Goffmanesque "presentation of self" could be read as a sexualizing, gendered class script. For example, Merlina told me she wanted to present herself as sufficiently well-educated so that potential employers would imagine she could teach their children English, and/or tutor them in other subjects. Yet, she also knew, from discussions with friends who had completed contracts in Hong Kong, that she would probably be hired by a male Chinese employer whose wife, her "lady boss," would have more limited education. So Merlina's challenge was to avoid any appearance of assertiveness or communicate other clues that might suggest class advantage. She also understood she should constrain her body language to minimize any sexualized readings. To this end she had deliberately tied her hair back and avoided make-up, including nail polish. She also recognized that skillfulness in this depiction of a "subordinated self" drew upon a cultural repertoire which here, as on other occasions, was presented to me with the offhand remark; "You see *Mam* Pauline, we Filipinos (she meant women) are like this; we know how to please people." Her acknowledged complicity in this cultural performance will serve her well in her employer's household, as it likely did in her parents', and in her Catholic training at school.

Class and Migrant Complicity

As noted, this discussion explores the politics of class and complicity that are necessarily engaged by Filipinos as they project themselves into foreign service-sector labor markets. Most of the sixty-some migration histories I have collected from the mid 1990s have been from women, many not unlike Merlina, others with less education but some with more. As can be seen from Merlina's self-representation, there is an ironic undermining of some aspects of her identity—education, knowledge, beauty, and sexuality—in a performance of subordination that is produced knowingly, in order to accomplish not just employment but a position with the most desirable employer under the circumstances. The idea of performed subordination draws attention to the manner in which migrants prepare themselves to fit particular labor market slots; a process that typically calls for them to highlight select features of their identities and personal skills, while downplaying other qualities they might otherwise be proud of. This produces contradictions that are at once deeply personal and also revealing of the necessity for accommodation to structural inequalities in global labor markets. Here we see Merlina "playing up" what she discerns to be desirable qualities; her gender, youth, education, and the cultural norms associated with being family-minded, to name but the most obvious. At the same time, she is "downplaying" less desirable features of these same qualities. The securing of an employment contract and meeting other institutional requirements for emigration/migration/immigration can be read as a classed performance of what we might also call an "economic subjectivity" responsive to new gendered geographies of class and power in commodified domestic labor. As feminist scholars have argued, such labor, frequently entailing emotional work (Hochschild 1983) is fundamental to spatially organized, racialized divisions of labor in contemporary global political economy (Anderson 2000; Ehrenreich and Hochschild 2003; Hondagneu-Sotelo 2001; Katz 2001; McDowell 2006; Sassen 2000; Parreñas 2001).

To advance my argument one step further, such subjective positionings are discordant not only with the insights that produce performances of class and gender, they also militate against the resolution of this discordant, or muted, class understanding through action. The development of an explicitly critical class understanding is thus occluded at this threshold moment in the migration process. Later, when employment is secured, any expression of class agency is even less likely to be publicly performed, to become collective, partly because of the isolating conditions of the workplace and also because of the economic stakes involved. As I will later clarify, migration involves indebtedness. Often, migrants' economic aspirations prove unrealistic as they struggle to manage multiple claims upon wages including debt repayment and ongoing requests from kin. Philippine cultural discourses, often with religious reference, promote family and group loyalties, a feature of daily life constantly reinforced in public media and institutions. In addition to their own needs, most migrants feel strongly obligated to financially support particular relatives such as parents; to risk losing employment is perceived as also placing others in jeopardy. Despite these disincentives, and sometimes in reaction to the sheer injustice of the conditions that have produced them, there are strong visible expressions of public militancy present in the Philippine labor diaspora. How might these alternate class expressions be reconciled?

It is not surprising that the literature on Philippine women migrants has tended to emphasize disciplined gendered subjectivities, the everyday dialectics of subordination (Chang and Ling 2000; Chin 1997; Constable 1997, 2004; Groves and Chang 1999; Parreñas 2001; cf., Barber 2006 and Zontini, chapter 5). But as I have argued elsewhere, class is also constituted through these very same relationships, actions, and understandings (Barber 2004). Eric Wolf (1999) astutely pointed out that power is both structural and relational. Further, in her interrogation of silence, spun off from Wolf's work on the modalities of power, Maria-Luisa Achino-Loeb (2006: 4) writes: "identity cannot be seen as a condition; rather it is an activity that ultimately depends on shades of silence for its successful realization." Complicity is implicated in silence. This is helpful for thinking through Filipino migrants' self-censorship in their subordinating performances and how discourses about Filipino gendered cultural identities are "naturalized" in ways that, taken at face value, privilege culture, thereby curbing an extension of the conversation into a more explicit classed analysis and perhaps politicized action.

Thus Merlina's ironic aside to me about Filipino submissiveness can be read as complicity while class remains part of the analytical agenda.

Class and Militancy in the Labor Diaspora

Yet one of the most striking aspects of the Philippine labor diaspora is the political activism that surfaces wherever Filipinos congregate. Usually, political expressions are directed at Philippine migration politics, but on occasion there have been well-developed examples of what Nina Glick Schiller and Georges Fouron (2001) describe as long-distance nationalism, where concerns target Philippine class politics more generally. Typically the activists are part of transnational political networks. At other times, the activists emerge out of local organizations, sometimes churches, concerned with migrant services. When such political voices challenge Philippine political structures, there appears a disconnection, or fracturing, of political consciousness between the lived experiences of the majority of migrants, women working in commodified domestic labor, and the radical actions of those who represent them. Some of the radical voices represent the diasporic reach of the fragmented Philippine left, further complicated by feminization and deskilling in Philippine migration flows (Piper 2008).

One Canadian example of diasporic militancy is the Philippine Women Centre of BC (British Columbia). Geraldine Pratt completed collaborative research in the BC Centre in 1995. Noting that domestic workers learn at the BC Centre to "see themselves as exploited third-world women and to understand their situations within a socialist feminist theory of imperialism" (2004: 63), she goes on to describe the BC Centre "as a source of a powerful and productive criticism of neo-colonialism, racism, and gender and class oppression in Filipino and Canadian societies" (65).[4] In a number of "campaigns" dating back to at least 1995, including web postings and press releases, the BC Centre has provided radical critiques about the Philippine political elite and labor export policies. For example, in commemoration of International Women's day in March 2005 they targeted the current Philippine president Gloria Macapagal Arroyo for her "trafficking" of Filipino women to 186 countries and the Canadian government's Live-in Caregiver program (LCP) for its collusion with this project. The 2005 activities of the BC Centre circulated posters calling for "international solidarity to bring down Arroyo's government, free Liza Maza [a Congresswomen associated with Gabriela—a militant Philippine women's activist organization with an international mandate and profile], and [to] scrap the LCP in Canada. Today we honor Filipino women and their continued struggle, demanding peace and justice for all Filipinos worldwide, genuine democracy towards our national liberation, and to cease our exploitation at home and abroad!" They conclude with the rallying calls:

> Stop political repression in the Philippines!
> Oust Philippine President Gloria Macapagal Arroyo!
> Scrap the racist and anti-woman Live-in Caregiver Program!
> Forward our struggle for genuine equality, development, and a just and lasting peace!
> Long live international solidarity! (e-correspondence from the BC Centre, March 2005)

Philippine women and men arriving in Canada under the caregiver visa program are considered "professional" caregivers. Program applicants must be functional in English or French and hold the equivalent of a Canadian high school education, plus six months of full-time training or twelve months (six months of which are continuous) of full-time paid employment in a related field. This experience must be within three years prior to application for the visa. Applicants must also secure a written employment contract, undergo medical tests, and navigate Philippine exit-visa requirements. Many migrants who target Canada submit to specialized "caregiver" training offered by an elite stratum of recruitment agencies (sometimes owned by diasporic Filipinos) that promise ease of placement and assistance with visa processing at home and abroad. The fees charged vary but are always burdensome for emigrants who are typically deeply in debt—to relatives or money lending agents. Loan agents present in most migrant sending communities are called "5/6ers"—meaning borrow 5,000 pesos, pay back 6,000. But the Philippine state now attempts more stringent regulation of the recruitment sector, mainly in response to political mobilizations from disgruntled migrants and their families. Despite regulation, placement fees remain problematically uneven. Even licensed agencies commit fee violations.

Within Canada caregivers are required to live with their employers for a minimum of two years after which they can apply for permanent Canadian residency. The logic for the live-in requirement is that there is no shortage of Canadians seeking employment as caregivers but they refuse to live with their employers. The caregiver's visa falls under Temporary Foreign Worker programs requiring a labor market assessment to prove there are insufficient Canadians available for a particular type of work. However, until recently caregivers were the only foreign workers selected with the idea of permanent resident status in mind, a feature built into the eligibility criteria for the visa to ensure their post-contract adaptability to Canadian labor markets and citizenship criteria. By 2008 significant changes in Canada's immigration policy saw a massive increase in contract-limited foreign workers across a wide variety of skill sets but primarily for "low-skilled occupations." Here again, Philippine workers comprise the majority of foreign workers, some of whom may take on a series of three-year contracts as a prelude to permanent citizenship under the more flexible arrangements worked out with individual provinces through Provincial Nominee programs (see Barber 2008). That the caregiver visa offers a more direct pathway to citizenship, if certain conditions are complied with, remains one of the features of the program that makes it attractive to potential migrants who are prepared to deskill themselves to enter Canada. It is also what makes the program so contentious to activists who charge the program with racist exploitation. Until recently, many immigrants who had entered Canada as caregivers, continued in this form of employment as permanent residents and citizens, proof to observers such as Pratt (2004) of the deskilling argument. People with caregiver visas must live with their employers and are prohibited from taking other employment even though there are labor regulations (variable by province) that restrict their hours of work while requiring paid overtime. This means that even with the restriction on live-in work, Canadian contracts include provisions for more "free time" than occurs in other international labor markets. Periodically, caregivers who have taken on extra paid employment have been caught and repatriated to the Philippines with much public protest. So the BC Centre is not alone in its condemnation of the program. Daiva Stasiulis and Abigail Bakan (2005) convincingly argue that the program is profoundly discriminatory and constitutes evidence of neoliberal policies that position Canada's migrant caregivers, now predominantly Filipina, into predefined local and global hierarchies of circumscribed citizenship.

Class, Compliance, and the Labor Process

From a transnational vantage point, however, the BC Women Centre, interesting as it surely is as an example of class mobilization in the diaspora, is not easily reconciled with ethnographic evidence showing acquiescence to the conditions of work and living for the majority of Filipina in the labor diaspora. Indeed, the BC Centre likely achieves its momentum from the labor campaigns associated with a variety of different employment structures and migration pathways, including a mix of skilled workers (nurses who entered as such) and deskilled caregivers. Pratt (2004) implies that this, along with the political motivation inspiring the activist leadership, generated the social space for creative dialogue and political mobilization for local and transnational projects. But potential migrants I have spoken with, both in the Philippines and Hong Kong, remain keenly interested in the Canadian caregiver program. This is because along with the promise of eventual citizenship, the employment seems better paid and regulated than is the case for many similarly deskilled gendered labor markets of which they have knowledge. Along with Merlina, these migrants must navigate the experiencing of class subordination through gendered cultural idioms that simultaneously permit and restrict critical action. Challenges to structural power are curbed by reminders of the relational nexus of power relating to economic needs (personal, familial, and national), through which migration is justified (see Sassen 2000). Such contradictions are fundamental to commodified domestic service work in Southeast Asian labor markets, where contracts typically require workers to be on duty for 16-hour days, and on 24-hour call.

Given the intensity of such exploitation, the possibilities of collective response to the indignities of the work are confined to migrant gatherings on their limited time off. Live-in work, by definition, also entails both 24-hour surveillance by the employer and host-state officials, and offers numerous possibilities for employers to use emotional leverage to extract more labor than the contract calls for, through appeals to emotional loyalty—as outlined in Arlie Hochschild's pathbreaking early work on emotional labor, "The Managed Heart" (1983). Intimidation is also an option often resorted to. Such conditions provide little opportunity for worker militancy and public spaces substitute for the workplace in providing possible sites for workers to organize; a reversal of the Marxian notion of the class-making potential of socialized workplaces. Much has been written about the gathering places of domestic workers in such regional labor markets as Hong Kong and Singapore (e.g., Chin 1997; Constable 1997; Groves and Chang 1999; see also Zontini, chapter 5). During a field trip to Hong Kong in 2001 I learned more about migrant militancy in collective actions organized by migrant support groups who spoke freely about various public demonstrations they had participated in than I had from the ethnographic literature (see Barber 2004).

Achieving social spaces and the political translation necessary for migrants to imagine collective agency always represents a significant but not insurmountable challenge, but all the more so for socially isolated service workers (a common theme for this volume, but Però's and Zontini's cases in chapters 4 and 5 are particularly relevant here). Put differently, complicity does not cancel out the possibility that such classed understandings are transferable into forms of collective class expression, under the right conditions, and despite the nature of migrant workers' contracts and labor process. However in addition to the subordinating conditions of work, migrants also contend with the lived tension of geographic displacement and social fracture. One relatively new way in which this social fracture is made visible concerns the use of cell phones. To shift register and locate some new coordinates, I will now explore the potential for this technology to alter individual and collective political expressions.

Transnational Communication

When I first visited the Philippines some fifteen years ago, I was resident on a university campus in Dumaguete city, also in the Western Visayas. My purpose at the university was to conduct a preliminary investigation of gendered livelihood activities in nearby coastal communities, basically to assess the possibilities for a more extensive ethnographic project. In order to call my family in Canada, I had to reserve phone time (on what I have since learned to call a "land line") in a campus administrative office. From the office in Dumaguete I would attempt to connect to a long distance operator in Cebu, a major urban center on a neighboring island. It often took several trips to successfully navigate a call that required strategic timing because of the volume of calls and the approximately twelve-hour time difference between the two countries. The same constraints on international conversations confronted the vast majority of Filipinos living outside metro Manila and indeed likely millions inside the city as well. In that period, working class and poor Filipinos, and even those relatively better-off who self-described as middle class, had to rely on public phones unless they had access to "patrons" with land lines. Raul Pertierra et al. (2002) document the history of Philippine mass media, noting the inadequacies of the Philippine Long Distance Telephone Company (PLDT), established with American capital in the 1920s. By 1993 there remained a huge backlog in meeting the public demand for services. Rural areas were worst off, with over 90 percent of all phones remaining in urban areas. Manila had 76 percent of these with only 13 percent of municipalities and towns having access to a phone system (33). Hence, access to communication technologies at this time was very much a matter of geography, class, and power.

The situation today has been radically altered by wireless technologies that offer much greater geographic range. They are also less costly to access and have had a significant impact in developing countries generally. But nowhere is the impact more powerful than in insular yet cosmopolitan Philippines, described in several commentaries as the text messaging center of the world. For example, Pertierra (2005) claims that over 200 million texts are sent daily in the Philippines. This represents ten times the per capita world average, and is not surprising given that in 2007 text messages could be sent from the Philippines to international diaspora sites for one peso. Within the Philippines, it costs fifteen to twenty times this amount, depending on the server, to receive messages from abroad.

By providing more Filipinos with international communication possibilities, cellular (mobile phone) technologies, in particular Short Message Services (SMS) messaging or texting, add new complexities to the personal and political resistance potential of Filipino migrant workers. However, cellular technologies, through a form of "time-space compression," in David Harvey's (1990, 1995) classic sense, also enable new immediacy in the demands from "home" for migrant domestic workers. This layers reproductive labor for their Philippine homes on top of the commodified domestic labor they provide abroad. Cell technologies also fuel further migration decision making through the more immediate transmission of labor market information provided by calling "home." Thus the technologies play a role in reproducing the labor force preparing itself for migration. Along with the BC Centre, many activists in the labor diaspora see this as a national loss as emigrants become increasingly well qualified.

My research suggests the increased levels in education can be directly connected to the remittance practices of overseas migrants who support higher levels of education for younger siblings, their own children, and the children of their siblings. Ironically, this pattern serves to reproduce migration in yet another generation of migrants partly because migration relates to increased expectations of consumer goods and also because of high rates of national unemployment. For example, Philippine employment statistics for 2004 show that 2 million, or nearly half of the recorded 4.2 million unemployed Filipinos were between fifteen and twenty-five years old. About 34 percent of the unemployed were college graduates, while 28 percent were high school graduates. Men now account for just over 60 percent of the unemployed (*Philippine Star*, 8 February 2005), in part because women have higher rates of overseas employment and are educating themselves accordingly. Migration has thus become a normative cultural expectation (Barber 2004) and labor export policies have become more deeply entrenched (Cohen 2006; Gonzalez 1998).

However, cell phones can also be mobilized in the service of political activism concerning national and/or migration politics, as was the case during 2004 when overseas workers became eligible to vote in the presidential elections provided they had access to voter registration in officially designated Philippine institutions. Hong Kong provided one particularly active site where Filipinos comprise around 80 percent of the 180,000 resident foreign contract workers. Ninety thousand Filipinos registered to vote in Hong Kong and several leading Presidential candidates made campaign stops there. Supporting migrant workers in their contractual struggles and "re-entry" concerns topped the political agenda for this particular labor diaspora (see Barber 2006).

We must also keep gender in mind. What happens to the articulations of class, place, and political expression when the migrants are typically women, deployed in socially isolating commodified domestic labor, working under contracts deliberately contrived to restrict civic mobility and citizenship rights? Here I am concerned with the implications for class politics and mobilization given the social, cultural, political, and geographic segregation, acting in combination with the character of labor process subordination for live-in domestic workers. Given the social isolation of the labor process, what are the implications of migrants' access to cell phones? In part my questions arise from my own observations about the increased significance of cellular phone use in Philippine society. However, research on transnationalism and new global media also indicates this to be a compelling, if theoretically challenging, line of enquiry.

In a general overview of issues in migrant transnationalism, Steven Vertovec (2004: 11) notes: "One of the most significant (yet under-researched) modes of transnational practice affecting migrants' lives is the ability to telephone family members." With more direct relevance to this chapter, albeit in a reverse sequence of gendered communication, Sarah Mahler describes how Salvadorian women line up for hours to make collect phone calls to "mobile husbands" abroad. Once connected the women have to persuade the party at the other end to accept the collect phone charges. Their next challenge is to persuade cash-strapped husbands to hear out their pleas (a relatively costly process on a collect call) and to send more in remittances. "It is an emotional drama that underscores how these women's unequal positioning vis-à-vis men along the continuum of social locations—in this case determined largely by migration status and economic standing—shapes their agency" (Pessar and Mahler 2003: 824). Again with relevance to the Philippines, Heather Horst (2006) discusses the shift from a relatively recent increase in telephone (house phone) availability in rural Jamaica in the 1990s, to widespread mobile phone use by 2004. The relatively immobile residents in her field site now rely on their mobile phones for communication with extended and transnational family members. While mobile phones are characterized in Horst's survey advantageously as a "blessing," some of the more burdensome aspects of the technology are also noted, as Jamaicans become more involved in transnational familial fields. Here again tension is associated with the possibilities for emotional leverage, sometimes providing the means to heal estrangement, but also allowing greater immediacy to the requests for remittances so commonly received in labor diasporas (see also Glick Schiller and Fouron 2001).

Writing directly on mobile phone use in the Philippines, Pertierra (2005) suggests cell phones mediate and shape social relations and cosmopolitan subjectivities. He also touches on examples of cell phone use in Philippine political mobilizations, a subject I shall return to as I attempt to link how we might construct Philippine overseas domestic workers as global political subjects with class agency sometimes realized in collective action, sometimes in individual acts of defiance. As feminist geographer Cindi Katz reminds us, a Marxist approach to social reproduction recognizes both fluidity and skill differentiation in the reproduction of the labor force in particular, context-specific ways. She writes: "Not only are the material social practices associated with its production historically and geographically specific, but its contours and requirements are the outcome of ongoing struggle. Apart from the need to secure the means of existence, the production and reproduction of the labor force calls forth a range of cultural forms and practices that are also geographically and historically specific, including those associated with knowledge and learning, social justice and its apparatus, and the media" (2001: 711).

Calling "Home" from Work: Double Day / Double Duty

Cell phones and SMS provide a powerful new means of sustaining transnational ties to "home," allowing for a "stretching of intimacy" and an "absent presence" (Pertierra 2005) over the time and space displacements in migrant's transnational families (see Parreñas 2005). Caring work undertaken for kin is not readily "switched off." Given women's gender-specific familial obligations, being more accessible from-and-to "home" must be examined in the light of the *content* of the correspondence. There are significant cultural pressures on women migrants as daughters, sisters, wives, and mothers to maintain economic and emotional support for relatives remaining in the Philippines. More regular contact with home can simultaneously relieve personal stress and guilt about being absent from the family's daily routines, even as it produces deeper anxieties about these same routines where face-to-face interventions are not possible. And women who are expected to perform familial work—social reproduction duties—for their Philippine households, do so in conjunction with their productive work, which for service sector migrants, also happens to be emotionally charged reproductive work in domestic service. Service—closely aligned with servitude (Parreñas 2001)—is a particularly apt descriptor for live-in labor contracts in various regional labor markets were official off-duty hours are restricted to twelve hours per week. For the majority, this is the only time they are able to leave the residences where they are employed without being monitored. Many employers do, however, seek to regulate the behavior of their employees during their "day off" (Constable 1997).

To maintain ongoing, sometimes daily "conversations" with "home" thus places migrants on twenty-four-hour "double duty" in their socially reproductive labor—in the homes where they work in domestic service abroad (their productive labor in commodified domestic labor) and in their Philippine homes. When cell phones "stretch intimacy," a temporal effect of simultaneity occurs as women work on two "home fronts." Double duty is intended to capture this simultaneity while also highlighting the feminized cultural scripts—referenced by Merlina—dictating how familial work should be performed. It also adds complexity to the idea of the "double day" conceptualized through a sequence of feminist debates (e.g., Kuhn and Wolpe 1978; Molyneux 1979; Young, Wolkowitz and McCullagh 1981) concerned to expose the connections between productive and socially reproductive labor; basically the linkages between wage work producing goods and services, and unremunerated work (typically domestic labor assigned to female members of households) that sustains life, labor power, and society itself. Social reproductive labor occurs daily with the provision of meals and care for workers, on a generational basis as children (future laboring bodies) are born and raised, and at the societal level as cultural and social relations are shaped through familial and institutional educational processes to replicate the social formation. For women wage workers, held responsible for domestic labor in addition to productive work, this produces a "double day" of labor. In the case of migrants abroad, the double day includes the directing from a distance, increasingly by cell phones, decisions concerning childcare, education, family health, and household budgets (Parreñas 2005), while they perform some of those very same tasks for their employers. Again, as Katz reminds us above, social expectations and cultural understandings are historically specific to particular configurations of political power and geographically specialized divisions. Nowhere is this more apparent in Philippine labor export that Joaquin Gonzalez (1998) claims to be one of the world's most studied migration flows.

Cell phones can play a significant role in the further consolidation of Philippine labor export beyond easing the strain on family members who anticipate continuity in emotional care. Saskia Sassen (2000) details "counter-geographies of globalization"; feminized global circuits made up of women migrants and those who depend upon and profit from them. The Philippines is a prototypical case. The Filipino diaspora was projected to remit $9 billion in 2005.[5] Recent surveys reveal the migration flow is not likely to cease anytime soon with one in five Filipinos reported to be actively considering migration (Bello 2004: 3). In the Philippines various migration-related industries have proliferated. Educational and recruitment agencies have become more specialized promising placements in niche contract labor markets. As noted, intensified political effort to regulate exploitative recruitment practices has failed to curb inflated and fraudulent charges and workers abroad remain vulnerable to unscrupulous foreign employers. However, the continuities and changes in the political economy of Philippine labor migration are less visible from abroad.

Texting communication intensifies dialogues between migrants and people at "home" and I have argued that this serves to remind migrants of pressing economic issues at home—a disincentive to any action risking employment loss. A further, more clearly positive aspect of cell phone communication is tied to the mechanics of the labor process of live-in workers. During 2001 I completed a series of interviews with migrants in Hong Kong. Many of the women I spoke to mentioned that their "lady bosses" required them to seek permission to use the household's telephone. It is striking to me now, just six years later, how rapidly communications technologies have changed. At that time, no one I spoke to mentioned owning a cell phone. Nor did I think to query this, even though there was, at that time, plenty of evidence of the regional popularity of cell phones. Instead, women spoke of their constrained labor process and how they would seize opportunities to use phones (land lines), even when forbidden, to contact each other and, more rarely because of the greater risk of discovery, their kin at home.

Phone calls home, using phone cards, were also an important component of the activities planned for their twelve-hour weekly leave. Even then, calls gave cause for concern if events at home were perplexing, as they often were. There were always issues with household budgets and seemingly endless requests for money from assorted kin. Related to this were the longer-term plans for any savings that migrants struggled to set aside. Some women kept their savings secret from kin; others lent funds to friends and acquaintances in need of immediate assistance. In one memorable case, a woman loaned her entire savings to a female friend for a failed business venture. When I met her, she was brooding about how to retrieve monies owed, perhaps through legal channels, without disclosing her misjudgment to family members.

Other women talked about friends who had acquired new debts more deliberately, sometimes from overspending. Some migrants, I was informed, resorted to gambling on their day's off "to relieve work stress," again a pastime not discussed with family members. Most women worried about the health of relatives, typically but not always parents. The education and disciplining of children also occupied the phone time of mothers and many were concerned about the sexual loyalty of distant partners. Such was the content of concerns to be negotiated in the occasional transnational communications prior to cellular technologies, typically conducted through discounted phone-card land line conversations. In an interesting comparison with the Philippine streetscape public phones described earlier, despite the different colonial pathways to modernization, Hong Kong calls were made under conditions no more conducive to private conversation. There were street phones in Central, the ferry-side bus terminal where thousands congregated on their days off. There were also call stations in a number of small stores adjacent to Central. All this has now changed. But again, any relief through closer monitoring of Philippine daily routines also enables greater access from the Philippines, including calls for remittances.

A further positive application of cell phones occurs in a published review of pre-migration scenarios within the Philippines (Asis 2005). The review records a researcher-led focus group that included two nurses preparing to travel to Saudi Arabia. Part of the attraction of Saudi Arabia to these women was that the Philippine Overseas Employment Administration had organized the placement so their fees were less than 5000 pesos (approximately $104) in contrast to 50,000 pesos for a UK placement fee. The nurses were warned by other workshop participants who had worked in the kingdom about potential problems associated with their personal security. One of the women preparing to leave was assigned to work in a dispensary, at a clinic rather than a hospital. The larger institution was, apparently, considered less troublesome than the clinic. The more experienced migrants advised the clinic-destined nurse to carry a cell phone and enter the embassy phone numbers so that she could call or text in an emergency. In this example, cell phone use offers a "lifeline" in a very real sense between an isolated worker and agents of the Philippine state charged with her protection. This also reveals the preoccupation of migrants with the processes of "subordination" they must contend with abroad.

As mentioned earlier, in 2004 I did not investigate whether and how Philippine migrants might use cell phones to seek help in instances of employer abuse. I did however learn about two cases of "escape and rescue." From these limited examples and from the literature I can only speculate the cell phones might be used to contact friends and family in cases where migrants feel comfortable disclosing the grim details of their circumstances. This represents a considerable challenge for all the reasons I have described above; that families are relying on migrants for economic support so admitting defeat is subject to the same kind of subjective tur-moil as political mobilization. Further, deep feelings of personal shame accompanied the few stories of abuse I received in first-hand accounts. This was also true for migrants who felt they had violated the trust of relatives, for example in gambling with their earnings, or in one serious case of migrant distress, a married woman bearing the child of her over-seas lover. Again, dignity and a sense of self-worth are subject to constant renegotiation, which cell phone usage might sometimes help preserve but can also hinder. Some migrants describe their decision to work abroad as based on the desire to remove themselves from troublesome home cir-cumstances. Perhaps cell phones are not "a blessing" for these women though they might provide a "lifeline" under the right circumstances.

Political Mobilization and Texting

Cellular technologies became more available to urban Filipinos during the period of political controversy associated with President Joseph Es-trada (the third post-Marcos president) in power from 1998 to 2001.[6] After a massive public demonstration dubbed People Power II, which saw one million Filipinos demonstrate on Epifanio de los Santos Avenue (EDSA)— the physical site of Marcos's deposition—President Estrada was forced out of office in 2001. In keeping with Howard Rheingold's arguments in *Smart Mobs* (2002: 157–158), many attribute the success of the mass mobilization to the use of text messaging structured through mobile-tree networks. The current president, Gloria Macapagal Arroyo, railed against in the diasporic example of the BC Women Centre campaign, assumed office at Estrada's ousting and won the 2004 election under contentious circum-stances (Barber 2006). She remains under constant challenge by her op-ponents who occasionally rally mass protests at the symbolic EDSA site. These expressions of political organizing, embodied in mass protests, are time and place specific inside the Philippines. They highlight the signifi-cant shift in technological capacities afforded Filipinos from all walks of life as a result of the flexibilities in use and cost from wireless technolo-gies. Most important these examples demonstrate the way in which Fili-pinos have rapidly adapted to SMS messaging.

According to Michael Dumlao:

> Text-messaging is (now) so deeply embedded within the communications practices of Filipinos that rebels who often resort to kidnapping for income send ransom notes via SMS. In response to the SMS-mediated demon-strations that brought her to power President Arroyo now offers a form of

digital-democracy: a direct text cell number of her administration and many governmental agencies. Police stations rely on citizens to report crimes via mobile messaging and soon these tools will become payment devices by allowing customers to pay for retail items with pre-paid minutes. (2005: 12)

Dumlao cites a news commentator named Ha, who argues that text messaging fits well within Philippine culture where direct confrontation is frowned upon. Pertierra et al. (2002) also explore the ways in which Filipinos use text messaging to circumnavigate authority structures, personal conflicts, and restrictions on sexual expression. Here again, the historical account returns us to the complex forms of colonial domination that implicate the repressive dictates of Roman Catholicism and elite political culture, the combined results of which continue to reverberate in Philippine institutional structures and political engagements (see also Anderson 2003; Bello 2004; Eviota 1992; Hedman and Sidel 2000; Rafael 2000) and in the class dynamics of global migration politics (Cohen 2006).

Conclusion

As argued, historically specific colonial geographies and cultural frameworks differentiate certain kinds of labor as more mobile and subordinated (see Katz 2001; Pessar and Mahler 2003; Pratt 2004; Sassen 2000). In this article I situated Philippine migrants such as Elmer Jacinto and Merlina in the relational geographies—workplaces, home communities, and diasporic organizations—that condition their migration experiences and actions, to examine how new media, particularly cell phones, mediate labor subordination and class expressions. I also identified some of the classed contradictions associated with those migrants, typically women, but not exclusively, who perform socially reproductive work fuelling the global economy. To the degree that women migrants have responded to the structuring of their nation's political economy by taking on the economic challenge of financial support for their families, cell phones are what Filipino's might call a "mixed blessing"; this aphorism holds more ambivalence than in Horst's (2006) earlier Jamaican example. Women migrants sustain emotional contact by being "on call," literally 24/7, for family members. This extends their reproductive work at home producing a spatially dispersed simultaneity to their doubled caregiver work, which, at least in terms of time, might have been attended to sequentially, although perhaps not subjectively and emotionally, prior to the take-up of more flexible wireless technologies. This is likely helpful for being in "both places at once" but it also leaves women vulnerable to more detailed accounts of the vagaries of life in the Philippines, including things they cannot attend to, do much about, or even wish to escape from.

Elsewhere, I have characterized Philippine migration as revealing a Janus effect (Barber 2002). Janus invokes the notion of the doorway where two "faces" are visible simultaneously; let us call these agency and exploitation. In the case of the former, migration provides a journey ripe with possibilities for migrants. Rather than exploitation, migrants prefer to imagine they might realize class mobility, locate themselves with compassionate employers, and have things go well back home during their absence. Some women also imagine a better future disentangled from messy familial (and national) politics left behind as they embark on an overseas adventure. All migrants speak of "hope and possibility" and many see the experience as "empowering" if for no other reason than their successful negotiation of the challenges of difficult, sometimes dangerous, and often demeaning work abroad. This is an important aspect of labor migration— as with all workers, dignity is critical to how work is subjectively rendered and communicated. Nonetheless, Philippine labor export policies, now normalized, arise out of an exploitative colonial history. Caregiver work is decidedly subordinating and exploitative. This is the negative optic of the Janus effect. Calling and texting allow moments of technologically mediated autonomy from the overseas workplace across a transnational familial divide (mapped by Parreñas 2005). Silences are also possible as certain subjects are not disclosed to "home." Further, political discussions with the potential to mobilize workers can ensue from these same communicative possibilities. But, as I have argued, the spaces for migrants to translate their class expressions into political mobilization are few and the disincentives are powerful.

Public demonstrations show that many Filipinos recognize the profound inability of the state to correct the deficiencies in the structuring of the nation's political economy. In responding to their class aspirations, individual migrants are activated by discourses interpreted as personally meaningful (or relational) and politically charged (or structural) and layered across the temporal and spatial contexts of their lives. The Philippine state faces the challenge of maintaining the transnational loyalty of its citizens living abroad, many of whom were exported strategically through a logic tied to economic and domestic politics. While cell phones and texting provide an interesting window into the machinations of gender and class in the political economy of migration, beyond agreeing with Perterria (2005) that the technologies allow Filipinos new political possibilities, it remains too early to predict how the labor diaspora's new connectivity, and "confidence" (Abinales and Amoroso 2005) might further the political and class struggles associated with nation building. But certainly gendered class processes are now more socially, temporally, and geographically complex.

People's lives and livelihoods, all over the world, continue to be dramatically reshaped by the mobilities of capital and labor, facilitated by contemporary economic and development policies variously described as neoliberalism and/or globalization (Harvey 1995, 2005). Historically grounded ethnographic studies of workers' political expressions, or their absence, draw attention to the complexities (and complicities) of class relations set within geographies of capitalism and the politics of "place" (see Kalb and Tak 2005; Lem and Leach 2002; Narotsky and Smith 2006; Sider 2003). These explorations of how class gets configured in the social, political, and cultural landscapes of capitalism emphasize the extraordinarily inventive capacity of capital and workers alike to deploy local cultural idioms to advantage in ways that can deflect the mobilization of workers. Such work is powerful for the extension of the complexities of class mobilization beyond shop floor politics into the terrain of social reproduction, orchestrated through gendered class practices and, in immigrant-reception locales, the casting of ethnic and racialized difference typically to the disadvantage of the immigrants. Transnational migrants' socially reproductive work is surely central to theoretical and ethnographic work on class and mobilization, as are the household relations so critical to migrant livelihoods and citizenships (for example, Giles, Rothstein, and Lem in this volume). Their histories, geographies, and workplaces should thus be considered in conjunction with productive workers whose histories are not fractured by geographic mobility, as Leach demonstrates in chapter 9.

Notes

This article maps the terrain for a comparative project with Belinda Leach. Our study, *Performed subordination: Global migration and new economic subjectivities*, is funded by the Social Sciences and Humanities Research Council of Canada (2006).

1. The gendering of discourse on Jacinto warrants more extended comparison given that the "generic" migrant is a women working abroad as a nanny or nurse.
2. Since the feminization of migration in the mid 1980s, national ambivalence about migration is reflected in foreign policy decisions. "Protecting" Filipinos *and* their labor markets abroad has become a top priority, for example in Iraq (Abinales and Amoroso 2005; Barber 2006; Gonzales 1998).
3. A different Iloilo agency specialized in recruiting nurses for nursing work. Pratt (2004) and Stasiulis and Bakan (2005) discuss the concerns of nurses and caregivers in Canada.

4. Curiously, Pratt (2004) provides no fleshed-out history of the BC Centre itself, which has spawned a range of activist organizations (including support groups for migrants, nurses, and youth), with some overlapping memberships, housed under the umbrella of the Kalayaan Resource and Training Centre. Kalayaan celebrated its tenth anniversary in 1996.
5. In 2005 one of the country's largest mobile service providers, Smart Co., launched a text-messaging remittance service. This service, which I have yet to review, is remarkable for its innovation but hardly surprising given the high economic stakes.
6. The Marcos regime was in power from 1965 until the forced resignation of the president in 1986 after a hastily called, rigged election. Corazon Aquino held power from 1986 to 1992, and Fidel Ramos from 1992 to 1998.

References

Abinales, Patracio N., and Donna J. Amoroso. 2005. *State and Society in the Philippines*. Lanham: Rowman and Littlefield.

Achino-Loeb, Maria-Luisa. 2006. "Introduction." In *Silence: The Currency of Power*, ed. Maria-Luisa Achino-Loeb, 1–19. New York and Oxford: Berghahn Books.

Anderson, Benedict, 2003. *Imagined Communities: Reflections on the Origin and Spread of Nationalism*. Revized edition. Pasig City: Anvil Publishing.

Anderson, Bridget. 2000. *Doing the Dirty Work? The Global Politics of Domestic Labour*. London: Zed Books.

Asis, Mauja M. B. 2005. *Preparing to Work Abroad: Filipino Migrants' Experiences Prior to Deployment*. Manila: Scalabrini Migration Center for Philippine Migrants Rights Watch and Friedrich Ebert Stiftung.

Barber, Pauline Gardiner. 2002. "Renvisaging Power in Philippine Migration: The Janus Effect." In *Rethinking Empowerment: Gender and Development in a Global/Local World*, eds. Jane L. Parpart, Shirin M Rai, and Kathleen Staudt, 41–59. London and New York: Routlege.

———. 2004. "Contradictions of Class and Consumption when the Commodity is Labour." *Anthropologica* 46: 203–218.

———. 2006. "No/Ma(i)ds: Silenced Subjects in Philippine Migration." In *Silence: The Currency of Power*, ed. Maria-Luisa Achino-Loeb, 92–112. New York and Oxford: Berghahn Books.

———. 2008. "The Ideal Immigrant? Gendered Class Subjects in Philippine–Canada Migration." *Third World Quarterly* 27 (7): 1265–1285.

Bello, Walden. 2004. *The Anti-Development State: The Political Economy of Permanent Crisis in the Philippines*. Quezon City: University of the Philippines, Department of Sociology and Focus on the Global South.

Chang, Kimberly, and L. M. H. Ling. 2000. "Globalization and its Intimate Other: Filipina Domestic Workers in Hong Kong." In *Gender and Global Restructuring: Sightings, Sites, and Resistances*, eds. Marianne Marchand and Anne Sisson Runyan, 27–43. London: Routledge.

Chin, Christine. 1997. "Walls of Silence and Late Twentieth Century Representations of the Foreign Female Domestic Worker: The Case of Filipina and Indonesian Female Servants in Malaysia." *International Migration Review* 31 (2): 353–385.

Cohen, Robin. 2006. *Migration and its Enemies: Global Capital, Migrant Labour and the Nation-State*. Aldershot: Ashgate Publishing Ltd.

Constable, Nicole. 1997. *Maid to Order in Hong Kong: Stories of Filipina Workers*. Ithaca: Cornell University Press.

———. 2004. "Changing Filipina Identities and Ambivalent Returns." In *Coming Home? Refugees, Migrants, and Those Who Stayed Behind*, eds. Lynellyn D. Long and Ellen Oxfeld, 104–124. Philadelphia: University of Pennsylvania Press.

Dumlao, Michael. 2005. "Balikbayan: Diffusion and Development through Remittances in Malinao, Philippines." Unpublished paper. www.michaeldumlao.com.

Ehrenreich, Barbara, and Arlie Russell Hochschild. 2003. *Global Woman: Nannies, Maids and Sex Workers in the New Economy*. London: Grant Books.

Eviota, Elizabeth. 1992. *The Political Economy of Gender: Women and the Sexual Division of Labour in the Philippines*. London: Zed Books.

Glick Schiller, Nina, and Georges Fouron. 2001. *Georges Woke Up Laughing: Long Distance Nationalism and the Search for Home*. Durham: Duke University Press.

Gonzalez III, Joaquin L. 1998. *Philippine Labour Migration: Critical Dimensions of Public Policy*. Manila: De La Salle University Press, Inc. and Institute of Southeast Asian Studies.

Groves, Julian McAllister, and Kimberly Chang. 1999. "Romancing Resistance and Resisting Romance: Ethnography and the Construction of Power in the Filipina Domestic Worker Community in Hong Kong." *Journal of Contemporary Ethnography* 28 (3): 235–265.

Harvey, David. 1990. *The Condition of Postmodernity: An Enquiry into the Origins of Cultural Change*. Oxford: Basil Blackwell Ltd.

———. 1995. "Globalization in Question." *Rethinking Marxism* 8 (4): 1–17.

———. 2005. *A Brief History of Neoliberalism*. Oxford: Oxford University Press.

Hedman, Eva-Lotta E., and John T. Sidel. 2000. *Philippine Politics and Society in the Twentieth Century*. London and New York: Routledge.

Hochschild, Arlie. 1983. *The Managed Heart: The Commercialization of Human Feeling*. Berkeley: University of California Press.

Hondagneu-Sotelo, Pierrette. 2001. *Doméstica: Immigrant Workers Cleaning and Caring in the Shadows of Affluence*. Berkeley: University of California Press.

Horst, Heather. 2006. "The Blessing and Burdens of Communicating: Cell Phones in Jamaican Transnational Social Fields." *Global Networks* 6 (2): 143–159.

Kalb, Don, and Herman Tak, eds. 2005. *Critical Junctions: Anthropology and History Beyond the Cultural Turn*. New York: Berghahn Books.

Katz, Cindi. 2001. "Vagabond Capitalism and the Necessity of Social Reproduction." *Antipode* 33 (4): 709–728.

Kuhn, Annette, and Annemarie Wolpe, eds. 1978. *Feminism and Materialism*. London: Routledge & Kegan Paul.

Lem, Winnie, and Belinda Leach, eds. 2002. *Culture, Economy, Power: Anthropology as Critique, Anthropology as Praxis*. Albany: State University of New York Press.

McDowell, Linda. 2006. "Reconfigurations of Gender and Class Relations: Class Differences, Class Condescension and the Changing Place of Class Relations." *Antipode* 38 (4): 825–850.

Molyneux, Maxine. 1979. "Beyond the Domestic Labour Debate." *New Left Review* 116: 3–27.

Narotzky, Susana, and Gavin Smith. 2006. *Immediate Struggles: People, Power, and Place in Rural Spain*. Berkeley: University of California Press.

Parreñas, Rhacel. 2001. *Servants of Globalization: Women, Migration, and Domestic Work*. Stanford: Stanford University Press.

———. 2005. *Children of Global Migration: Transnational Families and Gendered Woes*. Stanford: Stanford University Press.

Pertierra, Raul, 2005. "Mobile Phones, Identity and Discursive Intimacy." *Human Technology* 1 (1): 23–44.

Pertierra, Raul, et al. 2002. *Txt-ing Selves: Cellphones and Philippine Modernity*. Manila: De La Salle University Press, Inc.

Pessar, Patricia, and Sarah Mahler. 2003. "Transnational Migration: Bringing Gender In." *International Migration Review* 37 (3): 812–846.

Piper, Nicola, ed. 2008. *New Perspectives on Gender and Migration: Livelihood, Rights and Entitlements*. New York: Routledge.

Pratt, Geraldine. 2004. *Working Feminism*. Philadelphia: Temple University Press.

Rafael, Vincente L. 2000. *White Love and Other Events in Filipino History*. Quezon City: Ateneo De Manila University Press.

Rheingold, Howard. 2002. *Smart Mobs: The Next Social Revolution*. Cambridge, MA: Perseus Books/Basic Books.

Sassen, Saskia. 2000. "Women's Burden: Counter-Geographies of Globalization and the Feminization of Survival." *Journal of International Affairs* 53 (2): 503–524.

Sider, Gerald. 2003. *Between History and Tomorrow: Making and Breaking Everyday Life in Rural Newfoundland*. Peterborough: Broadview Press.

Stasiulis, Davia, and Abigail Bakan. 2005. *Negotiating Citizenship: Migrant Women in Canada and the Global System*. Toronto: University of Toronto Press.

Vertovec, Steven. 2004. "Trends and Impacts of Migrant Transnationalism." COMPAS Working Paper No. 3. Oxford: Centre on Migration Policy and Society.

Wolf, Eric. 1999. *Envisioning Power: Ideologies of Dominance and Crisis*. Berkeley: University of California Press.

Young, Kate, Carol Wolkowitz, and Roslyn McCullagh. 1981. *Of Marriage and the Market*. London: Methuen.

Part III

Complicity and Compliance

— *Chapter 8* —

MAKING NEOLIBERAL CITIZENS IN URBAN FRANCE

Winnie Lem

In the fall of 2005 and spring of 2006 the urban landscape of France was punctuated by a series of conflicts. In March and early April 2006, high school and university students took to the streets. The centers of cities were occupied, roads were blocked, university buildings were seized, and property, both public and private was destroyed. French youth, as it was widely reported in the international press, were provoked into action to contest the implementation of the CPE or Contrat Premier Embauche (First Employment Contract), a measure introduced by the government to deregulate the labor market. Their protests and demonstrations were preceded by a period of social unrest in the fall of 2005, when riots erupted in the suburbs (*les banlieues*) located on the fringes of many cities throughout France.[1] Between 25 October and 17 November 2005 and again for a brief spell in the fall of 2006 suburban youth torched cars, sacked public buildings, hurled fire bombs at police cars, and, in general, wreaked havoc.[2]

That France was again beleaguered by demonstrations and militancy was hardly new: the country has become accustomed to regular eruptions of mass protest and violent confrontations. The combativeness of students in 2006 was a continuation of the legacy of student and urban rebellion that reached an apogee in the heady days of Paris in 1968. The violent demonstrations located in the suburbs were also not new. Since the 1970s, the urban peripheries have been the locus of persistent acts of defiance and young men, in particular, have engaged in the notorious "rodeos" in their altercations with the police.[3] Nonetheless, what *was* new in 2006 was the scale and intensity of these suburban confrontations which many proclaim to be unprecedented in the long history of contention among the notoriously contentious French.[4]

In this chapter I examine the political and economic forces that engendered such forceful displays of protest in the fall of 2005 and in the spring of 2006. These then form the backdrop against which I explore the conditions that produced quiescence amongst the ethnic Chinese during a period of time in which many ethnic minorities, across different classes, were mobilized. In historical moments when social agents become political agents, the question of which classes and categories of people emerge, and with what kinds of subjectivities and agencies, has been at the core of studies of resistance and social movements. Writers from Marx and Engels (1930) to the later generations of Marxists, from E. P. Thompson (1963) to Eric Wolf (1969, 1982), and more recently Gavin Smith (1989, 1999) as well as Erik Olin Wright (1997), J. K. Gibson-Graham (1996), Susan A. Narotzky and Gavin Smith (2006) have been concerned with this issue. This question is also at the core of the contributions to this volume made by Peró, Zontini, Narotzky, and Barber. However, as Robert Fletcher (2001, 2006) has recently and provocatively remarked, contained within the question of why some resist is the analytically more demanding question of why others do not. Responding to Fletcher's provocation, I examine the forces that condition the political practices of the class of Chinese migrants who make their living as petty capitalists in contemporary France. I ask in particular why the children of Chinese migrant entrepreneurs, who are referred to as members of the "second" or "third" generation, abstained from engagement alongside their peers in the recent confrontations.[5] In both mobilizations it was notably young people—*les jeunes*—who were provoked into taking different forms of collective action. While in the center of the city, youth from the middle-class families, members of the bourgeoisie, and ethnic majority populations formed the backbone of the protest, the demonstrations themselves transformed into a struggle that cut across class, generation, and ethnic divisions. Ethnic minority youth or whom Azouz Begag (2007) has recently called *jeunes ethniques* were roused into action.[6] Not only were middle-class *jeunes ethniques* among the participants but also the *rouilleurs*—the young members of working-class minorities—were present.[7] The *rouilleurs* are the disaffected young people who participated in the conflicts in the suburbs. Working-class *rouilleurs* of many different visible minorities also took part in the confrontations in the in the spring. However, through my participation in and observations of the Paris protests in spring 2006, I noted that few if any East Asian *jeunes ethniques* were engaged in the confrontations.[8]

Sharing these observations with informants in my research on Asia–Europe migration in the summer of 2006, I asked why the school- and university-aged children in the Asian families did not attend the demonstrations. I asked why they did not join to defend their interests as members of the future workforce in France.[9] The explanations offered to me drew on two dimensions of the limits of possibility that define their agency. On the one hand, informants' responses drew on what they understood to be cultural values of being Chinese and their responses ran along the lines of "The Chinese don't like to make trouble" and "We tend to respect authority." On the other hand, they drew on the structural/material dimensions of their lives, explaining that their modes of making a livelihood precluded an engagement in the political sphere of civil society in general and more specifically in the recent mobilization of young students. Such explanations were encapsulated in the oft-repeated answer to my queries: "Chinese immigrants are too busy working to get involved in politics." Further, many informants responded by referring to ideas of belonging and exclusion by stating that: "This is not *our* country. This is *their* [the French's] country. So we should not get involved in their conflicts."

The long history of rebellion and revolution in China clearly belies attempts to explain the political immobility of the Chinese as an essential quality, supported by fundamental values of deference to authority and obedience in Chinese culture.[10] Recent incidents of uprisings among the diasporic Chinese populations also contradict the explanations about the effect of the values that informants glossed as being "Chinese."[11] Nonetheless, the disjuncture between the objective facts of history and subjectivity must be probed in order to understand the political abstinence of the ethnic Chinese, as well as the forces that produce different forms of agency during particular historical moments, and the discursive explanations offered by informants for why it prevails. This requires an attempt to navigate the complex terrain of the relationship between the objective and the subjective and I do this by drawing on Bourdieu's idea of habitus. (see also Narotzky, chapter 6)

Habitus is a concept that is central in Bourdieu's theory of social action. It allows a way of confronting the age-old question of structure and agency without conceptualizing the two as distinct entities. By collapsing those distinctions, habitus allows an understanding of the objective and subjective dimensions of social structures through an appreciation of how agents incorporate a practical sense of what can or cannot be achieved—the "objective possibilities"—based on their intuitions gained through past collective experience. According to Bourdieu, habitus "produces practices which tend to reproduce the regularities immanent in the objective conditions of production of the generative principle" (1977: 78). It is generally understood as a structure of dispositions that reflect a "field of objective possibilities open to agents at a particular historical moment" (Lane 2000: 25). In other words it is a system of internalized dispositions that mediate between social structures and practical activity (Brubaker

1985: 758). It refers to the implicit cultural assumptions transmitted by institutions, practices, and social relations that then generate action according to certain dispositions. What is possible or unlikely for a particular class is thus developed through socialization, especially in the form of sayings, commonplaces, or ethical precepts.[12]

By using this idea, I wish to propose that the position of Chinese migrants and their children of the second and third generation can be understood by exploring their habitus as a class of petty entrepreneurs. My argument overall is that the protests of the youth in both the periphery and the center are a subset of the many demonstrations that have taken place to contest the shifting norms of citizenship that prevail in a period of time characterized by a transition to neoliberalism. I suggest along similar lines as Narotzky (chapter 6) that the possibilities for action are conditioned by the different positions that different classes occupy within that transition. Before discussing how those possibilities have been realized by focusing on Chinese migrants and entrepreneurs as a case in point, a brief overview of the political and economic changes that characterize this period of transition as a "historical moment" in France is in order.

Neoliberalism and Citizenship in France

In the early 1970s the French economy, like the economies of many other developed nations, experienced a series of downturns triggered by the world oil crisis and the increases in the prices of raw materials, which in turn led to inflation and unemployment. These downturns in the economy followed on the heels of a thirty-year period of relative prosperity after WWII, widely known as "*les trente glorieuses*." During *les trente glorieuses*, state-led industrialization aimed at growth and the construction of a competitive industrial economy out of a largely agrarian economy assured the employment of the French working class. The members of the working class grew as migrants from the provinces as well as labor migrants from France's former colonies in North Africa arrived in industrial centers such as Paris and Lyon. During *les trente glorieuses*, the welfare state reached a mature phase of development and state expenditures were made to ensure the social welfare of its citizens. One example of this was the funds that were dispersed to build low-income housing for the burgeoning working class. These projects—the *HLM* (*habitations à loyer modéré*)—were erected on the peripheries of cities and towns and provided what at the time were relatively "modern" facilities for workers who hitherto lived in old, cramped, often poorly maintained quarters in the urban centers. The projects were a result of the idea of limitless growth that seemed to prevail in the post-WWII decades of rapid industrialization and modernization. However, with the end of classical Fordist industrial organization and the onset of the globalization of industrial production, growth tapered off and high unemployment followed.

In France as well as in other nations in Europe and North America neoliberal prescriptions were seen to be a way of remedying economic stagnation and crises (see also Leach, chapter 9, Rothstein, chapter 2, and Labrecque, chapter 10). But in France the spread of neoliberalism as a set of economic policies has proceeded more slowly and has been less extreme than in many other national contexts. This is due to what some have called France's "pragmatic" approach to neoliberalism in which the privatization of national industries has been more aggressively pursued than reductions in taxation and "social expenditures."[13] The French approach of "pragmatic neoliberalism" stands in contrast to the American or British approach of aggressive cuts in social spending, tax cuts, and rapid deregulation of industry. Albeit in a gradual manner relative to Britain and the US, France nonetheless embarked on the road to neoliberal transformations in all spheres. After a period of "proto-neoliberalism" in the 1970s in which the political elites introduced limited price controls and discussed but never implemented privatizations, the application of neoliberal policies grew apace. In the mid 1980s then–Prime Minister Jacques Chirac implemented a "first wave of privatization" along with cuts in taxes and social spending to revive a flagging economy.[14] In the 1990s neoliberalism gathered more force with a "second wave of privatization" and reductions in state spending.[15] The distinctively French character of liberalization strategies prevailed with privatization representing the central platform of the neoliberal program in contrast to the American or British example of extensive cuts to taxes and social programs as well as industrial deregulation (see Prasad 2005; Smith 2004).

With measures introduced by Chirac's government, this three-decade long program of liberalization continues into a fourth and increasingly has come to take on the characteristics of those undertaken in the American and the British neoliberal programs.[16] Those measures included the introduction of new laws to deregulate industry and the labor market. In September of 2005 the French government passed the *CNE* or *Contrat Nouvelle Embauche* (New Employment Contract). The *CNE* allows employers to dismiss employees without reason but it applies only to businesses with under twenty employees. In February of 2006 the French parliament approved the *CPE* or *Contrat Premier Embauche* (First Employment Contract). The provisions of the *CPE* have been well publicized. The implementation of this legislation would significantly reduce job security in favor of granting employers and firms flexibility. It would enable employers in large firms and businesses to arbitrarily terminate the employment of those under twenty-six years of age and during a trial period of two years of employment. The *CPE* was actually the second law introduced over the course of a few months to deregulate the labor market. Whereas the *CPE* was meant to apply to large firms, the *CNE* applies to small firms. It is interesting to note that while the second measure—the *CPE*—was met with protests and demonstrations all across France after its introduction in the spring, the *CNE*—the first measure—was passed in the fall by the French parliament with hardly any resistance from unions, workers, and the French population at large. While it would be purely speculative to suggest any explanation for the quiescence of the French population at large, over the *CNE* an exploration of how migrant livelihoods are sustained within the context of changing norms of citizenship that accompanied this period of neoliberal transition suggests some reasons as to why one group among France's ethnic minorities, the Chinese, remained immobile.

In France, a shift in citizenship regime has accompanied the program of liberalization. A citizenship regime, according to Jane Jenson and Susan Phillips (1996), refers to the institutional arrangements, rules, and understandings that guide and shape concurrent policy decisions and expenditures of states, problem definitions by states and citizens, and claims-making by citizens. Further, regimes are redesigned and undergo a process of transformation in moments of economic and political turbulence, when the inherent contradictions of capitalism can no longer be contained and new mechanisms of stability are required (Jenson 2007). In France, the economic turmoil of recent decades and the economic remedies that have been prescribed for the problems of unemployment and inflation have provided the conditions for redrawing the norms of citizenship and a fundamental restructuring of the role of the state, of the division of labor between state and market and between public and "private," and of the relations between civil society and the state (Jenson and Phillips 1996). In France this process of fundamental restructuring has involved a move away from social democratic government to neoliberal governance in the regulation of civil society. Governance refers to a decentralized mode of social regulation where solving problems takes place in the public realm through groups and networks. This contrasts with a mode of social regulation that is centralized through the state. Often encapsulated as the shift from government to governance, the fundamental restructuring of the modes of regulating civil society implies the "hollowing out" of the state through the "agentization" of government. In this process of hollowing out, the provision of services and utilities also undergoes a process of privatization and there is an increasing reliance on partnerships and networks (Meehan 2003). This shift then refers to a redefinition of state-citizen relations in which rights and entitlements guaranteed by the state are coming to be redefined as interests supplied by the market, for which citizens must compete. So a changing citizenship regime implies a process where markets in the place of the state are assigned more importance as a mechanism for solving problems that range from welfare service provision to employment.[17] Because a citizenship regime encodes within it a paradigmatic representation of identities, of the "national" as well as the "model citizen," the "second-class citizen," and the non-citizen, the redesigning of citizenship is also manifested in the growing attempt to establish a changing set of citizenship norms (Jenson 2007). In France this has meant navigating away from a conception of citizenship in terms of the social rights toward a system in which the basis for inclusion implies a willingness to accept more public duties and social responsibilities and the emergence of a model that is increasingly premised on the principles of neoliberal communitarianism (Bieling 2003).[18] Resembling the agenda of what is popularly known as the "Third Way," neoliberal communitarianism is an attempt to deal with the problems produced in the post-Fordist restructuring of economies by strengthening private community networks. For example, neoliberal communitarians are proposing an active form of citizenship in which "flexibility" and "adaptability" on the part of the workforce are seen to resolve the problems of unemployment and these values have become inserted into ideas of the model citizen and model migrant (see CEC 2002).[19] As the idea of model migrants is often refracted through ideologies of the model citizen, in what follows, I discuss the contemporary habitus that configures the Chinese and particularly Chinese migrant entrepreneurs in France as model migrants and ideal citizens under the conditions of changing citizenship regimes.

Ideal Migrants, Model Citizens, and Work

In contemporary France, where racist and exclusionary discourses are directed at many different immigrant groups, the Chinese are often presented and represented as "ideal immigrants" at best or "acceptable" immigrants at the very least (see White, Winchester and Guillon 1987; Pang 1998, 1999). In the popular press, the relative acceptability of the Chinese as immigrants has been fostered by articles that stress the profound work ethic that the Chinese possess, as well as their compliance and their tendency toward self-sufficiency.[20] In reinforcing the view of the Chinese as model immigrants, the French press has often used rhetorical devices to stress the harmlessness of Asians, citing that "the only yellow peril to fear is that of their incommensurable facility to adapt." So they will bring with them "a commercial success with a mysterious scent."[21] While the popular press may be accused of propagating such exotic but generally positive images of the Chinese, many scholars, most notably, Herman Kahn (1979) and particularly Gordon Redding (1993), have jumped into the fray to try to uncover what is often seen through an "orientalist" lens as the mystery of the commercial success of firms and enterprises run by the Chinese.

Their attempts to uncover the secrets of this success have emerged against the backdrop of the economic miracles that had been unfolding in East Asia since the 1960s and more recently in China since the 1990s. These analysts have observed that much of that growth has occurred in the specifically Chinese parts of Asia, like Hong Kong and Taiwan, or in parts of Asia where large groups of Chinese immigrants predominate. Claiming that businesses and family firms run by the Chinese have formed the backbone of those miracles, analysts have propagated the idea that certain essential features of Chinese culture, particularly a set of Chinese values, are especially conducive to capitalist growth.[22] Because of the prevalence of such discourses in the press and media images in France, the Chinese are thought to represent the ideal group of immigrants because they subscribe to values compatible with the imperatives of investment, innovation, and entrepreneurship that might drive the economy in France toward global competitiveness (CEC 2002). Because of the prevalence among the Chinese of what is assumed to be a cohesive set of values that have lead to capitalist growth, it is believed that by and large, the Chinese can be successfully integrated into French society where republican values prevail on the one hand and capitalist ideologies prevail on the other. The pursuit of livelihoods through self-employment and entrepreneurship based on petty capitalism therefore represents an ideal solution to the problem of employment of immigrants from Asia. It also serves as a way of solving the problem of the incorporation immigrants in a nation concerned with the questions of social, economic, and cultural integration.

The relative acceptability of the Chinese is often linked to the ways in which they are understood to insert themselves into host societies through a process of absorption into dense social networks. These are the bonds of trust and networks of social relations that are generally referred to by analysts and subjects alike as *guanxi* and that are used to sustain their economies and communities (Yang 1994; Gold, Guthrie, and Wank 2002). By navigating through autonomous social and economic networks the problem of the economic incorporation of immigrants can be resolved, as work can be found in the businesses run by relatives, friends, and fellow countrymen and women. The small family-owned and operated Chinese restaurant or restaurant caterer (*restaurant-traiteur*) is a case in point. In these Chinese establishments newly arrived legal and undocumented immigrants alike can find work in the kitchens cleaning and preparing food or washing dishes. Kew, the Chinese owner-operator of a restaurant serving sushi commented to me during one interview conducted in a mixture of French, Cantonese, and Mandarin:

> There is always a new arrival from China who is looking for work and all they need to do is to put the word out to a relative or a friend in the community and eventually they will find work. I did this myself when I first arrived. When I need someone to work for me, I do the same and someone eventually turns up. Helping out in the kitchen to prepare fish and vegetables and wash dishes is not particularly skilled work so an untrained worker or a new arrival is fine for that kind of work.

Such small businesses are often themselves established through navigating these networks. Loans acquired through rotating credit societies called *tontines* by the Chinese in Paris help set up businesses and different forms of self-employment.[23] Once established, small businesses like the Chinese restaurant are sustained by exploiting the labor of family members—adults and children alike—and also the labor of undocumented migrants who work extraordinarily long hours during the week and also on weekends and holidays. In many of the small establishments where I conducted interviews the owners of the enterprise tended to be first-generation migrants whose sons and daughters were born in France and in attendance in the *lycées* and universities in Paris. They form part of the force of temporary, occasional, and part-time workers in the family business. I came to know many of these workers and their work routines through interviews with them and also through regular visits to the many different restaurants owned by relatives of these workers. This was how I came to know Claire and Lorie. The flexibility of this force of family labor is illustrated in the routine and conditions under which these two young women work.

Claire is a high school student—a *lycéenne*—and her older cousin Lorie is a high school graduate who obtained a qualification in business and accounting. Both are often called upon to work in the small restaurant businesses run by their family. Their family owns and operates two small restaurants located in two different *arrondissements* of Paris. Claire's father and mother run one restaurant. The other restaurant is owned and operated by Claire's uncle (and Lorie's brother) and aunt. On some evenings after school and on weekends, depending on the need for help, Claire is sent to work in one or the other restaurant. She is often sent to help Lorie

172 I Winnie Lem

who works more than full-time between the two restaurants. Together they serve, clean, and close up the restaurant after the dinner hour, often late at night. On weekends, Claire is expected to show up early, well before customers arrive and work late, cleaning and setting up for the next day after diners leave. As a student Claire works occasionally but regularly. Lorie's occasional work in the family restaurants was transformed into permanent work when she was obliged by her family to exchange her job in a French accounting firm for work in the family business.[24] She travels between the different restaurants to work during the lunch service in one, then for dinner in another. In contrast to her previous job, which came with health and unemployment benefits, regular pay, regular hours, and a large degree of responsibility, she is now engaged in work in the family restaurant, which is demanding in terms of time and also menial relative to her former job. The work that is performed by Lorie and Claire is not registered and not declared to the state. As a high school student, Claire lives at home, with her parents and is dependent on the common family budget for her sustenance. As a young unmarried member of the family, Lorie also lives with her brother and his family and is also dependent on the common family budget to ensure her material welfare. In both their cases, taxes are not paid for their work, nor are deductions made for any state benefits.

These work routines and conditions of work form part of the habitus in which the Chinese migrants and their children are socialized to live and work.

Habitus and Chinese Migrant Entrepreneurs

Their work patterns and patterns of employment allow small firms to be self-sustaining and flexible in an age when such flexibility is required to assure profitability in a competitive neoliberal environment. The flexibility results from the organization and structure of small capitalist enterprises or petty enterprises. Because the organization of the enterprise is often based on kinship, family members serve as both owners and workers for the firm. The possibilities for hiring and firing workers are mediated by kin ties. A sharp distinction between capital and labor does not prevail. Where the organization of the firm is embedded in the organization of the family, the hierarchical structure of the family is reproduced in the power structure of the firm. The male head of the family is also the head of the business. As many have argued, Chinese family businesses tend to be largely male preserves in which men monopolize the high-paying positions and also positions of authority (Greenhalgh 1994). Male members of the family tend to become established as the managers and bosses who directly manage and oversee the day-to-day running of the business. The ability of managers to command is underscored not simply by a value system that supports obedience and deference to patriarchs, but also by the material dependence of the junior and the least powerful members of the family and the firm, as in the cases of Claire and Lorie. Their example also illustrates that within the hierarchical structure of the small family-based enterprise, the least favorable jobs with the lowest responsibility are allocated to daughters or sisters, who also form part of the flexible labor force to be called upon to work temporarily or to supplement the permanent force of workers and to be assigned to work for low or no wages as needed outside the regular hours of business operation, to ensure a steady rate of profit.

What also assures a steady rate of profit is undeclared work. Undeclared work, particularly of family members in the underground or informal economy, has been an effective strategy for the reproduction of petty capitalism in many different contexts.[25] When discussing the issue of undeclared work in the restaurant trade, many owners favored the principle of minimum state involvement in business and the economy in general. Restaurant owners explained that too much state involvement diminishes the rate of profits, which, so these entrepreneurs claim, is usually quite marginal in small businesses in the first place. Kew complained about the excesses of the state, which intervenes at every stage of running a business by suggesting that it was "government extortion." He gave an example: "In addition to this tax and that tax, I even had to pay a fee to the government to put up a little sign for my restaurant!!! Is this not extortion?"

When I asked him about hiring undocumented workers in restaurants, he said it was the only way to survive when the state in France is so involved in the economy. Many owner-operators have also commented that informal arrangements through social networks are preferable to formal contracts as a means of securing labor. This practice is followed by Kew, who informally employs two non-kin workers in his restaurant and says that the whole process of hiring is fairly simple and unimpeded by filling out all sorts of forms. The preference for the flexibility of communitarian ties over the rigidity of formal work contracts is reflected in the comments of another small restaurant owner, Meiqing, who owns and operates a restaurant that serves Japanese food on the first floor of an apartment block in a mainly residential area in the northern part of Paris. When I interviewed Meiqing in 2005 she discussed the ways in which employment of labor in the underground economy allows for the flexibility to weather crises, while describing how she engages in the practices in France:

It is not easy to manage one's own business. Look at the large restaurants of the 13th arrondissement, for example.[26] During the SARS[27] scare they suffered a lot because no one would come to eat in their restaurants and they lost lots of money. They had to keep paying their workers. But, they could not lay off their employees. Also, my friends in England who run a larger restaurant had to lay off ten people. In England the taxes are lower, one can both hire, fire, and lay off more easily. In France one cannot lay off workers so easily. So for this reason we do not hire many outside the family to work if we can. But *le travail en noir* [undeclared work] is punished heavily in France, so you must declare some of your workers and some of your hours of work. But because there are no formal contracts and friends of friends or distant kin work for you, some informal arrangements are always made. For example, paid employees who may be members of your family and many who are not tend to declare less hours worked, for example three hours instead of ten to six instead of twelve. In the restaurant business you tend to work long hours but what you declare is less than what you work. Your friends and family will do that particularly if you hire someone who has just recently arrived. Most of these recent arrivals will have no skills so can wash dishes for you. All they need is the ability to work long hours during the day and also the ability to work a long week.

While operators of these businesses complain of the high degree of responsibility and risk involved in running these independent operations, many laud the ideals of independent ownership, freedom, and autonomy. When I asked Kew if he preferred to be an employer or an employee, he comments: "It is better to be a boss—*patron*—than a worker. There is no one looking over your shoulder." In response to the same question, Meiqing, who worked as a seamstress in a textile factory until the mid 1980s, replied:

I often think I would prefer to be an employee—a worker—because you take fewer risks and have less responsibility. But then I think about what almost happened to me and I think again. You are vulnerable and it is also risky. I was employed in the textile industry when I first arrived in France. In 1986, the clothes industry began its decline, the prices had fallen and I began to worry that we would not always have work. Then someone I know—a distant relative—told me about a job that was available as a waitress in a restaurant. I went for an interview at the house of this relative who was the mother of a distant aunt who owned the restaurant and I got the job. For a while, I held down two jobs. In the morning I worked sewing clothes in a factory and in the evenings I worked as a waitress. And then finally I quit the factory job because the wages were so low and many were being let go anyway and so I worked full-time as a waitress for six years. Now I have my own restaurant with my husband and we can manage things on our own. We have certain responsibilities to our customers but essentially we are free to run the business as we like, make changes that suit us and our customers, and respond to changes in tastes in the market. We rely on our own hard work and the hard work of members of our family— our nephew who helps us in the restaurant after school and our niece and my mother-in-law who looks after our children when we have to work. We don't ask anyone for anything but can count on each other.

Fearing the possibility of being made redundant during the recession in the mid 1980s, Meiqing thus changed her work strategies, acquired new skills, and retrained to work as an entrepreneur in the restaurant trade. These examples of the social and cultural practices of small entrepreneurship operated by migrants embody the ideals necessary for the operation of small businesses in the kinds of economies advocated by the architects of neoliberal reform and designers of a new citizenship regime. The pursuit of livelihoods through self-employment and flexible forms of entrepreneurship based on petty capitalism and sustained through autonomous social and economic networks solves the problem of the unemployment created as a result of economic restructuring in France. Moreover, the ideas of freedom, autonomy, and self-reliance as well as risk with responsibility mentioned by Meiqing are precisely the ideas that underpin liberalizing economies and are promoted in neoliberal models of citizenship. Neoliberal communitarians therefore are proposing this form of citizenship in which "flexibility" and "adaptability" on the part of both workers and enterprises have come to be seen as the panacea to the problems of unemployment (Van Apeldoorn 2003). The value of seeking solutions to social and economic problems such as unemployment is realized by activating social networks and relying on the market. Moreover, the redesigned citizenship regime demands that its citizens become less reliant on the state for welfare protection and more "employable," which implies instilling or reinforcing skill sets such as entrepreneurialism and attitudes such as self-reliance in order to adapt to more flexible labor markets and working conditions.[28]

In small businesses, such as the Chinese restaurant, this flexibility is embodied in the elasticity of work hours that extends well beyond the thirty-five to thirty-nine hours of work legislated by the French state for workers in large public and private enterprises. It is also embodied by the practices of deploying young economically dependent female members of the family to work as a kind of reserve force of labor for the extended hours of restaurant work. These organizational attributes of operating a small business not only preclude time for leisure and the participation in community activities, but also political activities, for both workers and employers alike. That is not to say that participation or indeed non-participation in the political life of a country is simply a function of time. But it is to say that the time constraints and the work routine contribute toward structuring a disposition against creating disturbances in a society in which their sense of belonging is tenuous.

For young women, like Claire and Lorie, this disposition is also re-inforced by the material dependence on and living within the ideological world of the Chinese family business. Within this world a system of material rewards and benefits sustains a value system that emphasizes obedience to authority, deference to power, and respect to elders as the ethical precepts that inform an identity as Chinese. This system of material rewards also supports the values of entrepreneurialism and the idea that entrepreneurship is an effective strategy to pursue in order to navigate the difficult terrain of sustaining a livelihood under neoliberalism. In these ways, the habitus of Chinese migrant entrepreneurship produces an inclination toward political disengagement and refusing to forge alliances with other classes in their struggles in a country undergoing political and economic changes associated with neoliberal reform.

Habitus, Conjunctures, Class, and Contention

Four decades of neoliberal reform had different consequences for migrants of different classes and groups of immigrants whose means of incorporation into France responded to the economic exigencies of distinctive eras. This is reflected in the contrast between the experiences of Chinese migrants, many of whom have been incorporated as petty capitalists and those from North Africa arrived in France to join the ranks of the industrial working class. For many migrants from North Africa whose labor helped to fuel the industrialization of France during *les trente glorieuses* in the post-WWII decades, the economic policies of neoliberalism have meant increasing economic and social precariousness.[29] Privatization and de-industrialization have meant a drastic fall in the number of jobs available in industry, which had a severe effect on the descendents of migrant workers, who came of working age during the era of the post-Fordist transition.[30] Cuts in public expenditure have meant the deterioration of the *cités*, the housing estates where old worn-out buildings have been closed without being replaced by new structures.[31] Built by planners in the 1950s some writers have argued that they were constructed to purge the cities of the poor (Wacquant 1993). The isolation of urban poor by relocating affordable housing to the suburbs, so it is argued, is not simply a part of an official program to keep working-class immigrants on the outside, socially and economically, but it is also part of an effort to decimate the working class in France. Within this optic, the protests in the *banlieues* that have been a persistent feature of life in the *cités* since the 1970s are part of an effort by working-class migrants to contest their annihilation (Wacquant and Stovall 2005; Stovall 1990). While there is much merit in this view and in the arguments made by such scholars to explain the political consequences of the spatial segregation of the urban poor, I suggest that at minimum, the protests in the suburbs are an attempt by the *rouilleurs* to object to the social and economic conditions brought on by post-Fordist restructuring and the transition to neoliberalism.

While there are many differences that can be drawn between the actions taken up by the *jeunes* who inhabit the *cités* in the *banlieues* of France and those of the *lycéen*, and many differences among the groups themselves, my argument here is that both groups share a political purpose.[32] Apart from striking a blow to the continuing efforts made to deregulate labor, the protesters were engaged in a collective struggle to contest the transformation of the relations between the state and its citizenry under neoliberalism. Students, *jeunes ethniques*, *rouilleurs*, unemployed, and employed alike were objecting to the transition from government to governance in France and contesting the hegemony of a new model of citizenship to define the basis for inclusion and participation in French society. Their militancy challenges the application of the model of the market to the governance of society and a model of citizenship whereby citizens must be autonomous, self-governing, and reliant on the market to guarantee their "interests" rather than on the state to guarantee their "rights."

Conclusion

In this chapter I have been concerned to examine the immobility of the Chinese *jeunes ethniques* in the context of the mobilization of the youth belonging to many other ethnic groups. I have argued that the status of the Chinese as "model immigrants" is linked to the ways in which Chinese migrants are understood and also understand themselves to be inserted into the host societies. Much scholarship and many popular accounts have stressed that they do so by negotiating family relations and dense networks that are embedded in a set of values associated with being Chinese. While these networks and relationships have long been a feature of Chinese migration, the emphasis placed on them in many current accounts has acquired a deeper significance in the contemporary context when liberal democracies are undergoing neoliberal transformation. It has acquired an immediacy particularly in an era when exclusionary discourses have emerged that consistently emphasize the undue burdens posed by increasing flows of migrants on the institutions of civil society and the state.

France is a nation in which there are heated arguments about the relationship between immigration and citizenship. Models of citizenship are vigorously debated between left, center, and right (see, e.g., Feldblum 1999; Favell 1998). The views propagated by the popular press and certain schools of scholarship on the relationship between Chinese values, entrepreneurship, and immigration validate certain ideals in the model of citizenship advocated by the Left and the Right. Prevailing images of the Chinese appeal to a republican ideal of citizenship advocated by the Left and center, in which assimilation in the public sphere is promoted and multiculturalism in the private sphere is tolerated. On the other hand, Chinese immigrants are thought to live up to the communitarian ideal of citizenship advocated by the right. As a model that promotes civic participation through self-reliance, Chinese immigrants are thought to possess what is often called the valued "social capital" and therefore can rely on their own resources and not strain the resources of the state for their own reproduction.[33] Immigrants who have social capital can eventually become model citizens and rely on their own resources. Because the Chinese possess social capital, they represent the exception to the exclusionary discourses that are generally directed at immigrant groups discussed by Peró (chapter 4) and Zontini (chapter 5). Chinese exceptionality, then, serves as a justification for the exclusion of other immigrant groups by reinforcing the political and social barricades against those migrants whose ability to participate in the globally competitive market is not borne out by the evidence of a putative ability to produce "economic miracles." It also serves as a justification to further fortify the walls of "Fortress Europe," to make it more impenetrable to those whose ability to sustain themselves through "social capital" has yet to be determined. However, it also ironically serves as a means for the exclusion of Chinese immigrants themselves, whose subjective perception of "not belonging" in France converges with the objective conditions of discrimination in a national labor market that is highly segmented by ethnicity.[34] As this chapter has shown, it perpetuates enclaves of de-politicized polities who are compliant in the face of the forces that perpetuate exclusion and a form of integration that ultimately implies subjection and a non-deliberative stance toward the terms of neoliberal governance.

Notes

1. *Banlieue* has become a sobriquet in France for dense urban neighborhoods, populated by ethnic minorities
2. In the fall of 2005 the eruptions were triggered by the deaths of two youths who were burned scaling the walls of a power plant while fleeing police whom they thought were chasing them. Conflicts involving youth living in suburbs continued in 2006 and

erupted frequently in various locations throughout Paris immediately preceding the presidential election in spring 2007 (see "Heurts entre jeunes et policiers à la gare du Nord, neuf interpellations,"*Le Monde*, 28 March 2007; see also Angelique Chrisafis, "Trapped in Squalor, Young Voters Long for a Candidate to Give them Hope," *The Guardian*, 29 March 2007).

3. *Rodeo* is a term used by young male participants in the confrontations in the suburbs. It refers to the tactics of protest that typically involve stealing a car, engaging the police in a chase, abandoning and then torching the stolen car. Such acts tend to follow incidents in which members of the local population experience a clash or conflict with public authorities or agents of the state. For a discussion of urban violence, see Wieviorka (1999).

4. The reputation of the French for contentiousness has been the subject of much scholarship. For an important historical account, see Tilly (1986).

5. For discussions regarding the second generation in Europe, see Simon (2003), Crul and Vermeulen (2003), and Parker and Song (2007).

6. *Jeunes ethniques* is a neologism used by Begag (2007) to describe members of minority ethnic populations, whose grandparents immigrated and settled in France and whose life experiences are often contoured by a process of ethnicization and also stigmatization despite being born in France and being culturally French. These groups are often referred to as the "third generation" of immigrants.

7. Begag (2007) subdivides *jeunes ethniques* into two further categories: *dérouilleurs* (movers or literally "de-rusters") who have experienced social and geographic mobility and *rouilleurs* ("rusters") who have not experienced such mobility having grown up in the 1990s in the midst of economic recession. The latter have been called members of the "underclass" of unemployed or underemployed. See Roy (2005).

8. Because of the spatial specificity of the fall protests, which were confined to the suburban public housing estates inhabited largely by African, Turkish, and North African *rouilleurs*, and few Asian migrants, it is not surprising that Chinese migrants were not counted among the protesters.

9. My research focuses on the political economy of migration between Asia and Europe and it examines the significance of transnationalism in sustaining migrant livelihoods in France. The research has involved interviews with workers and owners of small-scale family-based enterprises in the restaurant and retail trades in urban centers in France.

10. These values are often discussed as part of the Confucian orthodoxy that defines social relations within the family and political relations between state and citizens in pre-republican China. Transposed to the economy by management specialists, they have been used to explain the success of Asian business in the era of globalization. For a discussion of what has been called Confucian capitalism, see Yao (2003).

11. See, for example, Rosenthal and Povoledo in the *International Herald and Tribune,* 26 April 2007, on the riots in Milan Chinatown that occurred in April 2007.

12. I thank Gavin Smith for this insight.

13. According to Prasad (2005), the differences between France and other nations in implementing neoliberal change must be understood as related to the fact that state interventionism in the political and economic spheres of France is higher than in, for example, the US and the UK (see also Fourcade-Gourchinas and Babb 2002). Also, as Esping-Anderson (1990) has pointed out, the welfare state in France was developed by the Right and has been based on the principle of social insurance for the middle classes and not on the redistribution of wealth between classes. Welfare policy and also tax policy are rooted in electoral interests and therefore less able to be reformed. Industrial policy is not so rooted, and so is an easier target for reform.

14. Corporate taxes and individual taxes were cut during his period and the tax structure in France was made more regressive. But only thirteen state-owned enterprises were privatized, instead of the sixty-one that Chirac originally proposed, as the stock market crash of 1987 brought a halt to privatization (see Theret 1991).
15. This was precipitated by the signing of the Maastricht Treaty in 1991, and fiscal reform was required to participate in the European Monetary Union. With Chirac as president and Alain Juppé as prime minister, France's tax structure was made more regressive and 12.6 percent of the workforce has been moved from the public to the private sector (Prasad 2005; Smith 2004).
16. With the election of Nicholas Sarkozy to the presidency in May of 2007, this program will likely continue into a fifth decade with harsher measures than those introduced by former governments as he imposes labor and pension reforms as part of a program to further liberalize the economy and tighten immigration controls. The tightening of immigration controls and different patterns of state action are currently being negotiated and attempted as France, like many other nation-states, grapples with the global financial and economic crisis of 2008–2009. Different logics of neoliberalism may be pursued.
17. For a discussion of the difference between government and governance, see Loughlin (2000) and Held (1995). See also Jenson (2007).
18. Communitarian ideas of citizenship stress community in its various forms as the foundation of civil society and the ideas of participation and identity are emphasized. Although there are various forms of communitarianism (see Delanty 2000), what is common to all is a repudiation of individualism and contractualism. Communitarians are on the one hand opposed to models of citizenship premised on the idea of individualism in liberalism. On the other hand, proponents of communitarianism also reject social democratic forms of citizenship in which citizenship is reduced to a formalistic relationship to the state as one of rights and duties (see also Shaffir 1998; Hager 2007; and Van Apeldoorn 2003).
19. For an example of how such changes are envisioned for France, see Lallement and Paillard (2007).
20. The Chinese are seen, for example, to "work noiselessly, night and day like bees in a well-enclosed hive." See Flé (1985), which contains numerous examples of media rhetoric used to portray the Chinese in France.
21. See Flé (1985).
22. Elsewhere (Lem, 2007) I have offered a critique of what appears in the literature as the thesis of Chinese culture to explain entrepreneurial "success" of Chinese businesses.
23. *Tontines* are an investment vehicle that is a mixture of group annuity, group life insurance, and lottery in which investors each pay a sum into the *tontine*. The funds are invested and each investor receives dividends. Usually the scheme involves an arrangement that is made upon the death of an investor so that when an investor dies his or her share is divided among all the other investors. This process continues until only one investor survives who receives all of the remaining funds. Among the Chinese in Paris what is called a *tontine* resembles more a rotating credit society, in which investors each advance small loans to the borrower, who repays each investor with interest according to a pre-determined schedule. The death of investors seems not to figure in the arrangements in a prominent way. For a detailed discussion of the ways in which *tontines* are organized among Chinese immigrants in Paris, see Pairault (1990).
24. For a fuller discussion of the case of Lorie, see Lem (2007).
25. For a recent discussion of petty capitalism, see Smart and Smart (2005).

26. The 13th arrondissement is where a large Chinatown is located and where many of the larger Chinese restaurants are situated. Some of the large restaurants seat well over five hundred and have a staff of over twenty.

27. This is a reference to the Severe Acute Respiratory Syndrome outbreak in 2003, thought to have originated in China and carried rapidly by the Chinese to other continents. The fear of contagion resulted in the loss of revenues for Chinese businesses and particularly restaurants as people sought to avoid contact with the Chinese in Europe, North America, and elsewhere.

28. These skill sets and attitudes are transmitted in proposed new job-training and skills-development programs and lifelong learning (Hager 2007).

29. Because of the deprivations that arose in developing countries due to programs of structural adjustment and stabilization imposed upon them by international financial institutions in the 1980s and 1990s, the nature of migration to France changed. Temporary migration became more permanent and many migrants, particularly from France's former colonies in North Africa, remained in France. New migrants, moreover, began to arrive in increasing numbers.

30. In the 1990s youth unemployment reached figures as high as 20 percent, twice that of the national average. In certain housing estates, where increasing numbers of new migrants settled, the figures have been even higher, with unemployment among young residents on average above 30 percent, and reaching as high as 85 percent (see Silverstein 2005).

31. This has resulted in increased overcrowding and squatting. In suburban *cités* this socioeconomic marginalization has been reinforced by spatial isolation. The development of the urban transportation network has failed to keep pace with the growth of the suburban population and nearly 60 percent of these suburban municipalities lack their own train station. The result is the relative physical and symbolic separation of *cités* from each other and from Paris proper. Urban peripheries have also been increasingly militarized since the mid 1990s and the declaration of the "war on terror" (Silverstein 2005).

32. Many journalistic, political, and also academic accounts of the protests in the *banlieue* repeatedly and mistakenly describe the youth as "foreigners" or "outsiders"—*les étrangers*. Such *jeunes ethniques* are, as I mentioned earlier, French-born citizens and perhaps the descendants of immigrant parents. By contrast, riots of the youth that began in late February and continued into the spring of 2006 have been discussed as the protests of the "insiders" (see Budgen 2006).

33. The usage of the term in this model follows Putnam's idea (1993) in which *social capital* refers to the collective value of all social networks and the inclinations that arise from these networks to do things for each other. Putnam sees this as a building block for neoliberal forms of civic participation (cf. Bourdieu 1986, 1987).

34. Labor market discrimination persists despite what has been discussed as the "success" of the French model of integration for the French-born descendants of immigrants. See Hargreaves (2007), Wacquant (1993), and Tribalat (1996).

References

Begag, Azouz. 2007. *Ethnicity and Equality: France in the Balance.* Lincoln and London: University of Nebraska Press

Bieling, Hans-Jürgen. 2003. "European Employment Policy Between Neo-Liberal Rationalism and Communitarianism." In *The Political Economy of European Employment: European*

Integration and the Transnationalization of the (Un)Employment Question, ed. Hans Overbeek, 51–74. London: Routledge.

Bourdieu, Pierre. 1977. *Outline of a theory of practice.* Cambridge: Cambridge University Press
———. 1986. "The Forms of Capital." In *Handbook of Theory and Research for the Sociology of Education*, ed. John G. Richardson, 241–258. New York: Greenwood Press.
———. 1987. *Distinction: A Social Critique of the Judgment of Taste.* Cambridge, MA: Harvard University Press.

Brubaker, Rogers. 1985. "Rethinking Classical Theory." *Theory and Society* 14: 745–775.

Budgen Sébastien. 2006. "Liberal Francophobia." *New Left Review* 39 (March/April): 150–160.

CEC (Commission of the European Communities). 2002. "Commission of the European Communities: The Lisbon Strategy—Making Change Happen." COM 14 final. Brussels: European Economic Commission.

Crul, Maurice, and Hans Vermeulen. 2003. "The Second Generation in Europe." *International Migration Review* (winter) 37 (4): 965–985.

Delanty, Gerard. 2000. *Citizenship in a Global Age: Society, Culture, and Politics.* Buckingham: Open University Press.

Esping-Anderson, Gosta. 1990. *The Three Worlds of Welfare Capitalism.* Princeton: Princeton University Press.

Favell, Adrian. 1998. *Philosophies of Integration: Immigration and the Idea of Citizenship in Britain and France.* Basingstoke: Macmillan.

Feldblum, Miriam. 1999. *Reconstructing Citizenship: The Politics of Nationality Reform and Immigration in France.* Albany: State University of New York Press.

Flé, Catherine. 1985. *L'insertion professionnelle des réfugiées du Sud-est asiatique Diplôme d'études approfondie.* Université de Paris 7.

Fletcher, Robert. 2001. "What are We Fighting For? Rethinking Resistance in a Pewenche Community in Chile." *The Journal of Peasant Studies* 28 (3): 36–67.
———, ed. 2006. *Beyond Resistance: The Future of Freedom.* Hauppage: Nova Science Publishers, Inc.

Fourcade-Gourchinas, Marion, and Sarah Babb. 2002. "The Rebirth of the Liberal Creed: Paths to Neoliberalism in Four Countries." *American Journal of Sociology* 108 (3): 533–579.

Gibson-Graham, J. K. 1996. *The End of Capitalism (as We Knew It): A Feminist Critique of Political Economy.* Oxford: Blackwell.

Gold, Thomas, Bough Guthrie, and David Wank, eds. 2002. *Social Connections in China: Institutions and the Changing Nature of Guanxi.* London: Cambridge University Press.

Greenhalgh, Susan. 1994. "De-Orientalizing the Chinese Family Firm." *American Ethnologist* 21 (4): 746–775.

Hager, Sandy Brian. 2007. "The Lisbon Agenda and 'Neoliberal Communitarian' Citizenship." Multicultural Center Prague. http://aa.ecn.cz/img.

Hargreaves, Alec G. 2007. *Multi-Ethnic France: Immigration, Politics, Culture and Society.* 2nd edition. London: Routledge.

Held, David. 1995. *Democracy and the Global Order: From the Modern State.* London: Polity Press.

Jenson, Jane. 2007. "The European Union's Citizenship Regime: Creating Norms and Building Practices." *Comparative European Politics* 5 (1): 53–75.

Jenson, Jane, and Susan Phillips. 1996. "Regime Shift: New Citizenship Practices in Canada." *International Journal of Canadian Studies* 14: 111–135.

Kahn, Herman. 1979. World Economic Development: 1979 and Beyond. Boulder: Westview Press.

Lallement, Rémi, and Sandrine Paillard. 2007. "The French Innovation System in the Knowledge-Based Economy." Commissariat général du Plan de France. http://www. asko-europa-stiftung.de/zukunftswerkstatt/deutsch/ResearchPolicyPaillard_Lallement.pdf.

Lane, Jeremy F. 2000. *Pierre Bourdieu: A Critical Introduction*. London: Pluto.

Lem, Winnie. 2007. "Daughters, Duty and Deference in the Franco-Chinese Restaurant." In *Restaurants: The Anthropology of Where We Eat*, eds. David Beriss and David Sutton. London: Berg.

Loughlin, John. 2000. "The Cross-Border Challenges and Opportunities Posed by the Transformation of European Governance." Paper presented at the International Conference on European Cross Border Co-operation: Lessons for and from Ireland, 29 September to 1 October. Belfast: Queen's University.

Marx, Karl, and Friedrich Engels. 1930. *The German Ideology*. New York: International Publishers.

Meehan, Elizabeth. 2003. "From Government to Governance: Civic Participation and the 'New Politics.'" Occasional Paper No. 5, Centre for Advancement of Women in Politics. Belfast: Queen's University.

Narotzky, Susan, and Gavin Smith. 2006. *Immediate Struggles: People, Power and Place in Rural Spain*. Berkeley: University of California Press.

Pairault, Thierry. 1990. *L'intégration silencieuse: la petite entreprise Chinoise en France*. Paris: L'Harmattan.

Pang, Chin Lin. 1998. "Invisible visibility: Intergenerational transfer of identity and social position. Chinese Women in Belgium." *Asian and Pacific Migration Journal* 7(4): 433–542.

———. 1999. "Why are the Chinese Invisible and/or Unproblematic? Exploring Some Viable Explanations." *Ethnologia* 9–11: 105–120.

Parker, David, and Miri Song. 2007. "Inclusion, Participation, and the Emergence of British Chinese Websites." *Journal of Ethnic and Migration Studies* 33 (7): 1043–1061.

Prasad, Monica. 2005. "Why is France so French? Culture, Institutions, and Neoliberalism." *American Journal of Sociology* 111 (2): 357–407.

Putnam, Robert. 1993. *Making Democracy Work: Civic Traditions in Modern Italy*. Princeton: Princeton University Press

Redding, Gordon. 1993. *The Spirit of Chinese Capitalism*. Berlin: Walter de Gruyter.

Rosenthal, Elizabeth, and Elisabetta Povoledo. 2007. "A Pushcart War in the Streets of Milan's Chinatown." *International Herald and Tribune*, 26 April.

Roy, Olivier. 2005. "The Nature of the French Riots." *Social Science Research Council Web Forum*. http://riotsfrance.ssrc.org.

Shaffir, Gershon, ed. 1998. *The Citizenship Debates: A Reader*. Minneapolis: University of Minnesota Press.

Silverstein, Paul. 2005. "Postcolonial Urban Apartheid." Social Science Research Council Web Forum, November. http://riotsfrance.ssrc.org.

Simon, Patrick. 2003. "France and the Unknown Second Generation: Preliminary Results on Social Mobility." *International Migration Review* (winter) 37 (4): 1091–1119.

Smart, Alan, and Josephine Smart, eds. 2005. *Petty Capitalists and Globalization: Flexibility, Entrepreneurship and Economic Development*. Albany: State University of New York Press.

Smith, Gavin. 1989. *Livelihood and Resistance: Peasants and the Politics of Land in Peru*. Berkeley: University of California.

———. 1999. *Confronting the Present: Towards a Politically Engaged Anthropology*. London: Berg.

Smith, Timothy B. 2004. *France in Crisis: Welfare, Inequality, and Globalization since 1980*. Cambridge: Cambridge University Press.

Stovall, Tyler.1990. *The Rise of the Paris Red Belt*. Berkeley: University of California Press.

Théret, Bruno. 1991. "Néo-libéralisme, inégalites sociales et politiques fiscales de droite et de gauche dans la France des années 1980." *Revue Française de Science Politique* 41 (3): 342–381.

Thompson, E. P. 1963. *The Making of the English Working Class*. London: Victor Gollancz.

Tilly, Charles. 1986. *The Contentious French*. Cambridge: Harvard University.

Tribalat, Michelle. 1996. *De l'immigration à l'assimilation: Enquête sur les populations d'origines étrangères en France*. Paris: La Découverte.

Van Apeldoorn, Bastiaan. 2003. "European Unemployment and Transnational Capitalist Class Strategy." In *The Political Economy of European Employment: European Integration and the Transnationalization of the (Un)Employment Question*, ed. Hans Overbeek, 113–134. London: Routledge.

Wacquant, Loic. 1993. "Urban Outcasts: Stigma and Division in the Black American Ghetto and the French Urban Periphery." *International Journal and Urban and Regional Research* 17 (3): 366–383.

Wacquant, Loic, and Tyler Stovall. 2005. "Burn Baby Burn, French Style? Roots of the Riots in Urban France." Webcast, 17 November. Berkeley: University of California.

White, Paul, Hilary Winchester and Michelle Guillon. 1987. "South East Asian Refugees in Paris." *Ethnic and Racial Relations*. 10 (1): 48–61

Wieviorka, Michel. 1999. *Violence en France*. Paris: Seuil.

Wolf, Eric. 1969. *Peasant Wars of the Twentieth Century*. Norman: University of Oklahoma Press.

———. 1982. *Europe and the People Without History*. Berkeley: University of California Press.

Wright, Erik Olin. 1997. *Class Counts: Comparative Studies in Class Analysis*. London: Cambridge University Press.

Yang, Mayfair. 1994. *Gifts, Favors, and Banquets: The Art of Social Relationships in China*. Ithaca: Cornell University Press.

Yao, Souchou. 2003. *Confucian Capitalism: Discourse, Practice and the Myth of Chinese Enterprise*. London: Routledge Curzon.

Chapter 9

A CLASH OF HISTORIES IN CANADA'S AUTO INDUSTRY

Belinda Leach

In countries with histories of immigration, class formation is deeply entwined with processes of racialization, debates and practices around citizenship, contested constructions of skill and professional credentials, and cultural expectations of gender and ethnicity. The relative significance and treatment of these varies, according to economic swings, technological developments, labor market demands, and ensuing generous or ungenerous entrance policies.

In this chapter I try to think through some of the implications of encounters between immigrant and non-immigrant[1] workers in the workplace. For countries with sizeable immigrant populations and restructuring economies like Canada, immigrants are often perceived by more-established workers as competing for scarce jobs; a position fueled by anti-immigration political parties and their supporters. Workers' encounters, then, are frequently perceived and experienced as competitive and as fragmenting fragile or potential workplace solidarities. I explore the meaning of workplace friction and constructions of difference, and their implications for worker unity and for understanding class formation in the context of the volatile Canadian automobile parts industry.

My exploration of these issues proceeds from Eric Wolf's insight that rather than examining the single case, we investigate *"processes* that transcend separable cases, moving through and beyond them and transforming them as they proceed" (1982: 17), such that we may "move from a consideration of connections at work in separate cases to a wider perspective, one that will allow us to connect the connections in theory as well as in empirical study" (19). What is needed, then, is an approach that pays attention to how, through the labor process, migration transforms the shape

186 I Belinda Leach

of labor-capital relations and thus capitalism itself, and considers how the incorporation of migrants into workplaces contributes to broader processes of class formation and perhaps to the "unmaking" of old working classes (Silver 2003: 20).

My argument is that, along with their lunch boxes, migrant and native-born workers carry with them personal and collective histories of disruptions in livelihoods and identities that shape their orientations to work, to political action, and to how they perceive each other. Their encounters at work contribute to shaping local economies, with far-reaching implications for class and labor politics, and political identities, as well as for neoliberal agendas. But far from being separate, their histories are linked through colonial and capitalist pasts. I argue that hope for working-class unity requires attention to the individual and collective histories that workers bring to the workplace, but on unequal terms. It demands an understanding of the ways that dominant gendered and racialized national(ist) discourses and narratives mask subordinate histories.

A considerable body of research on migration and economic processes, within and outside anthropology, addresses questions of class, migration, and history. Saskia Sassen has drawn attention to the new social division of labor within cities, a stratification of the labor market in terms of race, ethnicity, and gender as global capital is serviced by an enormous number of people engaged in lower-paid and lower-status work, which she argues has created a new class structure (1991). Many such approaches interrogate the history and construction of segmented labor forces, but tend to focus, as do many anthropological studies, on workplaces where immigrants are isolated from non-immigrants in ethnic or racialized enclaves, in other words, where encounters around the labor process are not taking place.

Anthropologists have contributed to understanding the intersections of class, history, and migration through ethnographic studies that insist on attention to how people live out the abstraction that is referenced by those terms. Josiah Heyman, for example, has produced a body of scholarship, including his contribution in this book (chapter 3), that analyzes processes of racialized class development in the US border area close to Mexico, where documented and undocumented, permanent and cyclical migration shapes and is shaped by border industrialization and resulting labor markets. Shifting relations among Mexican and Anglo workers contribute as well to new class structures. Heyman shows how immigration and citizenship laws and practices influence how labor is allocated to production in both Mexico and the US, and "redound onto labor markets and everyday societal treatment of migrants to encourage, support and justify exploitive class relations" (2001: 129f.).

Histories figure in these processes as people make "waged life" choices among available alternatives about employment in the future, especially when new economic circumstances arise, drawing on gendered experiences of production and consumption activities in the past (Heyman 1990). Histories can be brought to bear on the present "more or less intentionally" and selectively (Giordano 2005: 56), but may equally be marginalized and suppressed, existing only as silent memories (see Carbonella 2005; Sider and Smith 1997). For migrants especially, remembered collective histories help in finding one's bearings in new surroundings, reassuring one of belonging to a larger social body, even when a palpable connection is lost.

Shared histories across national borders are an element of the enduring transnational processes that underlie migration (Basch, Schiller, and Szanton Blanc 1994; Wimmer and Glick Schiller 2002). Migrants connect to their home regions through remittances and other forms of economic support, long-distance care of the young and the elderly, and political identifications and activism in multiple locations. Informed by common histories held dear over time, imagined transnational communities may be especially resilient when return to the actual region of origin is difficult for political or other reasons.

How migrants' histories become subordinated to dominant cultural and class narratives, and with what consequences, emerges as a key question for understanding class processes where large immigrant populations exist. Wolf shows us that ethnic identities are "historical products of labor market segmentation under the capitalist mode" (1982: 381), and following closely Marx's lead, directs us to investigate the labor process as the arena where distinctions among people—of gender, race, ethnicity, and class—are created and reproduced. Attention to the labor process provides a window on "how classes can be formed in specific practical circumstances" (Hales 1980: 112), emphasizing class formation and action on a day-to-day level. Although workers may occupy the same class location structurally, labor relations reproduce and transform identities, often disguising underlying similarities. Yet, as Steve Striffler (2002) and Roger Rouse (1995) suggest, the shared experience of the labor process that transnational migration produces for people from different places may create common class identities, despite ideological attempts to establish firm borders around national identities, allegiances, and citizenships.

Within the labor process, mechanisms of labor control draw on cultural configurations to constitute particular disciplinary regimes (Lee 1998). I argue that these include the strategic foregrounding and submerging of people's histories. In workplaces that employ immigrant and non-immigrant labor these regimes structure, and sometimes dissipate class power along multiple axes, which include constructions of masculinity and femininity, as well as race, ethnicity, language, and citizenship.

Classed Encounters

The point of departure for my exploration of these issues are stories of workplace encounters between workers who had come to Canada from El Salvador and were working in automobile parts plants and those working alongside them.[2] Management's actions to segment workers included making sure people were not positioned physically close to others who spoke the same language. But workers also actively made discursive distinctions between themselves, as immigrant workers, associated with particular nations of origin, and a perceived other they referred to as Canadian. Fernando, a 24-year-old Salvadoran (interview, 19 May 2002) talked about his line, which comprised seventeen people, fourteen of whom regularly worked overtime: "There's only one Canadian who works overtime. The others are Chinese, Hispanics, one from Armenia, one from Africa, one from India, and five Yugoslavians. They work overtime every day." Fernando accused the Canadians of overt racism, and of covering for each other's mistakes. Management, he claimed, ignored it when Canadians slacked off: "The supervisors allowed him, everybody is watching to see why the Canadian is allowed, while the others have to run the machines."

In Fernando's workplace, national origins, attributed or real, are not used merely as a referent to identify difference. They also position people differently in relation to the labor process. In other words, they imply that not all groups of workers carry out the same tasks within the labor process, even when hired to do the same jobs. This leads us to interrogate "the processes of *production* of difference in a world of culturally, socially, and economically interconnected and interdependent spaces" (Gupta and Ferguson 1992: 14; italics in the original), in this case at the point of production.

Anthropologists interested in questions of class have not often investigated workplaces where migrant and locally born workers encounter each other (Lamphere 1992; Lamphere, Stepick, and Grenier 1994), so that the implications—for capital and labor—of such encounters and how they transform workplaces and capitalist labor processes are lost. Nancy Green (1996) considers this issue in her comparative study of garment workers in New York and Paris. She rejects the usual focus on a particular ethnicized group within a specific industrial sector, because, she argues, this leads inevitably to socially constructed categories (hardworking, docile, ambitious, entrepreneurial) that can be applied interchangeably to most groups of immigrant workers. Rather, she calls for a "diachronic and comparative picture" to reveal the contingency of labor segmentation (426), and contribute to understandings of class processes.

Pursuing this particular problematic requires looking at immigrant and non-immigrant workers within the same analytical frame. It calls for an exploration of the political and economic relations of inequality that link refugee Salvadorans and other migrants, *and* the working-class Canadian men and women they meet at work. This means pursuing an examination of the historical constitution of both Canadian and immigrant worker identity. The point is that although these groups appear to encounter each other for the first time side-by-side on an assembly line or work cell, their histories have been entwined through decades of transnational capitalist expansion and contraction. Such material continuity (Lowe 1997: 364) comes into sharp relief when one considers how multinational capital exploits workers in El Salvadoran free-trade zones and, simultaneously, Salvadoran migrants in US and Canadian factories.

Immigrant workers connect to histories of economic forces and exigencies through the legal apparatus of immigration policy (Lowe 1997: 358) that regulates who may come and on what terms, and operates to sustain a global system of domination by clearly classifying the other, and ensuring only limited access to spaces of economic prosperity such as Canada (Gupta and Ferguson 1992). In this "conjuncture of the national and transnational" (De Genova 2005:7) the nation constructs itself, in the Canadian case, as open and compassionate, yet safe and responsible.

The Transnationalized Automobile (Parts) Industry

The context for examining the issues raised by Fernando's workplace relations is the turbulent automobile industry, which is exemplary in terms of the ways labor processes are restructured through transnational processes. Management and production-worker expertise is shared between plants, frequently across national borders. Managers from Japan or the US run Honda and General Motors plants in other countries. Production workers and skilled tradespeople spend weeks at a time in "sister" plants in other countries. There they teach and learn about different technologies and techniques. Sometimes such knowledge transfer prefaces the contraction or closing of the facility whose workers are dispensing their expertise. Hilary Silver argues that auto industry labor militancy in North America and Europe, combined with the competitive threat posed by the success of Japanese automakers, led to major innovations in the automotive labor process. This post-Fordist technological "fix" involved the worldwide adoption and modification of Japanese lean production techniques, including flexible work rules, just-in-time delivery systems, teamwork, quality circles, and the move from vertical integration to outsourcing and subcontracting (Silver 2003: 66f.; see also Rinehart, Huxley, and Robertson 1997). The result is a transnational labor process that looks very much the same from one facility to another, although the character of particular workforces and regimes of control employed varies considerably.

The volatile auto parts industry in Southern Ontario employs about 120,000 people in hundreds of production facilities. It is a major driver of the Canadian economy, spreading to the suburbs and reindustrializing declining rural communities.[3] Some jobs, in plants that long supplied American automakers, are unionized. Once owned by Ford, General Motors, or Chrysler, these were sold to specialized parts makers in the 1970s and 1980s. With few exceptions, more recently established facilities are not unionized. Plants produce the full range of components—engines and seat covers, plastic instrument panels and wiring harnesses—all in direct competition with producers in much lower-wage countries. Competition with Mexican maquila plants is particularly keen because of their physical proximity to US (and to a lesser extent Canadian) assembly plants, and because of NAFTA, and also because many Canadian plants have sister plants in Mexico. Workers hear about the competition they face from Mexican plants on almost a daily basis (Yates and Leach 2006). More recently competition comes from China, other parts of Latin America, and Eastern Europe.

Multinationals like Canadian-owned Linamar and Magna, as well as American, Japanese, and European firms with plants worldwide, are major players in the industry, but there are dozens of others. Parts move by road to Ontario and US assembly plants for just-in-time production, for which flexibility is essential. This means that production is organized, or in older plants re-organized, around assembly lines or "cells"—u-shaped production units where four or five people pass work from one to the next, each performing a different step in the process. Cells are common in the parts industry, usually combined with piecework targets for each shift. For management, cells ensure that workers police themselves and each other to maintain production speeds and meet targets, which form the basis for bonuses and future targets. While assembly lines control workers through repetition, regulated pace, and deskilling, cells rely on older forms of control: a combination of a relatively low hourly wage, piecework, bonuses, penalties for spoiled or reprocessed items, coworker pressure, and direct supervision.

Just-in-time production means that workers face fluctuating demands for their labor individually and collectively. Usually hired first as temporary staff, often through agencies, if they meet management's requirements over several months, they may be made permanent. Even then, the familiar ups and downs of the auto industry, especially for the American assemblers, can mean weeks of mandatory overtime (Saturdays, plus three or four hours following a regular shift, sometimes well into the night after an afternoon shift; Leach and Yates 2007), followed by weeks of short-time or layoff when contracts with those further up the supply chain fail to materialize.

Such turbulence ramifies for people's work lives as a sense of job insecurity for all parts workers. Newspapers report daily on the state of the industry, on the difficulties facing specific companies, and the closure of particular plants, such that workers know their jobs are subject to forces outside their control, or even that of local management. This insecurity itself produces a form of control over workers, which may be the ultimate source of control.

In auto parts labor, men are more likely to work at "heavier" industrial processes, women in sewing and wiring and, historically, women are more likely to be found in parts than assembly. In newer facilities, younger men and women are found in more or less equal numbers, women comprising 30–40 percent of the parts labor force (Yates and Vrankulj 2006: 36). Following historical patterns of settlement, new immigrants have been more likely to work in the larger cities than in smaller cities and towns. Recent studies, however, show that immigrants are moving to the smaller cities to take parts jobs. In 2001 more than half of the five thousand auto parts workers in Guelph, a city of one hundred thousand, were immigrants, and about half of those had arrived since 1991 (37).

The Salvadorans we talked to lived and worked in the many smaller cities west of Toronto where parts factories have proliferated. Kitchener-Waterloo, for example, has received about two thousand Latin American immigrants since 1990, most of them admitted as refugees (Survivors of Torture and Trauma 2000). Three churches in Kitchener offer Spanish services, and according to one parts worker, priests from these visit other communities informally. A Latin American market sells *pupusas* (El Salvador's national dish of thick tortillas). Salvadoran parts workers match the profile of those in the newer plants. Out of fourteen, all but two were under age 25, and most lived with working partners and had small children. Only one had a unionized position, with nine years' seniority, while the rest had worked in their present jobs for one to three years. Kinship networks were important in finding jobs. One man worked at the same facility as his brother and uncle, a woman worked near her daughter, and a husband and wife worked at the same factory as her brother. Given that El Salvador has in recent years become a major remittance economy, it is reasonable to assume that most Salvadorans in Canada must also fulfill obligations to family members at home. All those under age 25 had completed high school in Canada, and this was their first full-time, permanent job.

Histories of Dispossession, Migration, Disruption

Historically, early immigrants to Canada fled poverty and dispossession as capitalist relations engulfed the European countryside. The first Canadian working class was fashioned from "migrants and dispossessed farmers, Irish, English, and Scots, Yankee mechanics and *habitants* moving to the city" (Palmer 1992: 54). On arrival immigrants found themselves constructed as the lowest class of workers, the most super-exploitable, often greatly resented by the more-established working class, many of whom only a few years earlier had occupied just such a position in the labor market. The massive expansion of capitalist enterprises in the late nineteenth century precipitated enormous demand for skilled and unskilled labor. The sources for these workers were rural and urban regions of eastern, western, and southern Europe, fragmenting the more ethnoculturally homogeneous Canadian working class of the previous century (156). They "came from societies which offered little experience with either work discipline or with constitutionalism and trade unionism" (Morrison 1976: 148). Subsequent waves of migrants, as capitalist penetration spread to new areas and changed others, repeated the pattern. Many thousands of the new workers spoke no English or French, which when combined with different regional and sectoral experiences of work, undermined early twentieth century class unity (Palmer 1992: 161f.).

Longer resident and locally born workers have always faced competition from new immigrants willing to work for lower wages, often undermining struggles for improved conditions or pay. Immigrant workers have provided flexibility for employers because they tend to be cheaper, more malleable, and lack (or claim to lack) traditions of proletarianization. Migrant workers in the early Canadian steel industry, for example, saw steel work as temporary, intending to move to other jobs, their own businesses, or back home. In the short term they provided cheap labor, and the bosses intensified the labor process to extract the maximum labor power for the few years they stayed. These workers declined to support their coworkers' demands to shorten the work day at the turn of the twentieth century because they wanted to extract the maximum pay from their labor power (Heron and Storey 1986: 220f.). While immigrants were blamed for the economic ills that beset more established workers, from depressions to failed unionization drives, immigration policy was blamed for not controlling access to the Canadian labor market (Piva 1979: 77).

In the present context, men and women who came to Canada from El Salvador brought with them their particular work histories, and their experiences of the form that relations of political and economic inequality have taken there. The civil war of 1980 to 1992, which pitted left-wing guerrillas intent on revolution against a US-supported government defending the capitalist status quo, followed decades of peasant disenfranchisement. A small country with a large population and land tenure practices that disadvantage the poor, the expansion of cash crop production in rural areas was imposed prior to the war by armed forces and security police forces formed to enforce class divisions (Mahler 1995: 37). Deteriorating rural economic conditions and the civil war itself disrupted the "delicate cycle" of peasant survival, pushing peasants into the towns (38). Urbanization in El Salvador has been less rapid than in other parts of Latin America, but the conflict paved the way for multinationals operating now in El Salvador, presenting new opportunities for work. Peasants and urbanites who formed organizations like unions or were suspected of anti-government activities met quick and often deadly punishment. Ruth Milkman notes a high level of class consciousness among immigrant workers, and a willingness to take risks in union organizing that she attributes to experiences in the home country. One Salvadoran who participated in the Justice for Janitors campaign in California noted "There if you were in a union, they killed you. . . . Here you lost a job at $4.25" (Milkman 2000: 9).

Between 1981 and 2001 more than fifty thousand Salvadorans arrived in Canada, most coming from urban, working-class backgrounds (Garcia 2006). When the civil war ended, migrants continued to flee political and criminal violence and natural disasters, and to seek out their relatives abroad.

Despite oversimplifying the complexities of Canadian immigration histories, these points suggest how broader histories of capitalist expansion and migration, and the policies that support these, constitute relations of inequality and vulnerability lived out in the present and at the workplace. Salvadoran workers' experience of civil war, and what preceded and followed, constitutes a single strand of global economic connections and interdependencies. Salvadorans' personal histories left them with little more to lose. Many had already lost those they loved. They had lived with violence and danger. They left with few material possessions. Disruption in their customary forms of life, rather than the desire to move away from it (Mahler 1995: 55), impelled their journey to Canada.

On arrival in Canada, like other Latin Americans and Asians, Salvadorans fill the "immigrant slot" reserved for the latest embodiment of cheap labor. Constructed by non-immigrant workers as potentially undermining struggles to raise wages and improve work conditions and as actually stealing scarce jobs, these combine with their personal and collective histories, what they know about factory work in El Salvador, their commitment to support family members still living in El Salvador,[4] and their status and experiences as refugees, to contribute to their subjectivities.

Their histories contrast with those of the non-immigrant workers they encounter. Many of these grew up in a post-war period that promised steady jobs for men, encouraging them to develop appropriate work habits and, as Roger Rouse describes for American-born workers in the same era, to anticipate "stable, lifelong trajectories and (often) steady upward mobility" (1995: 374). Through their unions, traditional Fordist workers fought for improved pay and work conditions, gains that ramified more generally in workplaces across the country, but that in the 1980s and 1990s were rolled back through the efforts of neoliberal governments anxious to attract multinational capital and trade in a highly competitive global environment. During the same period, as Canada negotiated free trade agreements with the US and Mexico, capital flight to lower-wage regions, including the US "right-to-work" states,[5] contributed to a sense that Canadian jobs were at constant risk from workers elsewhere, willing and often desperate enough to work for starvation wages. In a free-trade environment, the notion that in Mexico workers gladly accept $5 for a day's work became part of popular discourse on the "new world of work" at the turn of the twenty-first century. In practice, flexibility and the growth of contingency across industrial sectors have made the conditions and pay traditionally associated with "women's work" observed across the spectrum of men's jobs (Armstrong 1996), while ideological campaigns, combined with tougher labor policies and the reorganization of the labor process to disrupt shop floor alliances, have made it difficult for workers to organize.

With the shift to flexible, transnational forms of accumulation, workers have come to realize that the promise of a better future through hard work has been broken. This constitutes a rupture in expectations for non-immigrant workers, albeit of a different kind from that experienced by newer immigrant workers. For both, dispossession—at different historical moments and taking very different forms—characterizes their histories and intersects with the present.

Entwined Histories and Disciplinary Regimes

Lisa Lowe (1997) argues that restructuring can be measured by the synchronous displacement of first-world workers and increase in migration. Yet, the global economy's apparently insatiable need for cheap labor is in tension with the nation-state's desire to control immigration. Cold War rhetoric, that divided the world neatly into two, created political alignments that echo in the contemporary movements and receptions of migrants. While the communist world was dangerous, other parts, like most of Central America, were contested and unstable. Through specific state policies some of those who fled such places could be admitted to countries like Canada. As Heyman (chapter 3) discusses, in particular national contexts migrants, especially undocumented ones, are constituted as a "risk" and as a threat to the state. Immigration, then, is a key site where the contradictions of the restructured global economy and the security-conscious nation-state are played out, and these tensions are evident not only at border entry points. They also converge on the shop floor and are lived out by workers who bring to work their specific histories of colonialism, decolonization, national struggles, capitalist development, and multinational incursions.

Contradictions play out in other ways as well. As Luin Goldring (1998) suggests, migrants may struggle against oppression in one place, yet be committed to forms of exploitation in another. Salvadoran workers we interviewed denied any experience with labor unions, a position that Linda Green (personal communication) suggests is a form of self-protection, and that fits with reports that at one plant, management was fighting unionization attempts and actively seeking the ringleaders. In this particular context, then, workers choose not to organize politically at their workplaces, in contrast to the Latin American workers Però discusses in chapter 4. Contradictions are lived also by Canadian-born workers, especially men, as they confront every day the disruption between the stable work life they expected and the one they live. Lowe points out: "The contradictions through which immigration brings national institutions into crisis produces immigrant cultures as oppositional and contestatory" (1997: 369).

These contradictions play into prevailing disciplinary regimes. To modify Ching Kwan Lee's (1998: 165) definition, factory regimes are institutions in which gender, racialization, and dominant discourses of progress and modernization are central and primary organizing principles of production politics. I argue that to be effective, regimes must mask connected histories and subvert class identification and solidarity. In the southern Ontario auto parts industry disciplinary regimes are constituted through the combination of worker insecurity (immigrant and non-immigrant, and all gendered and racialized), flexible labor processes with particular mechanisms for control, and dominant narratives that privilege the losses to labor in recent decades, especially to male workers, and silence subordinate histories.

Although the popular narrative is of loss, scholars debate whether native-born workers are *replaced* or *displaced* by racialized workers, that is whether they move willingly out of particular jobs as new ones became available or retire (Waldinger 1986; Milkman 2000), or, alternatively, are reluctantly pushed out as immigrants willing to take lower wages flood the labor market (Sassen 1988). Anthropological research suggests that a major factor here concerns the dynamics of the local labor market. Sarah Mahler (1995: 7–14 and 108–111) considers the displacement/replacement debate in the context of suburban Long Island, where the aerospace industry has generated work in core firms for fairly small numbers of skilled, white workers, and has indirectly created many more jobs in supplier firms, attracting newer immigrant workers away from the inner city while still, Mahler concludes, sustaining a well-differentiated and mutually exclusive dual labor market.

The expansion of auto parts in southern Ontario has also created a dual labor market structure, but I would argue that unlike Mahler's context, there is opportunity for mobility between them. Two rural and one suburban automobile assembly plants, all established since 1980, and despite the industry's volatility all expanding their labor forces since, have created hundreds of well-paid jobs within them, as well as thousands of lower-paid jobs in the supplier parts firms. Unlike Mahler's case where second tier jobs are at the very low end of the labor market, jobs in the second tier of the Ontario auto industry pay between $12 and $25 per hour, considerably more than the minimum wage of $8. In the present economic context, these jobs are quite desirable for immigrant and non-immigrant workers contending with a labor market saturated with minimum wage service jobs. Furthermore, as the assembly plants expand their workforces, workers in the parts sector feel well prepared to take those jobs. Immigrant and non-immigrant parts workers wait for word that one or other of the assembly plants "are hiring," joining thousands of other hopeful applicants at every round. And, unlike Mahler's case, my research indicates that immigrant parts workers do get hired into the assembly plants, where the best paid blue-collar jobs in the country command $30 per hour or more.

Processes of racialization, then, do not operate solely through the structuring of the labor market, rather they need to be effected through the day-to-day practices of workers and employers themselves, in the labor process. These practices work in combination with dominant class-based, masculinist, and nationalist narratives that mask the deep historical connections among different workers, including women and immigrants. Such processes cast immigrant workers and their histories as subordinate,[6] thus less likely to benefit from management's largesse in the present work situation, and to imagine themselves as highly paid assembly plant workers.

The capitalist labor process is fundamentally about ensuring exploitation through control. In the past, with stronger unions, Canadian workers exercized a degree of informal control over their own labor process, able to structure their work rhythms through manipulating elements of it, such as contriving stoppages for minor machine problems, or playing the system (Burawoy 1979). Such informal control has been undermined by labor process restructuring in recent decades, structuring the experience of class so as to limit its oppositional character (Thompson 1983: 232; see also Labrecque, chapter 10). New processes, like the cell system, are difficult to cheat and they further undermine class unity because they provoke a form of coworker policing that both relies on and fuels racialized differentiation among workers. Parts workers reported numerous arguments with coworkers over the pace of work, shift allocations, and access to and acceptance of overtime, conflicts frequently tinged in their reporting with ideas about ethnicity, race, and nationality.

Alicia Schmidt Camacho (1999) points out that under classic Fordism, white, male, and often skilled workers had a relatively high degree of control over the sale of their labor and their productivity. Loss of control at the individual workplace and in the labor market more generally, together with the state's withdrawal of many elements of the social safety net, contribute to a narrative of working-class loss that has become dominant, especially within the organized labor movement. Schmidt Camacho argues that the contemporary American labor movement relies on evocations of the past that focus on privileged workers' pre-eminence in the global labor market, and the moral basis of their pact with the regulatory state. For her, American labor leaders exhibit persistent faith in expansionary capitalism and market growth. A similar narrative of loss—of good pay and benefits, of union and state protection—is evident in the Canadian labor movement and among Canadian workers who have seen better times, as I have described for steelworkers threatened by shocks to their industry (Leach 1998, 2002).

Schmidt Camacho points out that North American labor's gains were, of course, contingent on exploitation of natural resources and labor in the developing world, aided by Cold War and pro-development policies. David Sheinin (1994) argues that Canadian policy in Latin America through the twentieth century was conditioned by adherence to American foreign policies, and that Canadian business interests collaborated with government in shaping Canada-Latin America relations, primarily as an opportunity for entrepreneurial expansion. An aid agreement between Canada and El Salvador in the 1980s, lauded as upholding regional stability, helped to entrench inequality through support to the non-democratic regime.

Through the 1980s and 1990s economic restructuring in Canada, connected to multinational expansion into cheaper labor markets, pulled the rug from under the feet of workers who had grown up with the idea of a steady lifelong job. As the lean workplace and contingent work became more common experiences, the popular target for blame—for workers and their managers—was the impoverished maquila worker, whose low daily wage drew work away from well-paid Canadians. Plant closures in Canada in the 1980s created a general sense of job insecurity, enhanced by actual threats that work could easily be moved "to Mexico" (Yates and Leach 2006). Schmidt Camacho argues that since the 1970s workers in developing areas have been the "other" of the white, male, skilled, and privileged worker. The dominant image for the international division of labor that emerged in the 1970s was the Third World woman, characterizing a feminized workforce associated with "capitalists' strategic maintenance of low levels of labor militancy and unionization, higher rates of turnover in jobs, weakened job security, high levels of surveillance and lower wages" (Schmidt Camacho 1999); in short, everything that Canadian workers had fought against for a century.

In this context, immigrant workers who now compete for work in a restructured economy, especially if they come from the maquila-friendly states of Central America, are constructed as a largely undifferentiated but feminized surplus labor force bearing devalued labor. The one unionized Salvadoran parts worker told us: "They keep calling me names, you know what I mean? But to my face, but it doesn't bother me. Like Mexican, or this and this, and how do you like to eat burritos?" Schmidt Camacho argues that even at union conventions American workers are exposed to racial and gender discourses that reduce workers from and in low-wage regions to "an endlessly renewable and disposable repository of surplus value" (1999: 7). This feminization combined with the racialization of immigrant labor is notably divergent from how immigrant workers in earlier waves were constructed. As the case of the Irish in North America clearly shows, earlier immigrants were racialized, but I would argue that they were simultaneously hyper-masculinized. The present combination of feminization and racialization in the insertion of migrants into labor processes in high-wage countries is new.

When non-immigrant workers are treated preferentially by management, as Fernando witnessed, their cross-class alliance puts on display the unequal power relations between immigrant and non-immigrant workers. From the other side, the presence of immigrant workers reminds non-immigrants that such an alliance is unstable, and they can be easily replaced. Class conflict, always inflected by race, gender, ethnicity, and citizenship, is distorted through the disciplinary regime to appear as crude ethnic conflict.

A Clash of Histories?

Maria, a 24-year-old Salvadoran (interview, 20 May 2002), has trained herself to be able to perform a number of jobs at her plant, because that way she feels more secure and gets more overtime. With determination she has worked out how to perform faster than her coworkers, so she can easily pass her targets. She blames an injury she sustained at work on her own lack of attention. Ana, who is also 24-years-old and also from El Salvador (interview, 18 May 2002) and who works at the same place, says that people who are lazy get fired, but "if they see you are a hard worker the job is secure." She says she works lots of overtime "so they don't close my line." Sometimes that backfires: "They don't mind if the person took a break or his lunch, they just see that the person did a certain number of parts in eight hours and that's what they are going to put as a target."[7]

Immigrant workers fight to construct themselves as "hard workers" in comparison to non-immigrants, as they have done historically, no matter where they have come from (Green 1996). Those overseas, who rely on remittances from Ontario, compel workers not only to work hard to hold on to their jobs, but may also inhibit political mobilization at the workplace.[8] Workers are supported in their desire to work hard by capital and the state. A *New York Times* article (Roger Cohen, "Vive la dolce vita," 16 April 2006) reported that the English dictation test for new US citizens includes the sentence "I plan to work hard every day." In this construction, immigrants are complicit in the intensification of the labor process, as they are when they take overtime as often as it is offered, allowing management a legal route to extend work hours beyond the regular eight and echoing nineteenth-century struggles between non-immigrant and immigrant workers around the length of the working day. Their actions allow the multiple forms of flexibility that employers use—overtime, piecework, and temporary work—to go unchallenged, and to be effective. Salvadoran parts workers try to ensure security in an unstable work environment by missing breaks and setting new piecework standards. Catching the attention of the supervisor because they work hard not only protects one's own job, it potentially creates jobs for friends and family as employers actively seek out new workers with similar work attitudes (sometimes, according to these workers, explicitly replacing less hardworking non-immigrant workers). But workers must also contend with conflicts that emerge from these work habits. Another Salvadoran woman (interview, 18 May 2002) described how a Philippine coworker criticized her and her husband for taking overtime when in her view they should be looking after their daughter.

Constructions of labor force segments and the practices that flow from those accrue immediate benefits to immigrant workers, as they always have, but ultimately the greater benefits are to capital. As immigrant workers acquiesce to flexible work (see also Lem, chapter 8) they reinforce neoliberal reconfigurations. The confrontations between immigrant and non-immigrant workers should be seen, then, not as a history of clashes as they are often represented, but rather as a clash of histories, a product and continuation of a process that has unfolded over a long period that meshes multiple histories of colonialism and capitalist expansion, but reduces these to simple difference. When certain histories are subordinated to dominant working class, masculinist, and nationalist narratives, the major loss is to class unity.

Roger Rouse (1995: 372f.) argues that immigrants are key players in the processes aided by ruling classes that determine how coalitions are formed, strengthening lines of difference and regulating forms of interaction. He stresses that encounters among immigrants and with those who are locally born provides two possibilities: for worsening tensions between groups and that people might develop new understandings and build broader and more effective coalitions. In Nicholas De Genova's ethnography of Mexican workers in Chicago a man rebuked his coworkers for their constant preoccupation with events in Mexico. He demanded they acknowledge the problem they all confronted at work: "Why worry about what's happening over there? You're here and here you have to worry about Tia Rita [the firm's personnel manager]" (2005: 149).

In some workplaces class unity emerges despite difference. Steve Striffler (2002: 312) reports how the following comment captured with humor and veracity the reality for workers in an American chicken processing plant, despite their different national origins: "We're all Mexicans here. Screwed-over Mexicans." "Mexican" becomes almost a synonym for "worker" at the plant, a classed term, but signaling a racialized identity for those doing the worst kind of work; those not racialized as much as those who are. In another Canadian auto parts factory, Luis, from El Salvador (interview, 3 June 2002) talked about the difficulties of working alongside people whose language he doesn't understand, and who, like himself, don't speak much English. After a minute or two he stopped the conversation with a hand gesture, refusing to submit to its logical direction. "We understand each other," he said.

For this to happen, and to contribute to more broadly effective forms of class unity, immigrant and non-immigrant workers must set to one side (but not forget) histories and historical differences and recognize both their shared pasts of capitalist dispossession and their present collective circumstances.

Notes

My thanks to Pauline Gardiner Barber, Winnie Lem, and anonymous reviewers for editorial advice. This is a slightly modified version of an essay originally published in 2008 in *Focaal: European Journal of Anthropology* 51: 43–56. The research on which this chapter is based has been supported by research grants from the Social Sciences and Humanities Research Council of Canada and the Tri-Council National Centre of Excellence on the Automobile in the Twenty-first Century.

1. Finding succinct terms to capture the complexities of migrant and non-migrant subjectivities while also speaking to the international literature on migration and fitting the Canadian context is a challenge. In Canada the term *migrant* usually refers to a person allowed entry to work on a short-term contract, for example in seasonal agricultural work or through the live-in caregiver program, distinguished from an *immigrant*, who has permanent resident status. I use the term immigrant here because the people I refer to have permanent resident status. The obverse of that category, those *perceived* as not-immigrants I refer to here as "non-immigrant." However it is quite likely that in popular usage this category includes people who came to Canada as immigrants but do not present as such because English is their first language, they have white skin, they have been here for many years, etc.

2. These encounters are reported in interviews carried out in 2002 by María Cristina Manzano-Munguia, research assistant for a multidisciplinary research project, Labour and Social Cohesion. Manzano-Munguia sought out Latin American auto parts workers who were known to be working in auto parts plants, mainly those without unions. All those she contacted had come to Canada from El Salvador. The interviews supplement the body of ethnographic data on the Ontario automobile industry that I have been gathering over the last eight years. They have stimulated the theoretical questions I explore here. Thus the article is not ethnography-based, but rather suggests a need for more ethnography on this subject.

3. For more on rural industrial restructuring in Ontario, see Winson and Leach (2002).

4. Overseas remittances support one in five families in El Salvador (Mahler 1995).

5. "Right-to-work" states are those that have enforced legislation that prohibits unions from compelling workers to join, i.e., workers have the right to work despite not

joining a union. This legislation makes it difficult to unionize workplaces and weakens existing unions' capacity to improve wages and working conditions.

6. This process is reinforced by broader practices of cultural subordination, such as recent municipal policies in one small town in Quebec, which explicitly target and ban practices like carrying a Kirpan and covering the face. Debates over "reasonable cultural accommodations" are now widespread in Canada, as they have been in Europe for some time.

7. These actions are consistent with what Pauline Gardiner Barber and I have called "performed subordination," as workers choose to present themselves as the kind of worker they perceive their managers desire. See chapter 7.

8. I thank a reviewer for pointing this out.

References

Armstrong, Pat. 1996. "The Feminization of the Labour Force: Harmonizing Down in a Global Economy." In *Rethinking Restructuring: Gender and Change in Canada*, ed. Isabella Bakker, 29–54. Toronto: University of Toronto Press.

Basch, Linda, Nina Glick Shiller, and Cristina Szanton Blanc. 1994. *Nations Unbound: Transnational Projects, Postcolonial Predicaments and Deterritorialized Nation States*. Langhorne: Gordon and Breach.

Burawoy, Michael. 1979. *Manufacturing Consent: Changes in the Labor Process Under Monopoly Capitalism*. Chicago: University of Chicago Press.

Carbonella, August. 2005. "Beyond the Limits of the Visible World: Remapping Historical Anthropology." In *Critical Junctions: Anthropology and History Beyond the Cultural Turn*, eds. Don Kalb and Herman Tak, 88–108. New York and Oxford: Berghahn Books.

De Genova, Nicholas. 2005. *Working the Boundaries: Race, Space, and "Illegality" in Mexican Chicago*. Durham and London: Duke University Press.

Garcia, Maria Cristina. 2006. *Canada: A Refuge for Central Americans*. Washington, D.C.: Migration Policy Institute.

Giordano, Christian. 2005. "The Past in the Present: Actualized History in the Social Construction of Reality." In *Critical Junctions: Anthropology and History Beyond the Cultural Turn*, eds. Don Kalb and Herman Tak, 53–71. New York and Oxford: Berghahn Books.

Goldring, Luin. 1998. "The Power of Status in Transnational Social Fields." In *Transnationalism from Below*, eds. Michael P. Smith and Luis Guarnizo. New Brunswick: Transaction Publishers.

Green, Nancy. 1996. "Women and Immigrants in the Sweatshop: Categories of Labor Segmentation Revisited." *Comparative Studies in Society and History* 38 (3): 411–433.

Gupta, Akhil, and James Ferguson. 1992. "Beyond 'Culture': Space, Identity and the Politics of Difference." *Cultural Anthropology* 7 (1): 6–23.

Hales, Mike. 1980. *Living Thinkwork: Where do Labour Processes Come From?* London: CSE Books.

Heron, Craig, and Robert Storey. 1986. "Work and Struggle in the Canadian Steel Industry, 1900–1950." In *On the Job: Confronting the Labour Process in Canada*, eds. Craig Heron and Robert Storey, 210–244. Montreal and Kingston: McGill-Queen's University Press.

Heyman, Josiah McC. 1990. "The Emergence of the Waged Life Course on the United States-Mexico Border." *American Ethnologist* 17 (2): 348–359.

———. 2001. "Class and Classification at the U.S.-Mexico Border." *Human Organization* 60 (2): 128–140.

Lamphere, Louise, ed. 1992. *Structuring Diversity: Ethnographic Perspectives on the New Immigration.* Chicago: University of Chicago Press.

Lamphere, Louise, Alex Stepick, and Guillermo Grenier, eds. 1994. *Newcomers in the Workplace: Immigrants and the Restructuring of the U.S. Economy.* Philadelphia: Temple University Press.

Leach, Belinda. 1998. "Citizenship and the Politics of Exclusion in a 'Post'-Fordist Industrial City." *Critique of Anthropology* 18 (2): 181–204.

———. 2002. "Class, Discipline, and the Politics of Opposition in Ontario." In *Culture, Economy, Power: Anthropology as Critique, Anthropology as Praxis,* eds. Winnie Lem and Belinda Leach, 191–205. Albany: SUNY Press.

Leach, Belinda, and Charlotte Yates. 2007. "Gendering Social Cohesion." In *Workers and Social Cohesion,* ed. Robert O'Brien., 21–37. Vancouver: University of British Columbia Press.

Lee, Ching Kwan. 1998. *Gender and the South China Miracle: Two Worlds of Factory Women.* Berkeley: University of California Press.

Lowe, Lisa. 1997. "Work, Immigration, Gender: New Subjectivities of Cultural Politics." In *The Politics of Culture in the Shadow of Capital,* eds. Lisa Lowe and David Lloyd, 364–375. Durham: Duke University Press.

Mahler, Sarah J. 1995. *American Dreaming: Immigrant Life on the Margins.* Princeton: University of Princeton Press.

Milkman, Ruth. 2000. "Introduction." In *Organizing Immigrants: The Challenge for Unions in Contemporary California,* ed. Ruth Milkman, 1–24. Ithaca: ILR Press.

Morrison, Jean. 1976. "Ethnicity and Violence: The Lakehead Freight Handlers Before World War I." In *Essays in Canadian Working Class History,* eds. Gregory S. Kealey and Peter Warrian, 143–160. Toronto: McClelland and Stewart.

Palmer, Bryan. 1992. *Working Class Experience: Rethinking the History of Canadian Labour, 1800–1991.* Toronto: McClelland and Stewart.

Piva, Michael J. 1979. *The Condition of the Working Class in Toronto, 1900–1921.* Ottawa: University of Ottawa Press.

Rinehart, James W., Christopher Huxley, and David Robertson. 1997. *Just Another Car Factory? Lean Production and its Discontents.* Ithaca: ILR Press.

Rouse, Roger. 1995. "Thinking Through Transnationalism: Notes on the Cultural Politics of Class Relations in the Contemporary United States." *Public Culture* 7: 353–402.

Sassen, Saskia. 1988. *The Mobility of Labour and Capital.* Cambridge: Cambridge University Press.

———. 1991. *The Global City: New York, London, Tokyo.* Princeton: Princeton University Press.

Schmidt Camacho, Alicia. 1999. "On the Borders of Solidarity: Race and Gender Contradictions in the 'New Voice' Platform of the AFL-CIO." *Social Justice* 26 (3): 79–102.

Sheinin, David. 1994. "Between War and Peace in Central America: Choices for Canada." Review article. *Journal of Canadian Studies* 29 (2): 176–188.

Sider, Gerald, and Gavin Smith. 1997. *Between History and Histories: The Making of Silences and Commemorations.* Toronto: University of Toronto Press.

Silver, Hilary. 2003. *Forces of Labor: Workers' Movements and Globalization since 1870.* Cambridge: Cambridge University Press.

Striffler, Steve. 2002. "Inside a Poultry Processing Plant: An Ethnographic Portrait." *Labor History* 43 (3): 305–313.

Survivors of Torture and Trauma Working Group. 2000. *Building Community Support for Refugees Community.* Kitchener, Ontario.

Thompson, Paul. 1983. *The Nature of Work: An Introduction to Debates on the Labour Process.* London: MacMillan.

Waldinger, Roger. 1986. *Through the Eye of a Needle: Immigrants and Enterprise in New York's Garment Trades.* New York: New York University Press.

Wimmer, Andreas, and Nina Glick Schiller. 2002. "Methodological Nationalism and the Study of Migration." *Archives of European Sociology* XLIII (2): 217–240.

Winson, Anthony, and Belinda Leach. 2002. *Contingent Work, Disrupted Lives: Labour and Community in the New Rural Economy.* Toronto: University of Toronto Press.

Wolf, Eric. 1982. *Europe and the People Without History.* Berkeley: University of California Press.

Yates, Charlotte A. B., and Belinda Leach. 2006. "Why 'Good' Jobs Lead to Social Exclusion." *Economic and Industrial Democracy* 27 (3): 341–468.

Yates, Charlotte A. B., and Sam Vrankulj. 2006. Labour as a Competitive Advantage in the Canadian Automotive Parts Industry: A Study of Canada and Four Local Labour Markets. Hamilton: Labour Studies Program, McMaster University.

— *Chapter 10* —

MEXICAN WORKER DEMOBILIZATION AND THE GLOBAL ECONOMY

Marie France Labrecque
Translated by Mary Richardson

As I was conducting research on maquiladoras in the state of Yucatán between 1995 and 2005, I found the lack of worker mobilization and the invisibility of unions in the maquiladora sector rather baffling. Part of an explanation for this state of affairs has been provided by specialists on the issue in Yucatán, such as Beatriz Castilla Ramos and Beatriz Torres Góngora (2007: 53–54), who have shown how Taylorism has gradually been supplanted in maquiladoras by new forms of work organization (NFWO). In their view these NFWOs have helped to create a new figure of the worker that is shaped by transnationally tested methods and transcends the local conditions of workers. The characteristics of NFWOs include a new labor-management style based on the organization of production in work groups and an emphasis on consensus rather than confrontation. In this context unions are considered virtually obsolete.

While labor organization in these companies seems to have changed the workers, the wages are not, however, quite so transformative. The Mexican department of labor (Secretaría del Trabajo y Previsión Social) issued a news item pointing out that in 2005 a maquiladora worker earned an average of 73 pesos a day (about $10 at the time). This was the lowest level of all Mexican states and was not enough to purchase a basic food basket[1]; it was far below the national average of 104.5 pesos a day or the maximum of 120 pesos a day in the state of Nuevo León (Presidency of the Republic 2005).

In other words (to use an unoriginal concept) the overwork of maquiladora employees goes beyond necessary labor to such an extent that, considering the wages they receive, they can be said to be exploited. It is true that the work conditions in maquiladoras are not always so bad: some companies even promote socializing between supervisors and workers on birthdays and other festive occasions and attempts are made to attract and hold on to workers by providing high-quality cafeterias, recreational facilities and opportunities to participate in sports tournaments (Castilla Ramos and Torres Góngora 2007: 59; Juárez Núñez 2007).

Exploitation clearly can take on different forms in the context of a global economy. It may even be mitigated by the possibility of receiving a bonus, incentives, and even gifts, but I would maintain that its effects remain much the same as they were under Taylorism. Are NFWOs a sufficient explanation for worker demobilization? What about unionism? Is it really obsolete in the context of maquiladoras? Does it not play a role in the demobilization that I felt I was observing in Yucatán?

Features of Mexican Unionism

Placing unionism and demobilization side by side may seem surprising, but it is less so when we consider the specificities of Mexican unionism. In studying the phenomenon, the issues of *charros*[2]—or corporatist unions— as well as the much talked-about "protection contracts" soon arise. Specialists in labor relations have defined corporatist unionism as "a conglomerate of relations and mutual support between unions, the State and entrepreneurs" (Hermanson and de la Garza Toledo 2005: 183). *Charros* unions are part of the national landscape, particularly in maquiladoras and transnational corporations such as Wal-Mart. Here is how the system works: "When a company decides to establish a maquiladora in Mexico, a meeting takes place with local authorities in which the company is presented with a catalog of central labor councils. The company proceeds to choose one, signs a collective contract committing to minimal conditions required by law" (Fernández 2002: 463).

According to Dale Hathaway (2002: 427) "over 90% of total collective labor contracts in Mexico are designed primarily to protect the interest of the employer." Protection contracts are so effective in demobilizing workers that the formula is spreading to other countries. In a recent issue of *Proceso*, a Mexican magazine, a representative of the Inter American Regional Organisation of Workers[3] declared that "in recent years, in addition to migrants, Mexico has been exporting protection contracts to Latin American countries such as Venezuela, Peru and Colombia."[4]

A criticism of Mexican corporatist unionism and its role in worker demobilization must take into account the specific historical features of the regions where it exists as well as their class structure. Other factors such as gender and race may also come into play, depending on specific situations. In tracing the development of maquiladoras in various regions of Mexico, such as Chihuahua[5] and Yucatán, the gradual demobilization of workers—or the absence of mobilization—becomes apparent. Regardless of their increasing heterogeneity, these enterprises of transnational corporations all have the same imperative: to produce commodities at the lowest possible cost while fulfilling highly time-sensitive supply contracts. Whatever the sector may be, they import parts or materials into the host country, assemble them, and export the finished product to the country of origin. They are therefore looking for the greatest possible comparative advantage, which varies depending on the generation of the maquiladora in question.[6]

The most important comparative advantage for first-generation maquiladoras, which require a large labor force, is precisely that of reduced labor costs. The importance of low-cost labor, however, tends to decrease with second- and third-generation maquiladoras. Many other factors may enter into the equation, but when a ready-made garment maquiladora chooses China over Mexico, for example, it is first and foremost because labor costs in China are sufficiently lower than in Mexico (even with the increase in transportation costs). The same scenario can also be played out within the country when maquiladoras choose one region over another. This was what happened in Mexico when clothing maquiladoras—typically first-generation and initially located on the northern border—began moving into southern states such as Yucatán.

For many years—even long after legislation allowed them to move further inside the country—maquiladoras were associated with the northern border. The association was so strong that when the Yucatán government began trying to attract maquiladoras, its advertising featured connections to the "other border" (an expression that was used explicitly) and emphasized its proximity to Florida or Louisiana by sea. In reality, Chihuahua and Yucatán are worlds apart, and about the only feature they have in common is that there are maquiladoras in both states. It is the differences rather than the similarities that make the comparison interesting and worthwhile. One of the differences is that the workers in Chihuahuan maquiladoras have come to the state mainly through waves of migration, whereas in Yucatán maquiladoras have been built in towns where workers were available on site or from nearby localities. It is a perfect opportunity to highlight the relation between worker mobility and mobilization. Although there are several ways to examine mobilization, I will do so through unionism (or the lack thereof). Unionism and maquiladoras will constitute the two strands of my argument, first for the country as a whole, then for each of the states being discussed.

Decline of Unionism and Multiplying Maquiladoras in Mexico

Internationally it seems clear that since the 1980s neoliberal globalization and capitalist restructuring have radically changed the working class and have weakened its power (Hodkinson 2005: 37). Almost everywhere in the world there has been a decline in the density of unionism since the 1980s (Ramasamy 2005: 13–14). As far as the labor market, the labor movement, and unionization are concerned, the situation in Mexico echoes the international situation. Between 1984 and 2000 the density of union membership in the formal sector dropped from 30 percent to 20 percent. Some researchers even estimate the current rate of unionization in Mexico to be 10 percent (Zepeda 2004).[7]

Although affected by neoliberal globalization, Mexican unionism has its own history. Since the vast majority of unions belong to large central trade unions founded between the 1930s and the 1950s—principally the Confederación de Trabajadores Mexicanos (CTM) and the Confederación Revolucionaria de Obreros y Campesinos (CROC),[8] which are under the umbrella of the Labor Congress (Congreso de Trabajo, or CT)—they have been controlled by the Partido Revolucionario Institucional (PRI). Particularly since the foundation of the CTM in the 1930s, a pact between the unions and the government has prevailed, resulting in the corporate system known as *charro*. Although this pact has been upset from time to time—most notably by the decrease in real wages after the peso crisis in the 1980s—until 2000 the social space continued to be controlled by organizations (including unions) connected to the State party (PRI; Bizberg 2003: 225–228).

With the defeat of PRI in the 2000 presidential elections, government control over the labor movement weakened, but the control of the older corporatist union elite did not. Currently, the Partido de Acción Nacional (PAN) continues to accept and even support the control of *charros* unions over workers (Roman and Velasco Arregui 2006: 96) and there is nothing to suggest that the situation has changed with the election of Felipe Calderón in July 2006. As De la Garza Toledo (2003: 20) has pointed out, "the interference of the Department of Labour in labour relations is part of a tradition that is hard to eradicate."

Despite the domination of corporatism, independent unionism was present throughout the twentieth century. In 1997 the Unión Nacional de Trabajadores (UNT) was created, the first independent confederation since the 1940s that brings together approximately one hundred and sixty independent unions.[9] The UNT, however, has not been able to constitute a significant counterweight to traditional unionism, nor has it been able to attract large unions. Under the Federal Labor Act (Ley Federal del Trabajo),[10] workers are not free to leave one union to join another and it is practically impossible for independent unions to recruit members from industries whose members already belong to another union. It is also difficult to form new unions because the department of labor still controls the registration of unions and their executive committees and it defines the legal terms for strikes (Bizberg 2003: 232–233). In short, it can be said that in spite of economic restructuring and the pressure workers feel on their living conditions, corporatist unionism continues to dominate the labor movement in Mexico.

Several researchers maintain that corporatist unionism, in particular, has in fact worsened workers' living conditions as official unions accepted a decrease in real wages to pre-1980s levels in an attempt to curb inflation. They also agreed to flexible collective labor contracts and they turned a blind eye to setbacks in social security for the sake of healthy government finance. Both union and non-union wages have declined, but union wages even more so (Hermanson and de la Garza Toledo 2005: 184). This means that union wages have been leveled downward, whereas the opposite would have seemed more likely. The labor movement is therefore facing a restructuring of social classes whereby the formal proletariat is getting poorer. What is more, and as Frances Rothstein (chapter 2) also shows with her own case study, as women move into the labor market in greater numbers, this class restructuring is also taking place along gender lines. Throughout Latin America there is an increasing parity between men and women in the formal proletariat. In Mexico it can be seen in the maquiladoras where women still represent over 50 percent of the labor force. Nonetheless, "women's increasing parity with men in terms of class position did not come from women's improving conditions . . . but rather from men 'falling down' the class ladder. . . . The increasing supply of women workers . . . may be one mechanism 'lowering the bar' for all workers, and perhaps 'emasculating' the Latin American work force, both literally and figuratively" (Bellone Hite and Viterna 2005: 78). More specifically, in maquiladoras "the workers . . . face conditions of superexploitation, but in situations and locations to which they are often newcomers" (Roman and Velasco Arregui 2001: 60). These companies first appeared on the northern border with the creation of the Programa de Industrialización Fronteriza in 1965. Under the program, inputs and components could be imported, assembled and exported without paying taxes, except on the value added in Mexico. The program's function was to create jobs for the hundreds of workers who became unemployed after the end of the Bracero Program (1942–1964), which gave seasonal job contracts in the United States to Mexican farm workers (de la O Martínez 2006a: 406).

Maquiladoras therefore first developed along the border with the United States.[11] In the late 1980s they began moving into the interior of the Republic after the government's export programs were changed (de la O Martínez 2006a: 406). Thereafter, NAFTA gave a new incentive for maquiladoras to set up shop in Mexico. The increase in the number of companies and workers lasted until the 2001 crisis in the United States and China's entry into the World Trade Organization. Today Mexico has almost three thousand maquiladoras that provide slightly more than one million jobs. The decline is more relative than what is generally maintained, especially in terms of the number of jobs, which still represents 91 percent of what it was in 2000, while the number of businesses is 76 percent of what it was in the same year (Contreras and Munguía 2007: 75).

The State of Chihuahua: Workers Flock to the Border

Chihuahua is one of six states on the northern border of Mexico with Baja California, Coahuila, Nuevo León, Sonora, and Tamaulipas. The territory of Chihuahua has been traveled for thousands of years by nomadic or semi-nomadic indigenous peoples who have been displaced and driven back by migrants either from within the country or from abroad, especially as of the nineteenth century (Chávez Chávez 2003: 60). Chihuahua's economic landscape has been dominated since that time by entrepreneurs in the agricultural and livestock sector, in mining or in logging. Under Porfirio Díaz[12] mining resources belonged to foreign interests. In fact, one of the high points in the labor movement in Chihuahua was in 1883 when the workers in a mine belonging to the Compañía Minera de Pinos Altos (a North American company) went on strike. The strike was put down by the army, which shot the miners considered to be leaders. This episode is considered to be the first formal effort by workers to defend their rights (Estado de Chihuahua 2005).

It was not until the 1960s–1970s that changes to production became increasingly apparent throughout the state. In that lapse of time the number of people employed in the industry experienced a relative increase of 53.5 percent. Workers in the commercial sector increased by 90 percent. Subsistence agriculture declined significantly in favor of mechanized irrigated agriculture. In other words wage workers made up a larger portion of the overall population. The historian Victor Orozco (2003) views this restructuring of social classes—in combination with political and ideological factors specific to the state—as the origin of the mobilizations of the period. Chihuahua experienced at least three successive waves of guerrilla activity, the first two in 1965 and 1968 related to rural demands, and the third in 1972, essentially urban but in continuity with the first two.[13] Both federal and state governments severely repressed the uprisings and the workers' movement never regained the power to mobilize that it had in the 1970s.

In the meantime the state of Chihuahua turned increasingly toward the United States for both industry and commerce, which led to the arrival of maquiladoras. At the end of 2006 there were 395 maquiladoras in Chihuahua employing a total of 306,828 workers out of an overall population of 3,241,444, which represents 23 percent of total employment. Of that number, 53 percent were women and 24 percent were technicians and administrators. The automobile and electronic sectors clearly dominate: they employ 67.3 percent of all maquiladora workers, while the textile and garment sectors employ 12.23 percent. The state's maquiladoras are concentrated in Ciudad Juárez on the border right across from El Paso, Texas (71 percent or 279 factories).[14]

As of the mid nineteenth century, Ciudad Juárez was an important site for migration. During WWII many European immigrants flocked to the city, as did a very large number of Mexicans, in the wake of the Braceros Program.[15] By 1942, at the beginning of the program, Ciudad Juárez had a population of 100,000 and was one of Mexico's main urban centers (Loera de la Rosa 2004: 247). At the time of the import substitution industrialization policies, the industrial development of Ciudad Juárez was based on Mexican businesses whose products were aimed at local and national markets, a trend that continued until the end of the 1970s.

Not only did maquiladoras displace local industries in Ciudad Juárez, but they also shaped a particular labor market in combination with trends in internal migration. Of the 400,000 people living in the city at the time, no less than 225,000—most of them migrants—had moved into temporary housing consisting of a single room with no access to public services (Flores Simental 2006: 18–19). Women were the main component of this migratory movement toward Juárez, particularly from the 1950s to the 1970s. They came mostly from within the state of Chihuahua and from the neighboring states of Coahuila and Durango, or from states farther away such as Zacatecas. Half of them were from rural areas and were less educated and less well-informed than non-migrants (Peña 2000: 129).

To this day migrants continue to move into Juárez and their presence continues to create additional difficulties for the city's labor movement. As of the 1980s large contingents of men began arriving from the center and south of Mexico, particularly from the state of Veracruz. There are currently more than 100,000 Veracruzanos (mostly from rural areas) in Juárez—to the point that they are referred to as "Juarochos," a contraction of Juárez and Jarochos (the name traditionally given to people from Veracruz; Ravelo Blancas and Sánchez Díaz 2006: 100; Juárez Núñez 2007). In the first six months of 2005 alone it is estimated that 10,000 Veracruzanos moved to Ciudad Juárez.[16]

In the mid 1980s migrant men began working more and more in maquiladoras. Whereas in 1982 there were 260 male workers for 1,000 female workers in maquiladoras, by 1993 the proportion of male to female workers had risen to 820 per 1,000 (Zamorano Villareal 2006: 49). This masculinization of the labor force in maquiladoras[17] can be attributed not only to the increasing presence of second- and third-generation maquiladoras but also to the scarcity of female workers, related in large part to women's family obligations (Bayon 2003). Still, maquiladoras remained the main source of employment for women (Quintero Ramírez 2003: 5–7). Women's presence in maquiladoras as well as their insecure job status was superimposed on and/or combined with the presence of migrants in influencing the rate of unionization in Juárez, which dropped from 33 percent in 1979 to 10 percent in 2004 (Quintero Ramírez 2006: 17).

As mentioned above, wages in general—and in maquiladoras in particular—were leveled down, notably as a result of corporatist unionism and protection contracts. The result is a high proportion of workers living in poverty. Of all workers, recent migrants have the worst living conditions and the lowest wages. They tend to settle on the city outskirts and a study on the rates of economic destitution has shown that the highest levels are in the zones of urban sprawl (Esparza, Waldorf, and Chavez 2004: 135). A study comparing the housing conditions among migrants in the 1980s with more recent migrants suggests that economic conditions have deteriorated, that their living conditions are even worse and that, unlike earlier migrants, their living situation does not improve over time (Zamorano Villareal 2006). It is harder and harder to find a job in Ciudad Juárez just as it is more and more difficult to cross the border—one of the migrants' goals. The city now has a floating population, a situation that combined with a large drug cartel contributes to the deterioration of the social fabric and is expressed in increased violence (Lasso Tiscareño 2005: 67).[18]

Between 2000 and 2006 the number of maquiladoras and jobs declined then rose back to a point where their current levels are respectively 12 percent and 8 percent of what they were in 2000.[19] This means that some maquiladoras have closed shop while others—especially second- and third-generation maquiladoras—have opened, providing a large number of jobs. On the other hand, the configuration of the maquiladoras and the types of jobs are shifting. The proportion of technicians and administrators, typical of these maquiladoras, is growing: as mentioned above, in November 2006 they represented 24 percent of all maquiladora workers in the state of Chihuahua. This means that newly arrived migrants—notably those from Veracruz with absolutely no training—either will not find as many jobs in the sector or will not be as well paid. Most likely the labor market will continue to fragment in the city, leaving little room for worker mobilization. Odds are that social classes will continue to be increasingly polarized.

The low rates of unionization and the lack of union power leaves but one recourse for workers who feel their rights have not been respected: direct individual negotiations before the Junta Local de Conciliación y Arbitraje (the local conciliation and arbitration board). Between 1995 and 2005 there were an average of 145 annual strike notices for all of Chihuahua, but there were only 3 strikes for the whole period. Meanwhile there were tens of thousands of individual claims[20]—no doubt to the great satisfaction of the lawyers hired by the workers to defend their cause.

The State of Yucatán:
"We Don't Like Unions, We Don't Want Them"

Like Chihuahua, Yucatán has undergone rapid economic changes since the 1970s. From the end of the nineteenth century until then, the north of the state—where the maquiladoras would later set up shop—was dominated by the production of henequen (or sisal), an agave plant containing a fiber that can be extracted to make rope and other derivatives, which constituted the region's main exports. In only thirty years, between 1970 and 2000, the tertiary (or service) sector overtook the primary sector. During those decades the growth of henequen declined along with the government subsidies that supported it, other crops replaced henequen, and subsistence farming decreased.

As subsidies for henequen production and processing ended in the mid 1980s, federal and local governments together took steps to encourage maquiladoras to move into the northern part of the state. They first set up in the industrial parks around the city of Mérida in 1985, twenty years after they first appeared on the northern border. Then, beginning in 1995, they began moving into the rural areas of Yucatán.[21] In November 2006 there were seventy-four maquiladoras in Yucatán employing some 25,760 people, that is, 3.2 percent of total employment. Of that number 51 percent were women and 16.4 percent were technicians and administrators;[22] 44 percent of the maquiladoras were in rural localities where they employed

68 percent of the workers in the sector (Castilla Ramos and Torres Góngora 2007: 56).

The number of maquiladoras and employees in the Yucatán dropped dramatically between 2001 and 2006: it reached 44 percent and 18 percent respectively whereas it was 12 percent and 18 percent in the state of Chihuahua. But the drop in the number of employees was lower than what might have been expected. This is due to the fact that most of the maquiladoras in Yucatán are in the clothing sector—first-generation maquiladoras requiring a large work force.[23] In Yucatán, labor generally could be found cheap. If the total employment is divided into four groups according to monthly income (no income, up to twice the minimum wage, between twice and five times the minimum wage, and over five times the minimum wage), the highest proportion of workers (50.8 percent) is in the second category and therefore earns less than twice the minimum wage per month. In Chihuahua the highest proportion (53.1 percent) is in the third category. In other words, on average Yucatán's total employed population earns *half* that of Chihuahua's.[24]

Maquiladoras arrived in the Yucatán with twenty years of transnational experience in labor relations. In Yucatán maquiladoras crystalized the characteristic power relations of the northern border in terms of both social class and gender relations while reinforcing deeply rooted relations in this southeastern state of Mexico. The position on unions not only among maquiladora directors but in the Yucatecan government was clearer than it had been during the first wave of maquiladoras on the northern border. In order to attract maquiladoras to the region, the governor at the time offered guarantees that no unions would be able penetrate maquiladoras.[25] The anti-union experience of the entrepreneurs was combined with the local union history, dominated by national central trade unions such as CTM and CROC—that is, by *charros* unions that would not stand up to the governor.

Yet one of the first unions in Yucatán (the rope-workers union) was an independent union and remained so from 1917 until the 1960s. Then in the 1970s several attempts were made to create independent unions, particularly among bus drivers, gas station employees, shoe makers, bakers, university employees, and construction workers (Echeverría V. 1999). These unions were created with the support of Efraín Calderón Lara, a law student at the University of Yucatán and member of a group founded in 1971 under the name Jacinto Canek, a Mayan leader who lived in the eighteenth century. Calderón Lara and his student companions had set up the Independant Unions'Advisory Office and had fought various attempts at corruption and threats by the government, bosses, and leaders of the CTM (El Rebelde 2007).

Calderón Lara was abducted on 14 February 1974. His body was found two days later in the neighboring state of Quintana Roo tortured and cruelly mutilated. Several observers believe that Calderón Lara was assassinated by order of the PRI-ist governor Carlos Loret de Mola with the complicity of large Yucatecan businessmen and leaders of the local CTM, "most certainly with the approval and support of the government of Luis Echeverría, national business bureaus and the national CTM" (El Rebelde 2007; see also Eiss 2003: 90; Echeverría V. 1999). Whoever was responsible, the assassination of Calderón Lara confirmed the hegemony of the national workers confederations. In spite of the "silent, popular and indigenous" resistance in present-day Yucatán pointed out by researchers and militants in the region (Macossay Vallado 2005: 31), independent unions are unable to survive—or only barely survive even if they do manage to get a foothold in a business or an area.[26] Though activists may like to refer to the centuries-old resistance of the Mayan people, or the fact that Yucatán was once (particularly in the 1920s) socialist, even "red,"[27] independent unions remain the exception in Yucatán. To date only one maquiladora— one of the oldest—is unionized with the CTM (Castilla Ramos and Torres Góngora 2006: 53). Independent unionization has not even been attempted in such companies.

The arrival of maquiladoras in rural localities in northern Yucatán beginning in 1995 has been a rewarding strategy for companies that are openly hostile to unionization. As Hathaway (2002: 431) points out, "the dispersion of maquiladoras to more rural settings throughout the country (has taken) away the small benefit to workers and made it even harder to organize unions." The general manager of the Canadian maquiladora Vogue Dessous, which operated in the Yucatán until 2001, summarizes the position of many entrepreneurs: "We don't like unions, we don't want them."[28] Not only do workers have to face such hostility, the fact that for most young maquiladora workers this is their first job in the industrial sector makes it all the more difficult to mobilize. As a result, they have no experience of labor relations. All they know about unions in general—and they are not mistaken—is that they are corrupt. What is more, the young women who were the first to be recruited into maquiladoras are the first generation of rural women to work in the industrial sector. Not only are they young women, they are young *indigenous* women.

One of the main differences between Yucatán and Chihuahua is that a high proportion of the Yucatecan population—of 1,818,948 persons[29]—can be defined as indigenous. In 2000 the indigenous population was estimated to be 58.57 percent of the overall state population (whereas nationally it is 10.5 percent; CDI 2002).[30] While the indigenous peoples of Chihuahua do not stand out much from the dominant population, Mayas dominate the Yucatecan landscape. The areas in which the Mayas live—close to the sites where maquiladoras have set up shop—are characterized by high levels of poverty and marginalization.[31] The poverty is such that maquiladoras can offer wages well below those paid almost everywhere else in the country.

In spite of these extreme conditions, in twenty years of maquiladora presence in Yucatán there have been only about twenty labor conflicts, most of which did not lead to full-fledged strikes (Torres Góngora N.d.). Indeed, strikes have virtually disappeared from the local scene: between 1995 and 2005 inclusively there were an average of sixty-eight strike notices per year but only two actual strikes—not per year, but for the entire eleven-year period (one in 1996 and one in 2003).[32] In Yucatán, as on the northern border, workers who let it be known that they wanted to form a union say they were threatened with being laid off.[33] And for those who do not believe that race is an additional factor, note this comment made by a manager concerning protesting workers: "Bloody Indians [*Indios de mierda*]—if you don't like working you can step aside, there are several starving people who can work" (Hernández Navarro 2006).

In summary, as I was able to see during my research in Yucatán, the only thing workers can do is to develop survival strategies. The members of rural households tend to diversify their activities by gender and generation and to pool their incomes. The older generation continues to farm; middle-aged women often work in domestic services; and the younger generation tends to work in maquiladoras (Labrecque 2005). All that is left for people in this situation are sporadic wildcat strikes and individual negotiations regarding work conditions.

Conclusion: Taking Advantages of Local Conditions

Comparing Chihuahua to Yucatán is a bold proposition. The simple fact that most of the maquiladoras in Chihuahua are located on the border between the United States and Mexico places them in a particular dynamic that has so far been studied only by specialists of the region. In order to make such a comparison and for it to be meaningful, it is important to take into account the many differences between the two states in terms of maquiladora size, the length of time they have been operating and various other characteristics in both regions. One of the most important differences is that 23 percent of total employment in Chihuahua is in a maquiladora whereas it is only 3 percent in Yucatán. The other difference that is significant for the purposes of this chapter is that the rate of unionization in Chihuahuan maquiladoras is 10 percent while it is zero in the Yucatán. Clearly, maquiladoras and unionism cannot be understood in the same way in both states.

Nonetheless, beyond the many quantitative differences, the processes are surprisingly alike. Take, for instance, the masculinization of the work force, the number of technicians and administrators, the presence of corporatist unionism and/or outright anti-unionism, and the spread of an individual approach to labor demands. In both states, these processes have led in sometimes contradictory ways to comparative advantages for the maquiladoras.

It is interesting to note that the maquiladoras in Chihuahua have relied on immigrant labor from the interior of Mexico, whereas the maquiladoras that opened factories in Yucatán did so because of the availability of a local work force that is both cheap and demobilized for reasons strongly related to gender. According to Rosita Villanueva Vargas (2006: 17), who has also studied the case of Yucatán, "it has been impossible to create bonds of solidarity or experience sharing between the 'old' male worker proletariat and its corporate independent union organization[34] and the 'new' female worker proletariat composed mainly of young women in the maquiladora export industry with no union base and no past references for forming an organized labour resistance." In Chihuahua migrant workers arrive in a polarized urban environment shaped by complex border dynamics, including delinquency and violence, where they make up an increasingly diverse population. There is no question that Chihuahua's proximity to the American market gives it an important comparative advantage with respect to Yucatán. It is therefore no surprise that in spite of the social decomposition, particularly in Ciudad Juárez (of which the still largely unpunished murders of women are a part), maquiladoras continue to occupy a large space. It is often said that maquiladoras are moving away from conflict zones, yet the high level of violence does not seem to come into play in Ciudad Juárez, on the contrary. Perhaps it is precisely this social decomposition that has enabled the labor market to become so fragmented and segmented, which itself results in low wages.[35] Thus, even in a context where the work force needed by second- and third-generation maquiladoras is more and more expensive, wages are still kept as far down as possible.

The fact that maquiladoras have moved into the Yucatecan countryside (unlike Chihuahua) gives pause to reflect on their ability to move into new spaces and to inflect social relations according to their needs and demands. The displacement of maquiladoras from urban to rural areas has divided the work force even further, this time on the basis of ethnicity, since the rural population is mostly indigenous while the urban population is not. On the other hand, Yucatán's rural population is fairly homogeneous in social, cultural, and ethnic terms. Whereas the comparative advantage on the northern border is founded on social decomposition, in Yucatán it is based on the integrity of the social fabric, a solidarity that is grounded in family survival strategies that I have been able to observe and that consist in diversifying the activities of household members and in pooling resources (Villanueva Vargas 2006: 19; Labrecque 2005). This explains why wages are among the lowest anywhere in the Republic.

Finally, the comparison between Chihuahua and Yucatán shows how in a globalized economy, the transnational capital underlying maquiladoras is able to adjust to the sociohistorical specificities of different places and to turn to its advantage some of the changes currently underway. This is but one illustration of the "flexible commitment of capital to particular places and workers," a process to which Frances Rothstein—as well as the majority of the authors in this volume for a diversity of cases—refers, also in the case of Mexico. In the two states compared here, the processes of fragmentation and segmentation of the labor force—which are both causes and effects of worker demobilization—were already well underway and even quite advanced when the maquiladoras arrived, either because of corporatist unionism or *charro* (in the case of Chihuahua) or because of the negative reputation that unionism had earned itself because of *charro* (in the Yucatán). In this sense, to answer the question laid out in the beginning of this chapter, worker demobilization clearly cannot be explained by NFWOs alone; rather, demobilization may explain why NFWOs were introduced into maquiladoras in the first place. As to whether unionism is obsolete in maquiladoras, the question must be reformulated in Mexico taking into account corporatist unionism or *charro*. Insofar as the question is not a hidden means of discrediting unionism in its more progressive historical dimensions, the answer is clearly "yes" from the workers' viewpoint. On the other hand, it seems that a certain portion of capital still needs some tried and true basic tools to protect its comparative advantage. Otherwise why would the protection contracts, the spearhead of *charro* unionism, be exported?

Notes

1. In Mexico, the minimum wage varies on the basis of three geographical regions that are set according to the cost of living. Yucatán is in zone C where the minimum wage until 1 January 2007 was 45.81 pesos. This means that 73 pesos a day is less than twice the minimum wage. The minimum wage covers only 25 percent of the basic grocery basket (Canasta Básica Nutricional). It would take at least four minimum wages a day to meet daily nutritional requirements. See the website of the Senate of the LX

legislature of Mexico: http://www.senado.gob.mx/sgsp/gaceta/?sesion=2007/03/15 /1&documento=23 (accessed 30 May 2007).

2. In the context of Mexican unionism, the term *charro* refers to a unionism that is subjugated to the government. Protection contracts are established in the context of *charro* unions. The leaders of such unions are *charro* leaders, hence the term *charrismo*.

3. The Inter American Regional Organisation of Workers (CIOSL/ORIT) is affiliated with the ICFTU (International Confederation of Free Trade Unions) representing trade unions from the Americas.

4. *Proceso*, issue 1591, 29 April 2007.

5. I received two successive research grants from SSHRC (Social Sciences and Humanities Research Council) for research in Yucatán from 1999 to 2007. Although my fieldwork in Chihuahua was not as extensive, I spent time there on several occasions between 1999 and 2005 doing follow-up on the murders of women in Ciudad Juárez, which are part of the context of violence in the city. I have discussed this subject elsewhere (Labrecque 2006).

6. Researchers define three generations of maquiladoras: the first, in which the labor force is employed largely for assembly (as is the case in the garment industry); the second, in which more technology is needed in the production process; and the third, in which research and development are applied to the production process (Contreras and Munguía 2007: 80). Although the three generations represent greater degrees of technical development, they continue to coexist. Recently this definition of three generations has been questioned and researchers have shown that factors other than the labor force must be combined to characterize the differences between *maquiladoras* (Carrillo and Gomis 2005).

7. The rates of unionization also seem to have dropped in the United States where the rate is 13.9 percent and in Canada where it is 30 percent (Zepeda 2004).

8. There are more than thirty such confederations or central labor unions.

9. In about 2001 the UNT had approximately 1.5 million members while the CTM had between 4 and 4.5 million (5.5 million according to the CTM), making it the largest workers organization in the country (US Department of Labor 2002: 5, 7).

10. There has been much discussion concerning the bill to reform the federal labor act. The bill was tabled in parliament in 2002 by the labor minister at the time, Carlos Abascal. The bill came mainly out of official union circles. According to observers, the bill was proposing greater flexibility in work arrangements and would be a clear step backward for workers' rights. The bill has still not been passed.

11. See also Buitelaar and Padilla Pérez 2000: 1631.

12. Porfirio Díaz was president of Mexico from 1876 to 1911, with a four-year interruption.

13. These protests also echoed the repression of the student movement in the center of the country with the 2 October 1968 massacre in Mexico City, and more immediately the 10 June 1971 massacre.

14. All the information in this paragraph comes from INEGI (Instituto Nacional de Estadística Geografía e Informática; www.inegi.gob.mx). The demographic data are from Comunicado núm. 087/06, 24 de Mayo 2006, Cuadro 1, "Población total por entidad y tasa de crecimiento 2000–2005." The information on maquiladoras is mostly from the page entitled "Personal ocupado en la industria maquiladora de exportación, Chihuahua" (accessed 14 February 2007). For Juárez, the page was accessed on 28 May 2007.

15. In 1955 alone, 369,000 *braceros* went to work in the United States (Flores Simental 2006: 15).

16. Information from the director of Casa del Veracruzano (Veracruzano's house) in Ciudad Juárez, as reported in the newspaper *Norte*, 23 June 2005.
17. De la O Martínez (2006b: 104) speaks of a gradual defeminization of the labor force.
18. Chihuahua is sixth out of thirty-two states plus the federal district for the proportion of presumed delinquents, while Yucatán is thirty-first. See "Estadísticas por proyecto, Integración de estadísticas, Perspectivas Estadísticas (by state)," www.inegi.gob.mx.
19. These are my calculations based on INEGI data for the two years in question.
20. The information on strike notices and strikes is available from the department of labor under the heading "Relaciones laborales" (http://www.stps.gob.mx), as well as from INEGI under "Emplazamientos a huelga registrados" (http://www.inegi. gob.mx). Concerning individual complaints, for 2005–2006 alone the Chihuahuan government has reported 5,625 resolved complaints (*demandas concluidas*), 21,170 complaints being processed, 43,269 notices (*notificaciones*), 1,739 arbitrations, 731 judgements for direct or indirect protection (*amparo*), and 3,942 agreements with a judgment (Gobierno de Chihuahua 2006: 301).
21. In 2005, 32.6 percent of Yucatán's population was rural. See INEGI 2006 Cuaderno de Información Oportuna Regional, no. 89, Tercer trimestre 2006.
22. See "Estadísticas por proyecto, Integración de estadísticas, Perspectivas Estadísticas" (by state; www.inegi.gob.mx).
23. The proportions for garment maquiladoras vary depending on the source. Castilla Ramos and Torres Góngora (2007: 57) say that they represent 61 percent of all maquiladoras in the state. INEGI, however, says that they were 71 percent in 2006.
24. These data are from INEGI and are for the end of 2006. See "Estadísticas por proyecto, Integración de estadísticas, Perspectivas Estadísticas" (by state; www. inegi.gob.mx).
25. See UNT, 7 November 2000, http://www.strm,org.mx/org/unt/ponenciasmer.htm (accessed 11 April 2006).
26. For a description and analysis of a relatively recent attempt at independent union organization that was unsuccessful, see Eiss 2003.
27. Political life in Yucatán was dominated by the PSSE (Partido Socialista del Sureste— The Socialist Party of the Southeast) in the 1920s. One of the founders of the PSSE was Felipe Carrillo Puerto, who was elected governor of Yucatán in 1922. At the time, the entire southeast was "red," as writers point out. Moreover, Yucatán was the location for the first feminist congress in the country. In fact, Felipe's sister, Elvia Carrillo Puerto, helped found the Feminist Resistance Leagues and was active in consolidating socialism in the state. However, Felipe Carrillo Puerto was executed in 1924 on behalf of Adolfo de la Huerta's counter-revolutionary movement, putting an end to the Yucatecan socialist dream (Lemaître León 1997).
28. A Toronto-based organization, the Maquila Solidarity Network, quoted this comment in one of its newsletters. Originally this quote belongs to Vogue Dessous' manager Denis Coutu as he was interviewed by journalist Linda Diebel. The article was published in the *Toronto Star* on 12 March 2000.
29. Source: INEGI, 2006, Comunicado núm. 087/06, 24 de Mayo, Cuadro 1, "Población total por entidad y tasa de crecimiento 2000–2005." The statistic therefore applies to 2005.
30. There is a difference between the estimate made by CDI (Comisión para el Desarrollo de los Pueblos Indígenas) concerning indigenous *persons* and that of INEGI, which refers to persons age five or more who *speak* an indigenous language, who accounted for 37.3 percent in Yucatán in 2000. See INEGI, "Estadísticas por proyecto, Integración de estadísticas, Perspectivas Estadísticas" (by state; www.inegi.gob.mx).

31. According to the Consejo Nacional de Población (CONAPO), 83 of Yucatán's 106 municipalities had high and very high levels of marginalization, which represents 35.5 percent of the state's population. See www.conapo.gob.mx/prensa/2003/discursos2003_04.htm (accessed 26 February 2006).
32. See the first part of note 20.
33. Diario de Yucatán, 28 January 2001. All our informants working in maquiladoras in Yucatán confirmed this statement (Labrecque 2005).
34. The author is referring to the rope-makers union.
35. In terms of the minimum wage Ciudad Juárez is in zone A. Until 1 January 2007, when the minimum wage was increased by 3.9 percent, minimum wage was 48.67 pesos a day. See the debates on whether this increase was sufficient on the web site of Infodemex: http://www.rel-uita.org/laboral/salario_minimo_mexico.htm (accessed 9 January 2007).

References

Bayon, María Cristina. 2003. "Trabajando en la frontera: Mujeres, mercado de trabajo y globalización." In *Las expresiones locales de la globalización: México y España*, eds. Carmen Bueno and Encarnación Aguilar, 49–66. México: Grupo Editorial Miguel Angel Porrua.

Bellone Hite, Amy, and Jocelyn Viterna. 2005. "Gendering Class in Latin America: How Women Effect and Experience Change in the Class Structure." *Latin American Research Review* 40 (2): 50–82.

Bizberg, Ilán. 2003. "El sindicalismo en fin de régimen." *Foro Internacional* 43 (1): 215–248.

Buitelaar, Rudolf M., and Ramón Padilla Pérez. 2000. "Maquila, Economic Reform and Corporate Strategies." *World Development* 28 (9): 1627–1642.

Carrillo, Jorge, and Redi Gomis. 2005. "Generaciones de maquiladoras: Un primer acercamiento a su medición." *Frontera Norte* 17 (33): 25–51.

Castilla Ramos, Beatriz, and Alejandra Quintanilla. 2006. "La industria maquiladora de exportación de Yucatán y su especialización en la rama de la confección." *El Cotidiano* 21 (136): 29–38.

Castilla Ramos, Beatriz, and Beatriz Torres Góngora. 2007. "Hacia nuevas formas de organizar el trabajo en la IME de Yucatán: análisis de dos empresas." *El Cotidiano* 22 (142): 53–63.

CDI (Comisión para el Desarrollo de los Pueblos Indígenas). 2002. "Indicadores socioeconómicos." http://cdi.gob.mx/index.php (accessed 12 November 2005).

Chávez Chávez, Jorge. 2003. "La cultura regional." In *Chihuahua Hoy 2003: Visiones de su historia, economía, política y cultura*, ed. Víctor Orozco, 49–80. Chihuahua: Universidad Autónoma de Ciudad Juárez.

Contreras, Óscar F., and Luis Felipe Munguía. 2007. "Evolución de las maquiladoras en México: Política industrial y aprendizaje tecnológico." *Región y Sociedad* 19, special issue: 71–87.

De la Garza Toledo, Enrique. 2003. "NAFTA, reestructuración productiva y relaciones laborales en México." Unpublished Paper. LASA International Congress, Dallas, TX.

De la O Martínez, María Eugenia. 2006a. "El trabajo de las mujeres en la industria maquiladora de México: balance de cuatro décadas de estudio." *AIBR: Revista de Antropología Iberoamericana* 1 (3): 404–427.

———. 2006b. "Geografía del trabajo femenino en las maquiladoras de México." *Papeles de Población* 049: 91–126.

Echeverría V., Pedro. 1999. "El gobierno de Loret y el asesinato del Charras: ¿Cómo pudo el gobernador controlar a la prensa?"*Revista Latina de Comunicación Social* 14. http://www.lazarillo.com/latina/a1999c/132echeve.htm (accessed 10 April 2006).

Eiss, Paul. 2003. "The War of the Eggs: Event, Archive, and History in Yucatán's Independent Union Movement, 1990." *Ethnology* 42 (2): 87–108.

El Rebelde. 2007. "Efraín Calderón Lara 'El Charras.'" http://imc-yucatan.espora.org/print.php?id=894 (accessed 13 February 2007).

Estado de Chihuahua. 2005. "Enciclopedia de los municipios de México: Estado de Chihuahua, Ocampo." http://www.e-local.gob.mx/work/templates/enciclo/chihuahua/Mpios/08051a.htm (accessed 17 February 2007).

Esparza, Adrian X., Brigitte S. Waldorf, and Javier Chavez. 2004. "Localized Effects of Globalization: The Case of Ciudad Juárez, Chihuahua, Mexico." *Urban Geograph* 25 (4): 120–138.

Fernández, Jorge Alberto. 2002. "Redesigning the Strategy of the Frente Auténtico del Trabajo in the Maquiladoras." *Labor History* 43 (4): 461–463.

Flores Simental, Raúl. 2006. "De Paso del Norte a Juárez: una ciudad del siglo XX." In *Sistema Socioeconómico y Geo-referencial sobre la Violencia de Género en Ciudad Juárez, Chihuahua: Propuesta para su Prevención*, vol. 2, ed. El Colegio de la Frontera Norte, 3–36. Ciudad Juárez: El Colegio de la Frontera Norte.

Gobierno de Chihuahua. 2006. *Segundo Informe de Gobierno. Administración 2004–2010.* México: Gobierno del Estado de Chihuahua.

Hathaway, Dale A. 2002. "Mexico's Frente Auténtico del Trabajo and the Problem of Unionizing Maquiladoras (Forum)." *Labor History* 43 (4): 427–438.

Hermanson, Jeff, and Enrique de la Garza Toledo. 2005. "El corporativismo y las nuevas luchas en las maquilas de México: El papel de las redes internacionales de apoyo." In *Sindicatos y nuevos movimientos sociales en América latina*, ed. Enrique de la Garza Toledo, 181–213. Buenos Aires: CLACSO.

Hernández Navarro, Luis. 2006. "Julio Macossay: Contra la corriente." Internet edition. *La jornada*, 16 May.

Hodkinson, Stuart. 2005. "Is There a New Trade Union Internationalism? The International Confederation of Free Trade Unions' Response to Globalization, 1996–2002." *Labour, Capital and Society* 38 (1/2): 36–65.

Juárez Núñez, Huberto. 2007. "El trabajo en la industria maquiladora de exportación." *Trabajadores* 11 (58). http://www.uom.edu.mx/trabajadores/58huberto.htm (accessed 28 May 2007).

Labrecque, Marie France. 2005. *Être Maya et travailler dans une maquiladora: État, identité, genre et génération au Yucatán,Mexique.* Québec: Presses de l'Université Laval.

———. 2006. "Féminicide et impunité à Ciudad Juárez, Mexique." In *L'autonomie des femmes en question: Antiféminisme et résistances en Amérique et en Europe*, eds. Josette Trat, Diane Lamoureux, and Roland Pfefferkorn, 71–89. Paris: L'Harmattan.

Lasso Tiscareño, Rigoberto. 2005. "Inercias y cambios en la cultura de Ciudad Juárez." In *Chihuahua hoy 2005*, ed. Victor Orozco, 61–95. Ciudad Juárez: Instituto Chihuahuense de la cultura.

Lemaître León, Monique J. 1997. "Elvia Carrillo Puerto: La 'Monja Roja del Mayab.'" http://www.actlab.utexas.edu/~geneve/zapwomen/forum/messages/39.html (accessed 28 May 2007).

Loera de la Rosa, Manuel. 2004. "Industria y libertad en la frontera mexicana del medio siglo—Un debate por conocer." In *Chihuahua hoy 2004*, ed. Victor Orozco, 241–275. Ciudad Juárez: Universidad Autónoma de Ciudad Juárez.

Macossay Vallado, Mauricio. 2005. "Tetíz, resistencia popular y obrera, 1980–2004." Unpublished paper. Oaxaca: Asociación Mexicana de Estudios Rurales.

Orozco, Víctor. 2003. *Diez ensayos sobre Chihuahua.* Chihuahua: Doble Helices Ediciones.
Peña, Leticia. 2000. "Retaining a Mexican Labor Force." *Journal of Business Ethics* 26 (2): 123–131.
Presidency of the Republic. 2005. "Lanza maquila yucateca 'bomba' de empleo." Website of the Presidency of the Republic. http://www.presidencia.gob.mx/buenasnoticias/ (accessed 1 January 2006).
Quintero Ramírez, Cirila. 2003. "Desarrollo maquilador precario y sus efectos laborales y sociales: El caso de Ciudad Juárez." Unpublished paper. 36th meeting of the South Council Latin American Studies, New Orleans, LA, 12–15 March.
———. 2006. "El sindicalismo en las maquiladoras: La persistencia de lo local en la globalización." *Desacatos* 21: 11–28.
Ramasamy, P. 2005. "Labour and Globalization: Towards a New Internationalism?" *Labour, Capital and Society* 38 (1/2): 5–35.
Ravelo Blancas, Patricia, and Sergio Sánchez Díaz. 2006. "Retroceso laboral, discriminación y riesgo en las maquiladoras: El caso de Ciudad Juárez, Chihuahua." *El Cotidiano* 21 (135): 71–77.
Roman, Richard, and Edur Velasco Arregui. 2001. "Neoliberalism, Labor Market Transformation, and Working-Class Responses." *Latin American Perspectives*, issue 119, 28 (4): 52–71.
———. 2006. "The State, the Bourgeoisie, and the Unions: The Recycling of Mexico's System of Labor Control." *Latin American Perspectives*, issue 147, 33 (2): 95–103.
Torres Góngora, Beatriz. N.d. "El trabajo femenino en las maquiladoras de exportación: Rostro emergente de la globalización en Yucatán." Unpublished manuscript. Centro de Investigaciones Regionales de la Universidad Autónoma del Estado Yucatán.
US Department of Labor. 2002. "Foreign Labor Trends: México." FLT 02–08. Mexico City: Bureau of International Labor Affairs and US Embassy. www.dol.gov/ILAB/media/reparts/flt/mexico-2002.pdf (accessed 8 July 2006).
Villanueva Vargas, Rosita. 2006. "Globalización y reestructuración productiva regional: La industria maquiladora de exportación en Yucatán." Unpublished paper. Mérida: 11° Encuentro Nacional del AMECIDER sobre Desarrollo Regional en México. http://www.sicbasa.com/tuto/AMECIDER2006/PARTE percent203/190 percent20Rosita percent20-Villanueva percent20Vargas.pdf (accessed 28 May 2006).
Zamorano Villareal, Claudia Carolina. 2006. "Ser inmigrante en Ciudad Juárez: Itinerarios residenciales en tiempos de la maquila." *Frontera Norte* 18 (35): 29–53.
Zepeda, Roberto. 2004. "Declive del sindicalismo y precarización del trabajo en Norteamérica: un análisis comparativo." *Trabajadores* 8 (42). http://www.uom.edu.mx/trabajadores/42zepeda.htm (accessed 8 July 2006).

LIST OF CONTRIBUTORS

Pauline Gardiner Barber is professor of social anthropology at Dalhousie University, Canada. Her research explores class and gender dynamics associated with Philippine migration, citizenship, and development. Recent articles on Filipinos as global migrants appear in Berghahn Books, Blackwell, and Routledge volumes, as well as journals such as the *Third World Quarterly, Focaal: European Journal of Ethnography*, and *Anthropologica*. She is coeditor of the Ashgate Press series *Gender in a Global/Local World.*

Wenona Giles is professor of anthropology at York University, Toronto, and publishes in the areas of gender, development studies, migration, globalization, ethnicity, and nationalism. Her books include: *Portuguese Women in Toronto: Gender, Immigration and Nationalism* (2002); *Development and Diaspora: Gender and the Refugee Experience*, coedited (1996); *Feminists under Fire: Exchanges across War Zones*, coedited (2003), and *Sites of Violence: Gender and Conflict Zones*, coedited (2004). Current research (with Jennifer Hyndman) on long-term refugee situations focuses on Somali refugees in Kenya and Afghan refugees in Iran.

Josiah Heyman is professor of anthropology and chair of the department of sociology and anthropology at the University of Texas at El Paso. He is the author or editor of three books and over forty journal articles and book chapters on borders, migration, states, police bureaucracies and illegal activities, working classes, and consumption. Recent publications include "The Inverse of Power," *Anthropological Theory* 3 (2), and editing with Hilary Cunningham a special issue of *Identities* 11 (3) on mobilities and enclosures at borders.

Susana Narotzky is professor of social anthropology at the University of Barcelona, Spain. She has done fieldwork in different regions of Spain (Catalunya, Valencia, Galicia). Her research focuses on the politics of social movements and memory in Spain as well as on the political economy of new forms of capitalism. In 2007 she published "The Project in the Model: Reciprocity, Social Capital and the Politics of Ethnographic Realism,"

Current Anthropology 48 (3): 403–424; and "A Cargo del Futuro: Between History and Memory An Account of the Fratricidal Conflict during Revolution and War in Spain (1936–39)," *Critique of Anthropology* 27 (4): 411–429; and coauthored in 2006 with Gavin Smith *Immediate Struggles: People, Power and Place in Rural Spain*, Berkeley: University of California Press.

Marie France Labrecque is professor of anthropology at Laval University, Quebec. Her recent work deals with the critique of the "women and development" approach in the area of international development, including income-generating projects in Mexico and participatory methodologies in Colombia. She is currently carrying out a research dealing with the gendering of production and the expansion of the maquiladoras in the rural areas of the state of Yucatan, Mexico. Out of this research, she published in 2005 a book: *Être Maya et travailler dans une maquiladora: État, identité, genre et génération au Yucatan, Mexique*, Québec: Presses de l'Université Laval. Her recent work in English includes an article, "Cultural Appreciation and Economic Depreciation of the Mayas of Northern Yucatán, Mexico," in *Latin American Perspectives*, July 2005, Issue 143, 32 (4): 87–105. She also is a member of the Quebec Committee for Solidarity with the Women of Ciudad Juárez.

Belinda Leach is professor in the department of sociology and anthropology at the University of Guelph. Her research investigates gender, economic restructuring and livelihoods in Canada and has been published in *Critique of Anthropology, Indentities, Labour—Le Travail and Signs*. She is currently carrying out research on migration from Trinidad to Canada. She is coeditor with Winnie Lem (2002) of *Culture, Economy, Power: Anthropology as Critique, Anthropology as Praxis* (Albany: State University of New York Press), and With Tony Winson (2002), *Contingent Work, Disrupted Lives: Labour and Community in the New Rural Economy* (Toronto: University of Toronto Press). She is also a co-editor of *Identities: Global Studies in Culture and Power*.

Winnie Lem is professor of international development studies and women's studies Trent University, Canada. Her research focuses on work, migration, urbanization, agrarian change, gender relations, ethnic economies, family enterprise, as well as the politics of exclusion, culture, and class. Among her publications are *Cultivating Dissent: Work, Identity and Praxis in Rural Languedoc* in 1997 (Albany: State University of New York Press); *Culture, Economy, Power: Anthropology as Critique; Anthropology as Praxis* in 2002 (coedited with Belinda Leach; Albany: State University of New York Press). She has also been editor-in-chief and editor of manuscripts in English of *Anthropologica*.

Davide Però is lecturer in sociology at the University of Nottingham and Research Associate at the Centre on Migration, Policy and Society, Institute of Social and Cultural Anthropology (Oxford University) where he previously worked. He has conducted ethnographic research on migration and politics in Italy, Spain and the UK. His book *Inclusionary Rhetoric/ Exclusionary Practices: Left-Wing Politics and Migrant in Italy* came out with Berghahn Books in 2007.

Frances Abrahamer Rothstein is professor of anthropology at Montclair State University in Montclair Heights, New Jersey. Her research focuses on globalization and gender. Currently, she is studying the conditions that encourage people to leave Mexico and whether, as some have argued, there is a new pattern of increased settlement. Her most recent book is *Globalization in Rural Mexico: Three Decades of Change* (Austin: University of Texas Press).

Elisabetta Zontini is a lecturer in sociology at Nottingham University. After completing her DPhil at Sussex University, she was research fellow in the Families and Social Capital ESRC Research Group at London South Bank University. Her recent publications include *Transnational Families, Migration and Gender: Moroccan and Filipino Women in Bologna and Barcelona* (Berghahn Books) and with H. Goulbourne, T. Reynolds, J. Solomos (2010) *Transnational Families, Ethnicities, Identities and Social Capital* (Routledge).

INDEX

CPSIA information can be obtained at www.ICGtesting.com
Printed in the USA
BVOW010748101212

307758BV00007B/75/P